Opening the American Mind

Opening the American Mind

The Integration of Biblical Truth in the Curriculum of the University

W. David Beck

BAKER BOOK HOUSE
Grand Rapids, Michigan 49516

Library of Congress Cataloging-in-Publication Data
Opening the American mind: the integration of biblical truth in the
    curriculum of the university / edited by W. David Beck.
            p.   cm.—(The Liberty series)
        Includes bibliographical references and index.
        ISBN 0-8010-0987-1
        1. Church colleges—United States—Curricula. 2. Church colleges—United
States—Philosophy. 3. Education, Higher—United States—Aims and objectives. I. Beck,
William David, 1947– . II. Series.
LC383.064   1991
378.1'00—dc20   90-48990
                                                                                      CIP

Unless otherwise indicated, Scripture references are from the Holy Bible, New International
Version. Copyright © 1973, 1978, 1984 International Bible Society. Used by permission of
Zondervan Bible Publishers. Other translations cited are the King James Version (KJV), the
New American Standard Bible (NASB), and the New King James Version (NKJV).

Contents

Foreword

In his best-selling educational blockbuster, a University of Chicago classics professor, Dr. Allan Bloom, speaks of "the closing of the American mind." He charges that higher education has closed its mind to absolute truth, absolute values, and the Bible as revelation. Bloom bemoans that "There is one thing a professor can be absolutely certain of: almost every student entering the university believes, or says he believes, that truth is relative." He further complains that "the best that can be done, it appears, is to teach 'The Bible as Literature,' as opposed to 'as Revelation,' which it claims to be."[1]

In this context, Christian higher education has an unprecedented opportunity for "opening the American mind." Its commitment to absolute truth, absolute values, and the Bible as God's revelation is the very foundation of its operation. Unlike many current suggestions such as Mortimer Adler's, who, as his recent book *Reforming Education* indicates, desires merely to open the American mind to the great classics, it is crucial that we open the mind to all truth, whether in great books or in the greatest Book. After all, if we are going to be really open-minded to all truth, then we must not be closed to the truth. Jesus said to his Father, "Thy Word is truth" (John 17:17 NASB). Many educators are open to all "truth" except God's truth. In the final analysis, then, they are closed to all truth, since all truth is God's truth.

Unlike professional schools geared to train one for specific service, the Christian liberal arts colleges and universities can open the Christian mind to a greater vista of human knowledge. We can

---

1. Allan Bloom, *The Closing of the American Mind* (New York: Simon and Schuster, 1987), 25, 374–75.

take seriously the divine imperative to "take every thought captive to the obedience of Christ" (2 Cor. 10:5 NASB). For it was Jesus who said, "You shall know the truth, and the truth shall make you free" (John 8:32 NASB).

Truth has a liberating effect on its recipient. By means of an education in the arts and sciences, the Christian is liberated from the bonds of provincialism and provided a freedom that knowledge of the Bible by itself does not provide. We need to know God's world as well as his Word. For understanding the truth is not sufficient until it includes an understanding of the times. Scripture commended the men of Issachar because they "understood the times and knew what Israel ought to do. . ." (1 Chron. 12:32). A truly Christian education, then, opens the mind not only to the content of Scripture but also to the context in which we proclaim it.

This book is an attempt by the faculty of Liberty University to set forth a model for accomplishing the reopening of the American mind to absolute truth, absolute values, and the Bible as God's revelation. It is an attempt, however imperfect, to integrate our belief in God's infallible and inerrant revelation in Scripture with the various disciplines in the university.

As we undertake our task, we are painfully aware of past failures. We contemplate with deep regret the unfulfilled desire of the evangelical founders of many of our first American universities. In its charter, Yale University (1745) acknowledged that it "under the blessing of Almighty God has trained up many worthy persons for the service of God in the state as well as in church." Almost a century earlier, the Statutes of Harvard University (1650) read: "Every one shall consider the main End of his life and studies, to know God and Jesus Christ which is Eternal Life." Today, this biblical heritage is scarcely a memory to most Ivy Leaguers. Let us hope and pray that the same fate will not befall the hosts of fine Christian institutions of higher learning God has raised up in America in our time.

Norman L. Geisler

Introduction:
Designing a Christian University

W. David Beck

Christian colleges are in jeopardy. In fact, if the current conditions of secular higher education in the United States persist, then I doubt that Christian colleges can continue much longer on their present course. The problem is this: How will these colleges continue to supply themselves with a sufficient number of fully qualified faculty who are theologically orthodox and capable of integrating biblical data with their subject matter at the highest professional level?

Background of the Current Problem

The difficulty stems from the dearth of doctorate-granting universities where Christian faculties operate with theistic worldviews and carefully integrate biblical material within their disciplines. There are, of course, Christian professors functioning in relative isolation at secular universities, but a sufficient variety of comprehensive Christian institutions, granting terminal degrees in every discipline, from biochemistry to Renaissance music, from Ugaritic to accounting, simply do not exist.

By itself, however, this fact does not account for the peril in which Christian higher education finds itself.[1] This lack of consistently Christian universities has been the case for a long time. It is the combination of this factor with the current shift in worldviews that has, I believe, brought about the situation.

Prior to recent changes in the dominant paradigms that govern the academic culture, the university, though certainly not explicitly Christian, was at least not entirely inimical to it. However, over the last fifty years or so a change has taken place. We are now faced with a dominant worldview that is diametrically opposed to Christian thinking, within which Christian thinking cannot even make sense.

As a result, new faculty at Christian colleges, with few exceptions, have never had a course, never worked through a research project, never been allowed to formulate solutions to a problem, or even work out the course content of a major within the framework of a theistic worldview. That is not to say that many have not attempted to do so on their own, or that the literature in many disciplines does not include examples and discussions based on a theistic model. Still, it is difficult to undo four or perhaps eight years of concentrated education. This will be especially true in fields where Christian thinking has no presence in the way of professional organizations, periodicals, conferences, or the like.

It is this situation that this book addresses. How is a Christian university defined in terms of the content of instruction? Of course, other contexts need definition as well. Everything from administrative styles to the role of sports, architecture, student rules, and external relations to the church needs careful discussion. Nevertheless, as important as some of these other matters are, none seem to me nearly as crucial to the character of a Christian institution of higher learning as the ingredients of the instruction provided by its professors.

Two changes, in particular, seem to me essential if the Christian college is to be rescued. First, it will be necessary to develop full-fledged Christian universities. Liberty University is not the only school to focus on that goal, and we hope there will be even more. It has, however, been too long since good models for a Christian

---

1. Two important studies of the history of Christian institutions are William Ringenberg, *The Christian College* (Grand Rapids: Eerdmans, 1984), and Manning Pattillo and Donald MacKenzie, *Church-Sponsored Higher Education in the United States* (Washington, D.C.: American Council on Education, 1966).

university existed in each discipline. In fact, some disciplines did not exist at all the last time around. Hence, we set out to define ourselves as a university in this book. Admittedly it is only a beginning. It is by no means a final statement, nor do we pretend to have reached our goal. We hope, however, to at least set a mark for ourselves and for others who will or already have started on the same route.

Second, Christian institutions must do more to help their faculties provide a thoroughly theistic education. A few schools are now establishing formal structures to accomplish that goal, but this is only a beginning. Here too, we hope that this book will offer some practical advice on how to be a Christian professor in each of the disciplines.

Two qualifications of this discussion should be mentioned here. It would, of course, be both pretentious and duplicative to include every discipline in the following chapters. We have tried to cover all the bases by grouping disciplines together where similar theoretical structures prevail. In other cases we have selected representative fields.

We also have tried to go beyond the traditional liberal arts and have included some of the professional fields that have become part of the contemporary mega-university. However, we have left out some of the more highly specialized—and expensive—areas such as law and medicine. Others will have to fill in the blanks.

The second qualification is that we are committed not only to biblical inerrancy, but also to the very concept that a Christian university is impossible without it. In several places we will argue only briefly for the latter point. The former is already the topic of many books and well beyond the parameters of this one.

Nevertheless, it is important to point out the difference that inerrancy makes for the whole topic of educational integration. Put simply, it is not enough to incorporate the sense of Scripture into the disciplines, that is, to put forth a Christian worldview. Inerrancy demands the full and equal incorporation of the data of Scripture: the propositions themselves.

In the remainder of this chapter, we need to set the stage for the specific discussions of the disciplines, first by summarizing the historical and philosophical context of the current Christian university and second by defining in the most general terms just what such an institution is.

The Current Setting

To understand what the Christian school is up against at the end of the twentieth century, we need a clear picture of the worldview that dominates current academic life in general, and especially how this worldview dictates the role of religion within education. This worldview is commonly referred to as naturalism. We can define its view of religion specifically as follows: "Religion" denotes our emotional need for security within a relativistic world. It is, therefore, nonrational, without relevance, and incapable of being true or false. As a result, it is different from, and must be radically separated from, the process of education that is concerned with knowledge.

Current Western society arrived at this view by the coincidence of a redefinition of religion spurred by theological developments in the nineteenth and early twentieth centuries on the one hand, and a redefinition of science initiated by philosophical developments moving into the current century on the other.

The Theological Scene

Although it was not without precedents, Kant's *Religion within the Limits of Reason Alone*[2] (1793) was a radically new construction of the concept of religion and dominated the theology of Europe and America during the nineteenth century. As liberalism developed, it completely internalized religion, locating its source in the autonomous choices of individuals and its content in a notion of religious experience.

Although some scholars have characterized liberalism as intellectual and elitist,[3] it clearly did have powerful effects on popular religious concepts and practice. One sees it clearly in the refocusing of evangelism from the demand of God to the desires of persons. Salvation is seen primarily as the conversion of the heart and less as divine justification. Church itself becomes more a matter of meeting human needs for fellowship and encouragement and less a matter of worship.

The real problem with liberalism, however, was its inability to provide any justification for either its method or its results. In

2. An excellent discussion of the background to Kant's work is found in Theodore Greene's "The Historical Context and Religious Significance of Kant's Religion" included in the Greene and Hort H. Hudson translation (New York: Harper and Row, 1960).

3. See, for example, Harvey Cox, *Religion in the Secular City* (New York: Simon and Schuster, 1984).

many ways William James's *The Varieties of Religious Experience*[4] marks the end of an attempt to find a science of religion.

Liberalism's replacement, neo-orthodoxy, seemed initially a return to objectivity. In fact, the long-term cultural result has been a total divorce of religion and rationality. Karl Barth's famous "no!" to natural theology has turned liberalism's failure to make religion an objective science into its complete dismissal from academic life. If liberalism made religion a distinct piece of the pie of knowledge, with a separate content and a unique process (religious experience), then neo-orthodoxy baked a whole new pie: the dimension of faith.

Ever since, not only theologians but also the entire academic community has been trying to find some function for religion outside of knowledge. Religious claims, including ethical pronouncements, do not express propositions, but rather encounters, feelings, beliefs, perhaps simply the determination to see one's world in a particular way.

As a result, academia is left wondering what religion has to do with education. The very word *God* has become unutterable in the process of science. Ethics may not intrude into politics (as in: "Personally I am opposed to . . . but I do not believe in legislating morality."). And divine activity has been banished from history entirely.

Theology itself has removed religion from the educational marketplace. It is not knowledge, but belief. It does not seek truth, but faith. It is not arrived at by argument, evidence, experiment, or proof, but by choice. It is hardly surprising, then, that our society in general has come to view religion as a matter of personal preference or even bias.

The Philosophical Setting

If theological developments have left academic culture with a view of religion as a totally separate domain from education, then philosophical directions in the twentieth century have rendered religion meaningless and irrational. Although it is true that until recently Anglo-American and European philosophy have gone their separate ways, the net result has been much the same.

In the earlier years of this century American and British philoso-

---

4. Delivered as the Gifford Lectures at Edinburgh and first published in 1902 by Longmans, Green and Company, New York.

phers largely succumbed to positivism. One of its clearest expressions can be found in A. J. Ayer's *Language, Truth, and Logic.*

> The principle of verification is supposed to furnish a criterion by which it can be determined whether or not a sentence is literally meaningful. A simple way to formulate it would be to say that a sentence had literal meaning if and only if the proposition it expressed was either analytic or empirically verifiable.[5]

> [I]t can not be significantly asserted that there is a nonempirical world of values, or that men have immortal souls, or that there is a transcendent God.[6]

By the fifties, several forms of language analysis replaced this view, both because it represented much too narrow a concept of language's functions and because the principle is self-contradictory. In respect to religion, much of the recent discussion has taken its cue from Ludwig Wittgenstein's concept of language as a toolbox in which there are many different tools, each with its own use.[7] One may not even be able to give any common definition to these many uses of language, much as one cannot for the word *game,* to use Wittgenstein's own example.

The task of the philosopher, then, is to identify the nature of the religious language game. Many earlier proposals, for example, that religious utterances are attempts to describe ethical commitments, were too simplistic and gave way to a more pluralistic view. Religion, perhaps, covers several different language games, which may or may not have anything in common, except that all of it is the language of the believer. That is, it is spoken out of a specific paradigm. But choices among paradigms are not matters of truth in much of current philosophical theory, and hence the believer's choice to speak of God cannot be said to be rational or objective in some universal sense.

This relativistic view of religion, which has been simmering within philosophy at least since W. O. Quine's works in the fifties,[8] finally caught fire in the more popularized work (at least within

---

5. Second ed. (New York: Dover, 1946), 5.
6. Ibid., 31.
7. See his *Philosophical Investigations,* trans. G. E. M. Anscombe (New York: Macmillan, 1953), especially §§10–19.
8. See, for example, the collection of essays in *From a Logical Point of View* (New York: Harper and Row, 1953).

the academic community) of Thomas Kuhn's *The Structure of Scientific Revolutions*,[9] Richard Rorty's *Philosophy and the Mirror of Nature*,[10] and others. It is now the dominating theory in most of the academic disciplines.

Religion, now, is simply a perspective, or, better, specific religious views are perspectives: ways of viewing one's world. One chooses it, or perhaps finds oneself already having it for pragmatic or sociological reasons, not by some fundamental analysis.

Revelation and Knowledge

A decade ago William Ringenberg had already noted that Christian colleges in decline have a tendency to define their Christianness in terms of carrying on a tradition and incorporating a Christian outlook or perspective.[11] This type of definition continues to dominate the current literature on the subject. Now there is clearly something to this. One characteristic of education that deserves the adjective *Christian* is surely that all that is taught is done so from a Christian perspective. But just how are we to define a Christian perspective or worldview?

We could, of course, resort to some form of sociological or historical explication. That, however, would fail to rationally justify its inclusion as knowledge, that is, as truth to be taught in the curriculum.

Some argue that a Christian worldview is rationally demonstrable on its own merits. I want to agree with this, but is seems totally insufficient. One can give arguments for God's existence, but how would one demonstrate that human beings are persons and valuable because they are in his image? One can argue for the reality of the past, but what premises imply the conclusion that history is the unfolding of an intentional and meaningful plan or that every event is under the sovereign dominion of God? Yet these latter items are absolutely essential to the complete understanding of psychology or history.

In fact, we cannot guarantee the content that identifies a Christian education apart from a knowably true revelation. That is, what gives a Christian institution its distinctiveness is the inclusion of the propositions of Scripture within the hard data of its instruc-

9. (Chicago: University of Chicago Press, 1962).
10. (Princeton: Princeton University Press, 1979).
11. "The Marks of a Christian College," *Christianity Today*, 2 Nov. 1979, 26.

tional content. But this inclusion is utterly unjustifiable apart from some argument, or evidence, or the provision of grounds for so doing.

It should be apparent, then, why the Christian college is in such difficult straits. Presenting any kind of rationale for its distinctiveness is impossible in the current setting. Academia has bought into a view of religion that makes any such enterprise out of bounds. Worst of all, this view has been aided by academic theology itself. It not only allows for but actually promotes the elimination of religion as truth from the academic marketplace. Religion remains only as an object for historical, sociological, and psychological examination.

Thus the Christian in each discipline is left to argue, not merely for the truth of specific biblical data, but for the very possibility of revelation being true at all. Here philosophers and theologians will have to bear the burden of providing an epistemology of revelation in general as well as an apologetic to substantiate the specific inclusion of scriptural data in course content. Without these instruments the very task of designing a Christian university is futile and illegitimate. With them we have to conclude that the very term *Christian university* is, in a sense, redundant. A university must be open to all truth, and if the revelation in Scripture is true then it must form part of the knowledge base of any university.

Defining a Christian University

To adequately describe the nature of a Christian university in a few pages is impossible. However, in order to provide a basic framework for the chapters to follow, it will be helpful to list a number of the essential characteristics. These distinctive qualities ground the Christian university in the past, direct the present, and provide a vision for the future.

The Effects of the Past

In a recent interview Carl Sagan, the self-proclaimed spokesman for American science, made the following distinction between religion and science:

> Despite sometimes similar goals, there is a major difference between science and religion: There are no sacred truths in science. . . . This is not the traditional approach in religion in which many assertions are never challenged.

At the very core of science and the core of religion there's a very similar objective, but their methods are very different.[12]

Sagan is right at least about this: If one defines the role of education as the advancement of knowledge free from religious preferences, then the university has no commitment to past absolutes, other than as historical curiosities. If, however, there are revelational data that must be included in the fund of knowledge, then a Christian university is tied to the past in several ways which will impact on how it does science and every other discipline.

Revelation Based

Education at a Christian university is based explicitly on divine revelation in Scripture.[13] This might seem obvious from the fact that a Christian university owes its existence to the Christian revelation. This fundamental dependence on its revelational basis must, nevertheless, not be overlooked.

In proclaiming that a Christian education is biblically based, we insist that the Word of God is normative in all disciplines. As such, it becomes the center around which all disciplines can and must be integrated. By this we do not mean that the Bible is used merely to inform the disciplines. This is certainly correct, but it is insufficient.

First of all, reducing biblical input to this meager level is unethical. It is unprofessional and improper to present materials without acknowledging the author or source. It is a form of stealing and blinds the student to the real means by which it was obtained. Likewise, the biblical data used by the Christian educator in any discipline must be carefully obtained and properly labeled.

Further, to reduce the Bible to a mere informant to the arts and sciences is to reject it as a revelation from God. It is to treat the Bible merely as a part of our culture or heritage, rather than as the revelation of God it claims to be and Christians accept it to be. The Bible is not only a cultural deposit, a part of our history, and a formative factor in a Judeo-Christian worldview. It is also absolutely critical truth that must be incorporated into our pursuit of knowledge. As such, it is not simply an influence; rather, it contributes essential data in every area of research.

12. *U. S. News and World Report,* 1 Dec. 1980, 62.
13. Much of the rest of this chapter is based on an earlier treatment of this topic that appeared as "What Is a Christian University" in Terry Miethe, *A Christian's Guide to Faith and Reason* (Minneapolis: Bethany, 1987).

Because the Bible is so crucial, it must be examined carefully in its own setting. Thus, it is imperative that the curriculum provide both the tools and the content of biblical studies. Students cannot learn how to apply biblical truth unless they know how to properly derive that truth from the Scriptures. For this same reason mathematics, logic, speech, grammar, research, and similar academic tools and skills should be studied and mastered on their own and not just applied in the pursuit of the various arts and sciences.

For example, a physicist will not know how to incorporate the Genesis use of "day" (*yom*) into his study of the origins of the universe unless this term is first understood in the biblical context and the ancient Hebrew language. And no one will have this knowledge unless part of the university faculty is dedicated entirely to biblical studies. Even baccalaureate students should be trained by biblical specialists in their field. Training in the Scriptures must never be viewed as merely passing a Bible course; rather, knowledge of Scripture is an authoritative basis for the acquisition of all other knowledge.

Doctrinally Correct

All the courses in a Christian university should be taught from a doctrinally correct point of view. This is not something that should be left simply to the theology or religion department. Because revealed data is true, no discipline can ignore it. The biblical revelation contains important truths concerning the origin and operation of the universe, the nature of human beings, the course of human history, and numerous other matters that bear on the various disciplines of a Christian university. Hence no area of study is spared and no department can relegate its obligation to speak with doctrinal correctness to some separate department of theological studies.

The event of creation, for example, is commonly regarded as a religious belief, a personal way of saying the universe has special order. Or it is claimed that *creation* is merely a religious term to describe how God used scientific evolution to accomplish his ends. This claim, however, is at odds with the descriptive nature of God's revelation about creation in Scripture. If indeed the Bible tells how God brought the first living things into existence, namely, by special historical act of creation, then this truth must radically transform all our thinking.

Once creation is taken as revealed fact, macro-evolutionary

models, which have been used to reinterpret virtually every discipline, must be rejected. This applies to social science models of human beings as stimulus/response organisms and to models of communication, including speech, literature, and writing, as the effects of social animals. And what is true of creation is also true of every item in Scripture. Once God has revealed a truth that impinges on his created order, it is our epistemic duty to include it in any discipline into which it intrudes.

Biblical data, then, are not an appendix to lectures. Each lecture, in whatever field, must be doctrinally correct. No teacher should end a course with "Now that we have looked at the facts, let me state my personal beliefs." Every department, not just the theology department, must teach doctrine. God's truth as historically revealed is normative for every area of research.

Philosophically Coherent

Education that is Christian must always be truth-conscious. It is not interested merely in what is current but in what is correct. Even though we recognize that our grasp on truth is less than ultimate, since God is truth, it cannot be any less absolute than he is.

God is a rational and coherent being. Thus, his truth is as rational and coherent as he is. If our ideas are incoherent, then they are faulty or incomplete. God is self-consistent, and his truth—which is all truth—must be as self-consistent as he is. God's created world reflects his orderly mind. This is what makes science and mathematics possible. The very concept of creation implies that there are descriptively accurate accounts of things. Mathematics and logic are not artificial constructs. Human reason and its linguistic expressions are not free-wheeling. The laws of science are not chance probabilities. Even the arts have an objective basis in reality. Beauty is not merely in the eye of the beholder. There is an order and unity in true beauty that reflects the order which God has imputed to his creation.

What is important here is that the faculty of a Christian university is committed to truth and to the consistency of that truth. Thus, when the results of a given discipline are placed in the larger body of knowledge, there must be rational coherence. No discipline is an island unto itself.

This view that all truth is consistent has far-reaching implications for our research and teaching. It means that when correct results are obtained in any two disciplines, they will always complement each other. This is not only true of biology and psychology, business and ethics, but also of Bible and geology. Conflicts between the data of revelation and the experiments of science have to be handled like apparent conflicts anywhere else in the university. This was one of the principal agendas in the early university and always must be. Such conflicts may not be dismissed as nonexistent because the data of revelation cannot, by definition, contradict any other data.

This, in turn, implies that a Christian university must always be characterized by a great deal of internal dialogue among disciplines. In this discussion the biblical studies department is an equal. But it is only an equal. Inerrancy implies that the biblical data are true, but not a superior truth that can avoid interaction. Truth is truth. The Bible does not contain all the data about human beings, and any theologian who thinks one can ignore the human and natural sciences in formulating a view of persons is not doing education.

On the other hand, one of the great destroyers of Christian institutions has been the attitude of some scientists that they must have the "academic freedom" to hold and to teach conclusions that contradict Scripture. They have, rather, an obligation to the truth to resolve the disagreement with divine revelation first. However, we should remember that the biblical interpreters have as often been proven wrong about their specific interpretations as have scientists about their experimental data.

Relation to the Present

A Christian university is not only rooted in the past but also related to the present. This is so in several important ways: ethically, spiritually, and ecclesiastically.

Ethical Integrity

Christian higher education is infused with a sense of ethical responsibility. Each member of the academic community, student as well as professor, is created in God's image. As such, they are free and morally accountable individuals. They will act freely on the basis of their knowledge; hence, they are responsible for what they do with what they learn. This ethical obligation may seem more obvious in "professional" courses, but it is just as important in the others. Courses in philosophy and psychology should discuss the possible ethical consequences of their ideas and actions as much as those in education or athletics. Law courses must place their concepts within the framework of moral responsibility.

No discipline exists in a moral vacuum. Both professor and student have a moral responsibility to find the truth as well as a moral responsibility with the truth. Not even science is excluded from the moral domain. With truth, no matter what area it is in, comes responsibility.

Spiritual Growth

Students have more than intellectual needs. They are also spiritual beings in need of spiritual growth. Hence, it is an essential obligation of a Christian university to help meet those needs. This can be accomplished in many ways, not the least of which is the spiritual model provided by a godly professor. The professor's prayer, use of Scripture, attitude, concern for student needs, and integrity of life should all contribute to the student's spiritual growth.

Beyond this, and more importantly, the very content of instruction must be spiritually uplifting. Every truth about ourselves and our universe is a reflection of God. Students need to know that to learn mathematics is to discover the very mind of God, that music communicates his creativity, that philosophy reveals God's rationality. For example, that two plus two equals four was a true description of how God's mind works before it was true of apples. In fact, that is why it is true of apples. Thus the description of God's mind itself is a mathematical truth, not a religious belief.

Church Relatedness

The Christian university exists to serve the Christian church and to help fulfill its ministry to the body of Christ and its mission to the world. It is unrealistic to expect this to be accomplished if students and faculty have no relation to the local church during their tenure in the university. Christian students at the university, no matter what their major or future vocation, are being trained to play effective roles within the church. To be sure, only some will be on the full-time staff of the church, but all the rest should be active lay leaders.

Vision for the Future

While recognizing its roots in the past and its obligation in the present, the Christian university must also lead into the future. This is accomplished in at least two ways: evangelistically and socially.

Evangelistic Outreach

Christ commissioned his followers to preach the gospel to the whole world. Since a Christian university is dedicated to training Christian leaders, it cannot escape its evangelistic obligation.[14] Of course, pastors and evangelists should be an important part of training in a Christian university. However, Jesus did not commission only the "clergy" to preach; he commanded all to make disciples (Matt. 28:18–19). Hence, in every course there must be a concerted effort to keep this sense of mission before the student.

Whether a doctor, lawyer, nurse, educator, scientist, artist, or athlete, we are all to communicate the gospel of Christ. Any education that fails to inspire students to take Christ to the world has failed to be Christian in one of its most important senses. A faculty that fails to model this desire to reach the world with the gospel of Christ has likewise failed to fulfill its Christian duty.

World Consciousness

God's concern is not only with building up the church but also with helping a world in need. Jesus spent much of his earthly ministry simply helping the needy. The church is to be light and salt to the world (Matt. 5:13–14). We are to "do good to all men" (Gal. 6:10 NASB). As such, our duty is not only spiritual but also social. We minister not simply to "souls" but to whole persons. We cannot expect the starving to listen to us speak about the Bread of Life. They need to be fed as well. Education at a Christian university, then, should inspire young men and women to become socially involved. This involvement needs to be concerned with meeting immediate needs as well as developing a long-term vision of preserving and creating those cultural conditions that conform to divine principles, thus allowing persons to live well and to be free to carry out the Great Commission.

---

14. A good discussion of this point is found in Ringenberg, *Christian College*, 28.

There is a pressing need for academically qualified professors who can integrate their subjects within a biblically based Christian worldview. But what is needed to make a university truly Christian is more than a Christian faculty and constituency. The greatest need is for a faculty and a student body committed to pursuing education, in whatever field, in accord with divine revelation. The data of Scripture must be incorporated into every discipline. Only an unashamed commitment to the absolute truth of that data can make a university truly Christian.

1   Biblical Studies

Norman L. Geisler

The Bible, the only divinely authorized source of written information we have, is basic to a Christian university. No discipline in the arts or sciences can operate independently of what the Bible teaches. However, much truth is not to be found in the Bible. Rather, God has chosen to disclose it in his general revelation. In this way the arts and sciences both complement the content of Scripture and are complemented by it. Thus, the relationship between God's special revelation in Scripture and his general revelation in nature, human beings, history, and the arts are of special concern for a Christian university.

Why the Arts and Sciences Depend on the Bible

The Bible is the written Word of God. As such it is absolutely unique and definitive for anyone in pursuit of truth, no matter what the discipline. God, of course, is the source of truth, and he has infallibly revealed truth in the Holy Scriptures.

The Biblical Claim for Inspiration

The Bible is the inspired Word of God and, as such, it is the last word on all the topics it covers, including the arts and sciences. Several important claims are implied by the term *inspiration of Scripture*.

The Bible Is Verbally Inspired

The Bible is a written revelation, not simply a record of revelation, as 2 Timothy 3:16 plainly affirms. Other texts are equally clear: "Moses then wrote down everything the LORD had said" (Exod. 24:4). Isaiah was instructed, "Take a large scroll and write" (Isa. 8:1) and "inscribe it on a scroll, that for the days to come it may be an everlasting witness" (Isa. 30:8). More than ninety times the New Testament introduces an authoritative citation of the Old Testament by the phrase *it is written*.

Jesus insisted that not even the smallest part of a Hebrew word or letter could be broken (Matt. 5:18). Paul testified that he spoke in "words taught by the Spirit" (1 Cor. 2:13). The New Testament constantly equates the Word of God with the Scripture (writings) of the Old Testament (see Matt. 21:42; Rom. 15:4; 2 Pet. 3:16). God exhorted the prophet: "Do not omit a word" (Jer. 26:2), and John pronounced anathema on all who would add to or subtract from the "words of the prophecy of this book" (Rev. 22:18–19). Often, the biblical author's words are identified with God's words, giving rise to the expression "What Scripture says, God says."[1]

The Bible Is Infallible

Inspiration also implies unbreakability, or infallibility. Jesus affirmed that the "Scripture cannot be broken" (John 10:35). Inspired writings are also irrevocable, as Jesus stated: "I tell you the truth, until heaven and earth disappear, not the smallest letter, not the least stroke of the pen, will by any means disappear from the Law until everything is accomplished" (Matt. 5:18; see also Luke 16:17). Scripture also has final authority, being the last word on all it treats. Jesus employed the Bible to resist the tempter (Matt. 4:4, 7, 10), to settle doctrinal disputes (Matt. 21:42), and to vindicate his authority (Mark 11:17). Sometimes a biblical teaching rests on a small historical detail (Heb. 7:4–10), a word or phrase (Acts

---

1. Sometimes the Old Testament gives what the human author said, and the New Testament quotes it as what God said (e.g., Gen. 2:24 and Matt. 19:4–5), showing that what God and the human author of Scripture said is interchangeable.

15:13–17), or even the difference between the singular and the plural (Gal. 3:16).

The Bible is also inerrant, that is, wholly true and without error. Jesus declared, "Your word is truth" (John 17:17). To those who denied the truth of Scripture he responded, "You are in error because you do not know the Scriptures" (Matt. 22:29). The psalmist said, "The law of the LORD is perfect," and, "All your words are true" (Pss. 19:7; 119:160). The Bible is God's Word, and God cannot err (Titus 1:2; Heb. 6:18). Scriptures are the utterances of the Holy Spirit (2 Tim. 3:16), and the Spirit of Truth cannot err.

The Extent of Inspiration

When we speak of the inspiration of all of Scripture we mean both Old and New Testaments. By the Old Testament we mean the thirty-nine books of the Jewish Bible.[2]

The Claim for Inspiration of the Old Testament

The whole Old Testament is a prophetic book (Heb. 1:1; 2 Pet. 1:20–21), and a prophet was the mouthpiece of divine utterance. For example, the Lord said to Moses, "See, I have made you like God to Pharaoh, and your brother Aaron will be your prophet" (Exod. 7:1). In Deuteronomy 18:18 God describes a prophet in these words: "I will put my words in his mouth, and he will tell them everything I command him." Moses was told, "Do not add to what I command you and do not subtract from it" (Deut. 4:2). The prophets demanded obedience to their message as to God himself (see Isa. 8:5; Jer. 3:6; Ezek. 21:1; Amos 3:1).[3] Moreover, the prophet was one who felt, as Amos, "The Sovereign LORD has spoken—who can but prophesy?" (3:8) or even as Balaam, who said, "I could not do anything great or small to go beyond the command of the LORD my God" (Num. 22:18).

2. The Protestant Old Testament and the Jewish Bible are identical but the books are numbered differently. The Roman Catholic Church added eleven books (seven full books listed in the table of contents and four portions added to other books) to the Jewish Bible in 1546. But this was unjustified, since these books do not claim to be inspired and were never accepted by Judaism as inspired. Jesus and the apostles never cited them as authoritative, the great Roman Catholic scholar Jerome rejected them, and they contain false doctrine, such as prayer for the dead (2 Macc. 12:45 [46]).

3. The prophets were the voice of God not only in what they said but in what they wrote as well. Moses was commanded, "Write down these words" (Exod. 34:27). The Lord ordered Jeremiah to "take again another scroll and write on it all the former words that were on the first scroll" (Jer. 36:28). Isaiah testified that the Lord said to him: "Take for yourself a large tablet and write on it" (Isa. 8:1; see also Hab. 2:2).

Further, the whole Old Testament is a prophetic message, as the prophets confirm by the oft-repeated "thus saith the Lord" or "God said." In addition, the entire Old Testament is described by the phrase *Law and Prophets*.[4] Moses, who wrote the Law, was also a prophet (Deut. 34:10). And, as Jesus said, the Law and Prophets are "all the Scriptures" up to the time of Christ (Matt. 5:17; Luke 16:31; 24:27). Thus it follows that the whole Old Testament is a prophetic writing.[5] Finally, the New Testament declares the entire Old Testament is a prophetic writing (Heb. 1:1; 2 Pet. 1:20–21); since all prophetic writing comes from God, then it follows that the whole Old Testament is the Word of God. Indeed, the Old Testament is called "the Word of God." Jesus called the Jewish Scriptures the "Word of God," adding that the Scriptures "cannot be broken" (John 10:35). He also excoriated the Pharisees: "Thus you nullify the word of God for the sake of your tradition" (Matt. 15:6).

The Claim for the Inspiration of the New Testament

The New Testament claims the Old Testament is inspired (2 Tim. 3:15–16). Likewise, Peter called Paul's epistles "Scriptures" when he wrote, "Our beloved brother Paul . . . wrote to you . . . as also in all his letters . . . which the untaught and unstable distort, as they do also the rest of the Scriptures" (2 Pet. 3:15–16 NASB). Further, in 1 Timothy 5:18 the apostle Paul quoted from Luke, placing Luke's Gospel on the same level with the rest of Scripture by using the introduction "for the Scripture says" (with reference to Luke 10:7). In brief, "all Scripture" is inspired (2 Tim. 3:16 NASB), the New Testament along with the Old Testament.

In addition, the New Testament is a prophetic writing. According to 2 Peter 1:20–21, prophetic utterances (or writings) come only by the moving of the Holy Spirit. Because the New Testament writings are pronounced "prophetic writings," they too must be included within the group of Spirit-moved utterances. Jesus promised to give his disciples a Spirit-directed ministry (John 14:26; 16:13), and

---

4. Even in the latter part of Old Testament times this designation referred to the entire canon of Scripture in existence (see Dan. 9:2, 13; Zech. 7:7, 12; Neh. 9:30). The same is true in the intertestamental literature (cf. 2 Macc. 15:9) and in the Qumran writings (1.3; 8.15; 9.11).

5. Of course, not every Old Testament author was a prophet by office, but each was a prophet by function. That is, each one who wrote was the instrument through which God spoke. Likewise, not everyone who wrote a book in the Bible was conscious that God was so using him when he wrote. Even Balaam's donkey and the unbelieving Jewish high priest Caiaphas were unwitting instruments through which God spoke.

the New Testament church claimed the prophetic gift (Acts 11:28; 1 Cor. 14:31–32; Eph. 4:11). Paul considered his writings to be prophetic (Eph. 3:3–5). He told the Corinthians his words were "taught by the Spirit" (1 Cor. 2:13) and were the "Lord's command" (1 Cor. 14:37).[6] John is classified with his "brethren the [Old Testament] prophets" (Rev. 22:9). John wrote, "I warn every-one who hears the words of the prophecy of this book: If anyone adds anything to them, God will add to him the plagues described in this book" (Rev. 22:18). In short, all prophetic writings are inspired (2 Pet. 1:20–21). The New Testament is a prophetic writing (Rev. 22:18; Eph. 3:5). Therefore, the New Testament is also the inspired Word of God. Indeed, the New Testament writers pro-claimed their writings as the Word of God. If the Word of God is inspired, then the New Testament is also the inspired Word of God.

The Scope of Inspiration

Some people suggest that Scripture can be trusted on moral mat-ters but not on historical matters. Or they trust the Bible as an authority in the spiritual domain, but not in the sphere of science. If true, this viewpoint would render the Bible ineffective as a divine authority for the various disciplines in the Christian univer-sity. Therefore, this position demands careful scrutiny.

First of all, a close examination of Scripture reveals that the sci-entific (empirical) and spiritual truths of Scripture are often insepa-rable. For example, one cannot separate the spiritual truth of Christ's resurrection from the fact that his body permanently vacated the tomb and later physically appeared (Matt. 28:6; 1 Cor. 15:13–19). Likewise, if Jesus was not born of a biological virgin, then he is no different from the rest of the human race, on whom the stigma of Adam's sin rests (Rom. 5:12). In the same way the death of Christ for our sins cannot be detached from his shedding literal blood on the cross, for "without shedding of blood there is no forgiveness" (Heb. 9:22). Adam's existence and fall cannot be a myth for if there were no literal Adam and an actual fall, then the spiritual teachings about inherited sin and eventual or physical death (Rom. 5:12) are wrong. Historical reality and theological doc-trine stand or fall together.

Furthermore, moral truths of Scripture are often based on or are inseparably connected with actual events. The depravity of man

6. See also 2 Cor. 4:2; Heb. 4:12; Rev. 1:2.

and his consequent physical death are based on the truth of a literal Adam (Rom. 5:12). The doctrine of the incarnation is inseparable from the historical truth about Jesus of Nazareth (John 1:1, 14). Jesus' moral teaching about marriage was based on his teaching about God's joining a literal Adam and Eve together in marriage (Matt. 19:4–5). In each of these cases the moral or theological teaching is devoid of its meaning apart from the historical or factual event. If one denies that the literal event occurred, then there is no basis for believing the scriptural doctrine built upon it.

Jesus often directly compared Old Testament events with important spiritual truths, such as his death and resurrection to Jonah and the great fish (Matt. 12:40) or his second coming to the days of Noah (Matt. 24:37–39). Both the occasion and the manner of the comparisons make it clear that Jesus was affirming the historicity of those Old Testament events. Indeed, Jesus asserted to Nicodemus, "If I told you earthly things and you do not believe, how shall you believe if I tell you heavenly things?" (John 3:12). In short, if the Bible does not speak truthfully about the physical world, it cannot be trusted when it speaks about the spiritual world. The two are intimately related.

Inspiration includes not only all the Bible explicitly teaches but also everything the Bible touches. This is true whether the Bible is touching upon history, science, or mathematics.Whatever the Bible declares is true, whether it is a major point or a minor point. The Bible is God's Word, and God does not deviate from the truth. All the parts are as true as the whole that they constitute.

The Character of Inspiration

As already noted, the inspiration of Scripture includes its inerrancy, for the Bible is the Word of God, and God cannot err (Titus 1:2; Heb. 6:18). To deny the inerrancy of Scripture is to impugn either the integrity of God or the identity of the Bible as the Word of God. This argument may be stated as follows:

> The Bible is the Word of God.
> God cannot err (Titus 1:2; Heb. 6:18).
> Therefore, the Bible cannot err.

Defining Inerrancy

By the inerrancy of Scripture we mean that the Bible is wholly true and without error. Thus we must specify more clearly what is

meant by "truth" and what would constitute an "error."[7] By *truth*
we signify that which corresponds to reality. An error, then, is
what does not correspond to reality. Hence, nothing mistaken can
be true, even if the author intended his mistake to be true. An
error is a mistake, not simply something that is misleading.
Otherwise, every sincere utterance ever made is true, even one
that is grossly mistaken.[8] Likewise, something is not true simply
because it accomplishes its intended purpose.

The Bible clearly perceives truth as corresponding to reality.
Error is understood as that which does not correspond to reality,
not as intentionally misleading. This is evident from the fact that
the word *error* is used of unintentional mistakes (Lev. 4:2). The
Bible implies that truth has its basis in reality. For example, when
the Ten Commandments declare, "You shall not bear false witness
. . ." (Exod. 20:16), they imply that misrepresenting the facts is
wrong. Likewise, this same view of truth is used when Tertullus
said to Felix, "By examining him [Paul] yourself you will be able to
learn the truth about all these charges we are bringing against him"
(Acts 24:8).

Misunderstandings of Inerrancy

What the Bible says about itself is manifest by what the Bible
shows in itself. That is, the doctrine of Scripture must be understood in light of the data of Scripture. This is called the "phenomena" of Scripture. No definition of inerrancy is complete unless it
includes both the declarations and these manifestations. When
both are considered, they reveal what is meant by inspiration.

The Bible is not verbally dictated. With the exception of small sec-
tions like the Ten Commandments, which were "written by the finger of God" (Exod. 31:18), the Bible is not verbally dictated.[9] The
writers were not secretaries of the Holy Spirit. They were com-
posers employing their own literary styles and idiosyncrasies. These
human authors sometimes used human sources for their material
(Josh. 10:13; Acts 17:28; 1 Cor. 15:33; Titus 1:12). In fact, all the
books in the Bible were compositions of human writers (nearly

---

7. For further consideration of this see my discussion in "The Concept of Truth in the
Inerrancy Debate," *Bibliotheca Sacra* 137, n. 548 (October–December 1980): 327–39.

8. This is the mistake of G. C. Berkouwer, *Holy Scripture* (Grand Rapids: Eerdmans,
1975) and Jack Rogers, ed., *Biblical Authority* (Waco: Word, 1978). By defining error as
what misleads, rather than what is mistaken, they make all sincere errors unfalsifiable.

9. For a proponent of the verbal dictation view of Scripture, see John R. Rice, *Our God-
Breathed Book—The Bible* (Murfreesboro, Tenn.: Sword of the Lord, 1969).

forty in all). The Bible also manifests different human literary styles, from the mournful meter of Lamentations to the exalted poetry of Isaiah, from the simple grammar of John to the complex Greek of the Book of Hebrews. Scripture also manifests human perspectives: David spoke in Psalm 23 from a shepherd's perspective; Kings is written from a prophetic vantage point, and Chronicles from a priestly point of view; Acts manifests a historical interest and 2 Timothy a pastor's heart. Writers speak from an observer's standpoint when they write of the sun rising or setting (Josh. 1:15). They also reveal human thought patterns, including memory lapses (1 Cor. 1:14–16) and emotions (Gal. 4:14). The Bible also discloses specific human interests. For example, Hosea possessed a rural interest, Luke a medical concern, and James a love of nature.[10]

The Bible does not approve of all it records. The whole Bible is true (John 17:17), but it records some lies (e.g., Satan's [Gen. 3:4; cf. John 8:44] and Rahab's [Josh. 2:4]). Inspiration encompasses the Bible fully and completely in the sense that it records accurately and truthfully even the lies and errors of sinful beings. The truth of Scripture is found in what the Bible reveals, not in everything it records. Unless this distinction is held, it may be incorrectly concluded that the Bible teaches immorality because it narrates David's sin (2 Sam. 11:4), that it promotes polygamy because it records Solomon's (1 Kings 11:3), or that it affirms atheism because it quotes the fool as saying "there is no God" (Ps. 14:1).

The Bible incorporates diverse perspectives. Occasionally the Bible expresses the same thing in different ways, or at least from different viewpoints, at different times. Hence, inspiration does not exclude a diversity of expression. The four Gospels relate the same story in different ways to different groups of people and sometimes even quote the same sayings with different words. Compare, for example, Peter's famous confession in the three synoptic Gospels:

Matthew records it: "You are the Christ, the Son of the living God" (Matt. 16:16).

10. The biblical authors include a lawgiver (Moses), a general (Joshua), prophets (Samuel, Isaiah, et al.), kings (David and Solomon), a musician (Asaph), a herdsman (Amos), a prince and statesman (Daniel), a priest (Ezra), a tax collector (Matthew), a physician (Luke), a scholar (Paul), and fishermen (Peter and John). With such a variety of occupations represented among biblical writers, it is only natural that their personal interests and differences should be reflected in their writings.

Mark records it: "You are the Christ" (Mark 8:29).

Luke records it: "The Christ of God" (Luke 9:20).

Even the Decalogue, "written by the finger of God" (Deut. 9:10), is stated with variations the second time God gave it (cf. Exod. 20:8–11 with Deut. 5:12–15). There are many variations between the books of Kings and Chronicles in their description of identical events, yet they harbor no contradiction in the events they narrate. If such important utterances can be stated in different ways, then there is no problem in extending to the rest of Scripture a diversity of expression within the concept of a verbal inspiration.

The Bible employs nontechnical language. Inspiration certainly does not necessitate the use of scholarly, technical, or so-called scientific language. The Bible is written for the common people of every generation, and it therefore uses their common, everyday language. The use of observational, nonscientific language is not unscientific, it is merely prescientific. The Scriptures were written in ancient times by ancient standards, and it would be anachronistic to superimpose modern scientific standards upon them. However, it is no more unscientific to speak of the sun standing still (Josh. 10:12) than to refer to the sun rising (Josh. 1:15). Contemporary meteorologists still speak daily of the time of "sunrise" and "sunset."

The Bible utilizes round numbers. Like most ordinary speech the Bible uses round numbers. For example, it refers to diameter as being about one-third of the circumference of something (2 Chron. 4:2). It may be imprecise from the standpoint of a contemporary technological society to speak of 3.14159265 as three, but it is not incorrect for an ancient nontechnological people. Round numbers are sufficient to describe a "cast metal sea" (2 Chron. 4:2) in an ancient Hebrew temple, even though they would not suffice for a computer in a modern rocket. But one should not expect scientific precision in a prescientific age.

The Bible makes use of literary devices. Finally, an "inspired" book need not be composed in one, and only one, literary style. Man is not limited in his modes of expression, and there is no reason to suppose that God can utilize only one style or literary genre in his communication to man. Several whole books are written in poetic style (e.g., Job, Psalms, Proverbs). The synoptic Gospels are filled with parables. In Galatians 4, Paul utilizes an allegory. The New

Testament abounds with metaphors (e.g., 2 Cor. 3:2–3; James 3:6) and similes (e.g., Matt. 20:1; James 1:6); hyperboles may also be found (e.g., Col. 1:23; John 21:25; 2 Cor. 3:2). And Jesus himself employed satire (cf. Matt. 19:24 with 23:24).

Errors exist in copies. God uttered the original text of Scripture, and God's words are inerrant. Thus, as Augustine noted, "If we are perplexed by any apparent contradiction in Scripture, it is not allowable to say, The author of this book is mistaken; but either the manuscript is faulty, or the translation is wrong, or you have not understood."[11] To be sure, discrepancies are present in Scripture, but not errors.[12] However, while present copies of Scripture are good, they are not without error. For example, 2 Kings 8:26 gives the age of King Ahaziah as twenty-two, whereas 2 Chronicles 22:2 gives forty-two. The latter number cannot be correct, or he would have been older than his father. This is obviously a copyist's error, but it does not alter the inerrancy of the original.

Defending Inerrancy

As God's Word, the originals cannot err.[13] However, some object to the inerrancy of Scripture because, as the poet put it, "To err is human." While the Bible is truly a human book, it does not follow that it errs, for even humans can write some books without errors. Furthermore, while mere humans usually err, the Bible is not a mere human book. It is also inspired by God. If the Bible had to err because it is human, then Jesus would have had to err (and sin) because he is completely human.

Take the following form of faulty reasoning: Humans err, and Jesus was human. Therefore Jesus erred. Or, Jesus was human, and humans sin. Hence, Jesus sinned. It is evident that Jesus did not have to sin because he was human and equally clear that the Bible does not have to err because it is a human book. Just as Jesus was truly human yet without error, even so the Bible is truly human yet without error. Jesus is both God and man, yet without sin (Heb. 4:15), and the Bible is both a Divine and human writing, yet without error.

11. Saint Augustine *Reply to Faustus the Manichaean* 11.5 in Philip Schaff, *A Select Library of the Nicene and Ante-Nicene Fathers of the Christian Church* (Grand Rapids: Eerdmans, 1956), vol. 4.

12. For a complete treatment of all the alleged errors and contradictions in Scripture, see Gleason L. Archer, Jr., *The Encyclopedia of Bible Difficulties* (Grand Rapids: Zondervan, 1982).

13. For a more complete defense of the inerrancy of Scripture see *Inerrancy*, ed. Norman L. Geisler (Grand Rapids: Zondervan, 1982).

So the Christian educator is in possession of an inspired and infallible book that expresses itself without error whenever it touches upon the arts or sciences. Thus, the Bible is the indispensable final authority for all that we think and teach. It is God's Word, and God has the last word on every topic he addresses.

Why Biblical Studies Depend on the Arts and Sciences

The Bible does not make pronouncements on every topic. For in addition to the Bible, God has revealed himself outside the Bible in nature (Rom. 1–2), in history (Dan. 2, 7), and in human beings made in his image (Gen. 1:27). This is called general revelation and is very important for understanding what a Christian university does.

The Nature and Scope of General Revelation

God's general revelation is manifest in several areas, including nature, history, humans, art, and music.[14] In each case God has disclosed something specific about himself and his relation to his creation.

God's Revelation in Nature

The psalmist wrote, "The heavens declare the glory of God; / the skies proclaim the work of his hands" (Ps. 19:1). Indeed, "The heavens proclaim his righteousness, / and all the peoples see his glory" (Ps. 97:6). Job added,

> "Ask the animals, and they will teach you
>   or the birds of the air, and they will tell you;
> or speak to the earth, and it will teach you,
>   or let the fish of the sea inform you.
> Which of all these does not know
>   that the hand of the LORD has done this?" [Job 12:7–9]

Paul introduced to the pagans at Lystra "the living God, who made heaven and earth and sea and everything in them. In the past, he let all nations go their own way. Yet he has not left himself without testimony: He has shown kindness by giving you rain from heaven and crops in their seasons; he provides you with plenty of food and fills your hearts with joy" (Acts 14:15–17). And he

---

14. The most comprehensive recent book on general revelation is that by Bruce A. Demerest, *General Revelation: Historical Views and Contemporary Issues* (Grand Rapids: Zondervan, 1982).

reminded the Greek philosophers that "the God who made the world and everything in it is the Lord of heaven and earth and does not live in temples built by hands. And he is not served by human hands, as if he needed anything, because he himself gives all men life and breath and everything else" (Acts 17:24–25).

Paul informed the Romans that even the heathen stand guilty before God, "since what may be known about God is plain to them, because God has made it plain to them. For since the creation of the world God's invisible qualities—his eternal power and divine nature—have been clearly seen, being understood from what has been made, so that men are without excuse" (Rom. 1:18–20). Little wonder the psalmist concluded, "The fool says in his heart, / 'There is no God'" (Ps. 14:1).

God is revealed in nature in two basic ways: as Creator and as Sustainer. He is both the cause of the origin as well as the operation of the universe. Note the following verses, parts of which I have emphasized: "By him all things *were created*" and "in him all things *hold together*" (Col. 1:16–17); God "*made* the universe" and he also *sustains* "all things by his powerful word" (Heb. 1:2–3); he "*created* all things" and by him all things "*have their being*" (Rev. 4:11). So God can be seen not only in the universe coming to be but also in its continuing to be. The psalmist saw this latter function when he wrote of God:

> He makes springs pour water into the ravines; . . .
> He makes grass grow for the cattle,
>   and plants for man to cultivate—
>   bringing forth food from the earth. . . . [Ps. 104:10, 14][15]

God's Disclosure in Human Nature

God created human beings in his image and likeness (Gen. 1:27). Hence, something about God can be learned from studying human beings (Ps. 8). Humans are so much like God that it is wrong to murder them (Gen. 9:6) and even to curse them (James 3:9–10). Even the redeemed are "renewed in knowledge in the image of . . . [their] Creator" (Col. 3:10). Paul insisted that God created "so that men would seek him and perhaps reach out for him and find him, though he is not far from each one of us. 'For in him

---

15. I have elaborated this point more fully in *Knowing the Truth about Creation*, ed. J. I. Packer and Peter Kreeft (Ann Arbor, Mich.: Servant, 1989).

we live and move and have our being.' As some of your own poets have said, 'We are his offspring.'" He adds, "Therefore since we are God's offspring, we should not think that the divine being is like gold or silver or stone—an image made by man's design and skill" (Acts 17:26–29). So by looking at the creature we can learn something about the Creator. For

> Does he who implanted the ear not hear?
>   Does he who formed the eye not see?
> Does he who disciplines nations not punish?
>   Does he who teaches man lack knowledge? [Ps. 94:9–10]

Even Christ in the flesh is said to be an image of the invisible God (John 1:14; Heb. 1:3).

God is manifested not only in the intellectual nature of human beings but also in their moral nature. God's moral law is written in human hearts. For "when Gentiles, who do not have the law, do by nature things required by the law, they are a law for themselves, even though they do not have the law, . . . their consciences also bearing witness . . ." (Rom. 2:12–15). Moral responsibility involves the ability to respond, or free choice. Being a free moral creature is also part of the image of God (Gen. 1:27; see also Gen. 2:16–17).

God's Revelation in Human History

History has been called the "footprints" of God in the sands of time. Paul declared about the nations that God "determined the times set for them and the exact places where they should live" (Acts 17:26). It was revealed to Daniel that "the Most High is sovereign over the kingdoms of men and gives them to anyone he wishes and sets over them the lowliest of men" (Dan. 4:17). In fact, God disclosed to Daniel that all of human history is moving toward the ultimate goal of God's kingdom on earth (Dan. 2, 7). So history is literally his-story. Thus, a proper study of history informs us about the plan and purpose of God.

God's Revelation in Art

God is beautiful and so is his creation. The psalmist declared: "O LORD, our Lord, / how majestic is your name in all the earth!" (Ps. 8:1).

Isaiah witnessed a spectacular display of God's beauty when he "saw the LORD seated on a throne, high and exalted, and the train of his robe filled the temple" (Isa. 6:1). Scripture exhorts us to "worship the LORD in the splendor of his holiness" (Ps. 29:2; see also Ps. 27:4).

God has also made everything in his world "beautiful in its time" (Eccles. 3:11). He speaks of his city of Zion as "perfect in beauty" (Ps. 50:2). Indeed, what God created is good like himself (Gen. 1:31; 1 Tim. 4:4). And God's goodness is beautiful. Hence, insofar as creation reflects God, it too is beautiful. God not only is beautiful and made a beautiful world, but also has created beings who can appreciate beauty and, like him, make beautiful things. Human beings are, as it were, "sub-creators." In fact, God endows certain humans with special creative gifts.

God's Revelation in Music

God loves music. He orchestrated the angelic choir at creation when "the morning stars sang together and all the angels shouted for joy" (Job 38:7). Angels chant the tersanctus continually in his presence, "Holy, holy, holy" (Isa. 6:3). Moreover, angels gather around the throne in heaven and "in a loud voice they sing: 'Worthy is the Lamb, who was slain . . .'" (Rev. 5:12).

Miriam led the triumphant Israelites in singing after God delivered them through the Red Sea (Exod. 15). David set up a choir for the temple and wrote many songs (psalms) to be sung in it. Paul admonished the church to "speak to one another with psalms, hymns and spiritual songs. Sing and make music in your heart to the Lord" (Eph. 5:19).

The human voice is not the only God-ordained instrument of music. The Jewish high priest entered within the holy of holiest with bells on his garment. The psalmist exhorted us to praise God with trumpet, harp, lyre, tambourine, and cymbals (Ps. 150:3–5). In heaven the angels play trumpets (Rev. 8:2) and others on harp-like instruments (Rev. 14:2). So music is a gift of God. Like the rest of his creation, it is a manifestation of his glory.

The Relationship of General and Special Revelation

God's general revelation in nature, man, history, art, and music offers vast opportunities for continual exploration, and it is here that the Christian university plays a unique role. To appreciate this role, we must spell out the relationship between general and special revelation (see table 1.1).

Table 1.1
Relationship between Special and General Revelation

Special Revelation	General Revelation
God as Redeemer	God as Creator
Norm for Church	Norm for Society
Means of Salvation	Means of Condemnation

The Role of Special Revelation

Special revelation contributed uniquely to Christian education. The Bible alone is infallible and inerrant. Further, the Bible is the only source both of God's revelation as Redeemer and of his plan of salvation. Thus Scripture is normative for all believers.

The Bible alone is infallible and inerrant. The Bible is normative for all Christian thought. It is a revelation of Christ (Matt. 5:17; Luke 24:27, 44; John 5:39; Heb. 10:7). The task of the Christian university, then, is "to take captive every thought to make it obedient to Christ" (2 Cor. 10:5) as revealed in Scripture. We must think as well as live Christocentrically (Gal. 2:20; Phil. 1:21).

The Bible alone reveals God as Redeemer. While general revelation manifests God as Creator, it does not reveal him as Redeemer. The universe speaks of God's greatness (Ps. 8:1; Isa. 40:12–17), but only special revelation reveals his redeeming grace (John 1:14). The heavens declare the glory of God (Ps. 19:1), but only Christ declared God's salvation (Titus 2:11–13).

The Bible alone has the message of Salvation. In view of God's general revelation all men are "without excuse" (Rom. 1:20). "All who sin apart from the [written] law will also perish apart from the law . . ." (Rom. 2:12). General revelation is sufficient grounds for man's condemnation. However, it is not sufficient for salvation. One can learn about the heavens by studying general revelation, but one cannot discover from that experience how to go to heaven. For "there is no other name under heaven [except Christ's] given to men by which we must be saved" (Acts 4:12). To be saved, a person must confess that "Jesus is Lord" and believe in his heart "that God raised him from the dead" (Rom. 10:9). People cannot call upon someone they have not heard of, "and how can they hear without someone preaching to them" (Rom. 10:14)? Thus, preach-

ing the gospel in all the world is the Christian's Great Commission
(Matt. 28:18–20).

The Bible is the norm for believers. Without the truth of Scripture
there would be no church, for the church is "built on the foundation of the apostles and prophets . . ." (Eph. 2:20). The revealed
Word of God is the norm for faith and practice. Paul said "all
Scripture is God-breathed and is useful for teaching, training,
rebuking, correcting and training in righteousness . . ." (2 Tim.
3:16). However, not all unbelievers have access to a Bible.
Nonetheless, God holds them responsible under his general revelation. For "all who sin apart from the [written] law will also perish
apart from the law," since they show that the requirements of the
law are written on their hearts (Rom. 2:12, 14).

The Role of General Revelation

While the Bible is all true, God has not revealed all truth in the
Bible. Whereas the Bible is only truth, some truth lies outside the
Bible. All truth is God's truth, not all God's truth is in the Bible.
General revelation, then, plays an important role in God's plan,
and as such it has several unique roles.

General revelation is broader than special revelation. General revelation encompasses much more than special revelation. Most of the
truths of science, history, mathematics, and the arts are not in the
Bible. The bulk of truth in all these areas is found only in God's
general revelation. While the Bible is everywhere scientifically
accurate, it is not a textbook on science. The mandate for doing
science is not a redemption mandate; it is a creation mandate.
Right after God created Adam he commanded him to "fill the
earth and subdue it" (Gen. 1:28). Likewise, there are no mathematical errors in God's inerrant Word, but then again there is very
little geometry or algebra and no calculus in it either. Similarly,
the Bible records accurately much of the history of Israel, but has
little on the history of the world, except as it bears on Israel. The
same is true of every area of the arts and sciences. Whenever the
Bible speaks in these areas, it speaks authoritatively, but God has
largely left the discoveries of his truths in these areas to a study of
general revelation.

General revelation is essential to human thought. God is a rational
being, and man is made in his image (Gen. 1:27). Just as God
thinks rationally, even so man was given the same capacity. Brute

beasts, by contrast, are called unreasoning (Jude 10). Indeed, the highest use of human reason is to love the Lord with "all your mind . . ." (Matt. 22:37).

The basic laws of human reason are common to believer and unbeliever. Without them no writing, thinking, or rational inferences would be possible. But nowhere are these laws of thought spelled out in the Bible. Rather, they are part of God's general revelation and the special field of philosophers.

General revelation is essential to government. God has ordained that believers live by his written Law, but he has written his law in the hearts of unbelievers (Rom. 2:12–15). Divine law in Scripture is the norm for Christians, but natural law is binding on all men. Nowhere in Scripture does God judge the nations either by the law of Moses he gave to Israel (Exod. 19–20) or by the law of Christ he enjoins on Christians. To think otherwise is the central error of theonomists.[16] The law of Moses, for example, was not given to the Gentiles. Paul said clearly, "the Gentiles who do not have the law" (Rom. 2:14). The psalmist said, "He has revealed his word to Jacob, his laws and decrees to Israel. He has done this for no other nation; they do not know his laws" (Ps. 147:19–20).[17] That the Law was not binding on the Gentiles is confirmed by the fact that, in spite of the many condemnations of Gentiles' sins in the Old Testament, never once were they condemned for not worshiping on the Sabbath or not bringing sacrifices or tithes to Jerusalem. This does not mean there is no law of God for nonbelievers; they are bound by the law written on their hearts. While they have no special revelation in holy Scripture, they are responsible to general revelation in human nature.

Interaction between General and Special Revelation

Since the university is a principal center of intellectual interchange, general revelation has a special role to play in its curriculum. However, the interaction between general and special revelation must be discussed. God has revealed himself in his Word and in his world. His truth is found both in Scripture and in science.

16. See Greg Bahnsen, *Theonomy in Christian Ethics* (Nutley, N.J.: Presbyterian and Reformed, 1977).

17. Moses made it clear that the law was not given to Gentiles. He said to Israel, "What other nation is so great as to have such righteous decrees and laws as this body of laws I am setting before you today?" (Deut. 4:8).

What do we do when two truths seem to conflict? To conclude that the Bible is always right and science is wrong is too simplistic. The Bible is always right, but our interpretation of it is not.

Distinguish between Scripture and its interpretation. When dealing with conflicts between Christianity and culture we must be careful to distinguish between God's Word, which is infallible, and our interpretation of it, which is not. God's revelation in his world is always true, but man's understanding of God's revelation is not always correct.[18] The progress of scientific understanding indicates that what was once held to be true is no longer believed to be so.

We can be sure of this: God's revelations in his Word and his world never contradict each other. God is consistent; he never talks out of both sides of his mouth. Whenever there is a conflict, it is between a human interpretation of God's Word and a human understanding of his world. Either one or both of these are wrong, but God has not erred.

Which realm gets the priority? When conflicts in understanding God's general and special revelations occur, which understanding takes priority? The temptation might be to give precedent to the biblical interpretation because the Bible is infallible, but this over-looks the crucial distinction just made. The Bible is inerrant, but our interpretations of it are not without error. The history of inter-pretation reveals that man can understand God's infallible Word just as he can misunderstand anything else. Likewise, the history of the arts and sciences exposes human misunderstandings of God's general revelation.

Are we then at an impasse? Not really. There is a workable solu-tion to the difficulty. When a conflict between an interpretation of the Bible and a current understanding in the arts or sciences occurs, priority should be given to the interpretation that is more certain. Sometimes this is our understanding of special revelation, and sometimes it is our understanding of general revelation, depending on which one is more thoroughly proven. A few exam-ples will help illuminate the point.

Some interpreters have wrongly concluded on the basis of bibli-cal references to "the four corners of the earth" (Rev. 7:1) that the

18. The correct meaning of a passage is what the author meant by it, not what it may mean to the reader. As E. D. Hirsch aptly noted, "As soon as the reader's outlook is permit-ted to determine what a text means, we have not simply a changing meaning but quite pos-sibly as many meanings as readers." See *Validity in Interpretation* (New Haven: Yale University Press, 1967), 213.

earth is flat. However, science has proves with certainty that this is wrong. Therefore, in this case the certainty in interpreting God's general revelation takes precedence over whatever uncertainty there may be in interpreting these biblical references. "Four corners" can be understood as a figure of speech, and, as already noted, the Bible uses such literary devices.

Others have claimed that the sun moves around the earth on the basis of biblical references to sunrise (Josh. 1:15) or the sun standing still (Josh. 10:13). However, this interpretation is not necessary. The language merely describes appearance from an observer's point of view. Furthermore, since Copernicus there is good reason to believe that the sun does not move around the earth. Hence, we assign a higher probability to the heliocentric interpretation of God's world at this point than to a geocentric interpretation of his Word.[19]

Still others are willing to believe in a given interpretation of God's Word, even if it involves a logical contradiction. But general revelation demands (by way of the law of noncontradiction) that opposites cannot both be true. Hence, we cannot believe that God is both one person and also three persons at the same time and in the same sense. Both monotheism and trinitarianism cannot be true. We can, and do, believe that God is three persons in one nature (trinitarianism). For even though this is a mystery, it is not a contradiction.[20] Therefore, we can be absolutely certain that any interpretation of Scripture that involves a contradiction is false.

However, there are times when an interpretation of Scripture should take precedence over even highly popular views in science. Macroevolution is a good example. It is virtually certain that the Bible cannot be properly interpreted to accommodate macroevolution.[21] Or to put it another way, it is most evident that the Bible

19. We say the heliocentric view has a higher "probability" because the geocentric view has not been disproven. Furthermore, there is no fixed point from which the measurements can be made. Hence, it is empirically unverifiable. Mathematically, everything works out both ways. The geocentric view was rejected largely because it was a simpler explanation.

20. A mystery goes beyond our reason but not against reason. It is beyond our ability to comprehend but not against the law of noncontradiction. We can know that both statements are not contradictory without knowing just how they are complementary.

21. For example, the Bible says man was created from dust (and returns to it), not from lower animals (Gen. 2:7). It also declares that Eve was made from Adam's rib, not from lower forms of life (Gen. 2:21). Furthermore, God created different "kinds" of life and each reproduce their kind (Gen. 1:21). To accept evolution one has to reject any kind of literal understanding of Genesis 1–2, as well as numerous New Testament teachings based on a literal understanding of it (e.g., Rom. 5:8; Matt. 19; 1 Tim. 2:22. See Geisler, *Knowing the Truth*, chaps. 1, 2, appendix 1.

teaches that God brought the universe into existence out of nothing (Gen. 1:1), that he created every basic kind of animal and plant (Gen. 1:21), and that he specially and directly created men and women in his image (Gen. 1:27).[22] Hence, in spite of the prevailing and popular (though not highly probable) evolutionary views to the contrary, the Christian must give priority to this highly probable interpretation of Scripture over the improbable theory of macroevolution.[23]

Biblical studies and arts and sciences enrich each other. Most often there is no serious conflict between biblical studies and the arts and sciences. Rather,there is mutual enrichment. For example, a knowledge of the content of the Bible is essential for understanding much of western art and literature. Furthermore, biblical history and world history overlap significantly, so that neither should be ignorant of the other. More neglected is the connection between modern science and the biblical idea of creation. The Christian university should stress the Christian motivation and ideas that led to the rise of modern science.[24] Of course, in the study of origins there is a direct overlap and mutual enrichment of the scientific and biblical data.

In a Christian university, the interaction between biblical studies and other disciplines should always be a two-way street. No one provides a monologue for the other; all engage in a continual dialogue. Although the Bible is infallible in whatever it addresses, it does not speak to every issue. Furthermore, while the Bible is infallible, our interpretations of it are not. Thus, those in biblical studies must listen to as well as speak to their colleagues in other disciplines. Interdepartmental dialogue, team-taught courses, and cooperative research projects are just some of the many ways this interaction can be implemented.

Summary

The Bible is essential to a Christian university. It is the only infallible writing we have. It speaks with unerring authority on

---

22. See Geisler, *Knowing the Truth*, chaps. 1, 2, appendix 1.

23. For a good recent analysis of the implausibility of evolution see Michael Denton, *Evolution: A Theory in Crisis* (New York: Adler and Adler, 1986). As to the high implausibility of the chemical evolution of life, see Charles B. Thaxton, Walter L. Bradley, and Roger L. Olsen, *The Mystery of Life's Origin* (New York: Philosophical Library, 1984).

24. See Norman L. Geisler and J. Kerby Anderson, *Origin Science: A Proposal for the Creation-Evolution Controversy* (Grand Rapids: Baker, 1987), chap. 2.

every topic it covers, whether spiritual or scientific, whether heavenly or earthly. However, the Bible is not God's only revelation to mankind. God has spoken in his world as well as in his Word. It is the task of the Christian university to appropriate the information from both and form a worldview that includes a theocentric and christocentric interpretation of science, history, human beings, and the arts. However, without God's revelation at the basis, this task is as impossible as moving the world with no place to put one's fulcrum.

2   Philosophy

J. P. Moreland

In his seventeenth-century work of art entitled *The Triumph of the Eucharist,* Peter Paul Rubens attempted to capture a widely held view of faith and reason.[1] In his painting, Rubens depicted religion as a person seated in a triumphal chair on a cart pulled by two angels. Walking behind the cart are different figures. Among those figures are a young man and an old man representing, respectively, science and philosophy. This painting conveys the notion of an integrated worldview where faith and reason are in harmony, theology is queen of the sciences, and the discipline of philosophy is the wise, old, long-standing friend of theology.

Throughout the history of the Christian church, philosophy has played an important role in the life of the church and the spread and defense of the gospel of Christ. The great theologian Saint Augustine (354–430) summarized the views of many early church fathers when he said, "We must show our Scriptures not to be in

---

1. Franklin L. Baumer, *Modern European Thought* (New York: Macmillan, 1978), 62–65.

conflict with whatever [our critics] can demonstrate about the nature of things from reliable sources."[2] Philosophy was the main tool Augustine used in this task.

Unfortunately, today things are different. Theologian R. C. Sproul has called this the most anti-intellectual period in the history of the church, and former president of the United Nations and Christian statesman Charles Malik warns that the greatest danger facing modern evangelicalism is a lack of cultivation of the mind, especially as it relates to philosophy.

This trend within the church is coupled with two unfortunate features of Western culture: the rampant pragmatism in society with the concomitant devaluation of the humanities in university life and the nonexistence of philosophy in our pre-college educational curricula. The result is that philosophy departments are endangered species in Christian colleges and seminaries, and serious philosophical reflection is virtually absent from most church fellowships. This, in turn, has contributed to intellectual shallowness and cultural insensitivity in the body of Christ.

But is philosophy really that important for the life, health, and witness of the church? Are we not warned in Scripture itself to avoid philosophy and worldly wisdom? And just what is philosophy, anyway? How does it help us form an integrated Christian worldview? How does philosophy relate to other disciplines taught at the university? To these and related questions we now turn.

The Nature of Philosophy

Scholars generally are agreed that there is no airtight definition that expresses a set of necessary and sufficient conditions for classifying some activity as philosophical. But this should not trouble us. In general, we do not need a definition of something before we can know features of the thing in question and recognize examples of it.[3] One can recognize examples of historical study, love, a person, art, matter, sport, and a host of other concepts without possessing an airtight definition. Nevertheless, definitions are useful, and we can offer a reasonably adequate definition of philosophy.

How might we go about formulating such a definition? Three

2. Augustine *De genesi ad litteram* 1.21. Cited in Ernan McMullin, "How Should Cosmology Relate to Theology?" in *The Sciences and Theology in the Twentieth Century*, ed. Arthur R. Peacocke (Notre Dame, Ind.: University of Notre Dame Press, 1981), 20.

3. See Roderick Chisholm, *Theory of Knowledge* (Englewood Cliffs, N.J.: Prentice-Hall, 1977), 119–34.

ways suggest themselves. First we could focus on the etymology of the word *philosophy*. The word comes from two Greek words: *philein*, to love, and *sophia*, wisdom. Thus, a philosopher is a lover of wisdom. Socrates held that the unexamined life is not worth living, and the ancient Greek philosophers sought wisdom regarding truth, knowledge, beauty, and goodness. In this sense, then, philosophy is the attempt to think hard about life, the world as a whole, and the things that matter most in order to secure knowledge about these matters. Thus, philosopher Ed Miller defines philosophy as "the attempt to think rationally and critically about the most important questions."[4]

Second, our understanding of philosophy will be enhanced if we observe that philosophy often functions as, among other things, a second-order discipline. For example, biology is a first-order discipline that studies living organisms, but philosophy is a second-order discipline that studies biology. In general, it is possible to have a philosophy of *x*, where *x* can be any discipline whatever, for example, law, mathematics, education, science, government, medicine, history, or literature. When philosophers examine another discipline to formulate a philosophy of that discipline, they ask normative questions about that discipline, analyze and criticize the assumptions underlying it, clarify the concepts within it, and integrate that discipline with other fields.

Consider biology again. Philosophers ask questions like these: Is there an external world that is knowable and, if so, how do we know it? What is life, and how does it differ from nonlife? How should we form, test, and use scientific theories and laws? Is it morally permissible to experiment on living things? When biologists talk about information in DNA, how should we understand this talk? How does the biological notion of us as *homo sapiens* relate to the theological notion of us as the image of God or to the legal and political notion of us as a person with legal/political rights? These questions are all philosophical in nature, and by examining them we see that philosophy asks and seeks to answer presuppositional, normative, conceptual, and integrative questions about other fields of study. Thus, by its very nature philosophy is, perhaps, the most important discipline in the task of integrating Christian theology with other fields of study. We will examine this claim in more detail later.

4. Ed L. Miller, *Questions That Matter* (New York: McGraw-Hill, 1984), 15.

One more observation is important. Because philosophy operates at a presuppositional level by clarifying and justifying those
presuppositions, philosophy is the only field of study that has no
unquestioned assumptions within its own domain. In other words,
philosophy is a self-referential discipline, for questions about the
definition, justification, and methodology of philosophy are themselves philosophical in nature. Philosophers keep the books on
everyone, including themselves. The justification of the assumptions of any discipline, including philosophy, is largely a philosophical matter.

A third way to characterize philosophy is to simply list the various sub-branches of philosophy. In addition to the various second-
order branches of philosophy, such as philosophy of law or science,
a number of standard areas of study are parts of philosophy.
Metaphysics is the study of being or reality. It asks questions such
as: What does it mean for something to exist? What are the ultimate kinds of things that exist? For example, what is a substance?
What is a property? Is matter real? Is mind real? What are space,
time, and causation? What is linguistic meaning?

Epistemology is the study of knowledge and justified belief.
What is knowledge? Can we have it? How do we know things and
justify our beliefs? What are the kinds of things we can know?
Value theory is the study of value, for example, ethical value and
aesthetic value. What does it mean to say something is right or
wrong, beautiful or ugly? How do we justify our beliefs in these
areas? Logic investigates the principles of right reasoning. When
can a conclusion legitimately be drawn from premises and why?

These sub-branches combine with the various second-order
areas of investigation to constitute the subject matter of philosophy.
In these areas of study, philosophy serves both a critical and a constructive function. Philosophy is critical because it examines
assumptions, asks questions of justification, seeks to clarify and
analyze concepts, and so on. Philosophy is constructive because it
attempts to provide synoptic vision; that is, it seeks to organize all
relevant facts into a rational system and speculate about the formation and justification of general worldviews.

We have briefly examined the different aspects of philosophy in
order to get a better grasp on what the discipline is and the sorts of
issues within its purview. Let us now look at the importance of philosophy for the Christian church in general and the Christian university in particular.

A Christian Justification of Philosophy

The history of the church reveals that philosophy has always played a crucial role in the nurture of believers and in the proclamation of a Christian worldview in general and the gospel in particular. The first universities in Europe were, of course, Christian, and the study of philosophy was considered of central importance to the health and vitality of the university. This is no less true today. In fact, there are at least seven reasons why philosophy is crucial to the texture, curricula, and mission of the Christian university.

First, philosophy is an aid in the task of apologetics. Apologetics is the art of giving a reasoned defense of Christian theism in light of objections raised against it and of offering positive evidence on its behalf.[5] Scripture commands us to engage in apologetics (see 1 Pet. 3:15; Jude 3).

The Old Testament prophets often appealed to broad arguments from the nature of the world to justify the religion of Israel. For example, they would chide pagan idols for their frailty and smallness. The world is too big, they claimed, to have been made by something this small (see Isa. 44–45). Arguments like this assume a philosophical position on the nature of causation, for example, that an effect (the world) cannot come from something of lesser reality or power than itself (the idol). Again, the Old Testament prophets often appealed to general principles of moral reasoning in criticizing the immorality of pagan nations (e.g., Amos 1–2). Arguments like this utilize natural moral law and general philosophical principles of moral reasoning.

In the New Testament, the apostles used philosophical argumentation and reasoning to proclaim Christ to unbelievers (see Acts 17:2–4, 17–31; 18:4; 19:8). Their practice was consistent with that of the Old Testament prophets in this regard.

Philosophy aids a person in stating arguments for God's existence, clarifying and defending a broad view of what it is for something to exist so as to include nonphysical and nonspatiotemporal entities, for example, God, angels, and perhaps disembodied souls. When an objection against Christianity comes from some discipline

5. For a basic treatment of the biblical nature and justification of apologetics, see Frederic R. Howe, *Challenge and Response* (Grand Rapids: Zondervan, 1982). Two overviews of the role of philosophy in apologetics in the history of the church are J. K. S. Reid, *Christian Apologetics* (Grand Rapids: Eerdmans, 1969) and L. Russ Bush, *Classical Readings in Christian Apologetics: A.D. 100–1800* (Grand Rapids: Zondervan, 1983).

of study, that objection almost always involves the use of philosophy. When Freud argued against religion on the grounds that our ideas of God are mere illusions, grounded in and caused by our fears and need for a father figure, his attack, while rooted in psychology, nevertheless involved the discipline of philosophy. He was considering the basic question of how the source of our belief relates to our justification for that belief.[6]

Second, philosophy aids the church in its task of polemics. Whereas apologetics involves the defense of Christian theism, polemics is the art of criticizing and refuting alternative views of the world. For example, in the field of artificial intelligence and cognitive psychology there is a tendency to view a human being in physicalist terms, that is, as a complex physical system.[7] Despite protests to the contrary from some Christian thinkers, dualism (the view that we are composed of both a physical and a mental aspect) is the view taught in Scripture (see 2 Cor. 5:1–8, Phil. 1:21–24).[8] Part of the task of a believer working in the areas of artificial intelligence or cognitive psychology is to develop a critique of a purely physicalist vision of being human, and this task includes issues in the philosophy of mind.

Third, philosophy is a central expression of the image of God in us. It is very difficult to come up with an airtight definition of the image of God, but most theologians have agreed that it includes the ability to engage in abstract reasoning, especially in areas having to do with ethical, religious, and philosophical issues. God himself is a rational being, and we are made like him in this respect. This is one of the reasons we are commanded to love God with all of our minds (Matt. 22:37).[9] Since philosophy is a discipline that chiefly

6. A popular treatment of psychological objections against Christianity is R. C. Sproul, *The Psychology of Atheism* (Minneapolis: Bethany, 1974).

7. For an overview of the philosophical and scientific aspects of the mind/body problem written from the point of view of a committed physicalist, see Paul M. Churchland, *Matter and Consciousness*, rev. ed. (Cambridge, Mass.: MIT Press, 1988). Two good critiques of physicalism are Richard Swinburne, *The Evolution of the Soul* (Oxford: Oxford University Press, 1986) and Richard J. Connell, *Substance and Modern Science* (Notre Dame, Ind.: University of Notre Dame Press, 1988).

8. See George Eldon Ladd, *A Theology of the New Testament* (Grand Rapids: Eerdmans, 1974), 457–78; Robert H. Gundry, *Sōma in Biblical Theology* (Cambridge: Cambridge University Press, 1976).

9. For treatments on the importance of the mind for the Christian life, see John R. W. Stott, *Your Mind Matters* (London: InterVarsity, 1972); Roger Trigg, *Reason and Commitment* (Cambridge: Cambridge University Press, 1973); Harry Blamires, *The Christian Mind* (Ann Arbor, Mich.: Servant, 1963).

focuses on ultimate questions near the very heart of existence and religion, then philosophical reflection about God's special and general revelation are part of loving him and thinking his thoughts after him.

Fourth, philosophy permeates systematic theology and serves as its handmaid in several ways.[10] Philosophy helps to add clarity to the concepts of systematic theology. For example, philosophers can help to clarify the different attributes of God, they can show that the doctrines of the trinity and incarnation are not contradictory, they can shed light on the nature of human freedom, and so on.

Further, philosophy can help to extend biblical teaching into areas where the Bible is not explicit. For example, several areas currently under discussion in medical ethics (active/passive euthanasia, genetic screening, artificial food and hydration, artificial insemination) are not explicitly mentioned in Scripture. The philosopher can, however, take the language and doctrines of the Bible and appropriately recast them in the relevant categories under discussion. In this way the philosopher can help to shed biblical light on an issue not explicitly mentioned in Scripture by providing conceptual categories and analysis that fit the situation and preserve the tenor and substance of biblical teaching.

Fifth, the discipline of philosophy can facilitate the spiritual discipline of study. Study is itself a spiritual discipline, and the very act of study can change the self. One who undergoes the discipline of study lives through certain types of experiences where certain skills are developed through habitual study: framing an issue, solving problems, learning how to weigh evidence and eliminate irrelevant factors, cultivating the ability to see important distinctions instead of blurring them, and so on. The discipline of study also aids in the development of certain virtues and values, for example, a desire for the truth, honesty with data, an openness to criticism, self-reflection, and an ability to get along nondefensively with those who differ with you.

Of course, the discipline of study is not unique to philosophy. But philosophy is among the most rigorous of fields, and its approach and subject matter are so central to life, close to religion, and foundational to other fields of investigation, that the discipline

10. See Winfried Corduan, *Handmaid to Theology: An Essay in Philosophical Prolegomena* (Grand Rapids: Baker, 1981).

of philosophical study can aid someone in the pursuit of truth in any other area of life or university study.

Sixth, the discipline of philosophy can enhance the boldness and self-image of the Christian community in general. It is well known that a group, especially a minority group, will be vital and active only if it feels good about itself in comparison with outsiders. Further, there will be more tolerance of internal group differences, and thus more harmony, when a group feels comfortable toward outsiders.

In a fascinating study, John G. Gager argues that the early church faced intellectual and cultural ridicule from Romans and Greeks. This ridicule threatened internal cohesion within the church and its evangelistic boldness toward unbelievers. Gager argues that it was primarily the presence of philosophers and apologists within the church that enhanced the self-image of the Christian community because these early scholars showed that the Christian community was just as rich intellectually and culturally as was the pagan culture surrounding it. Says Gager:

> Whether or not the apologists persuaded pagan critics to revise their view of Christians as illiterate fools, they succeeded in projecting for the group as a whole a favorable image of itself as the embodiment of true wisdom and piety. . . . Whatever we may say about the expressed purpose of these apologies, their latent function was not so much to change the pagan image of Christians as to prevent that image from being internalized by Christians themselves.[11]

Gager's point could and should be applied to the value of Christian scholarship in general, but the applicability of his remarks to the field of philosophy should be obvious. Historically, philosophy has been the main discipline that has aided the church in its intellectual relationship with unbelievers. Because of the very nature of philosophy itself—its areas of study and their importance for answering ultimate questions, the questions it asks and answers, its closeness to theology—the potential of this discipline for enhancing the self-respect of the believing community is enormous.

It seems clear that evangelicalism in America is having a serious

11. John G. Gager, *Kingdom and Community: The Social World of Early Christianity* (Englewood Cliffs, N.J.: Prentice-Hall, 1975), 86, 87.

self-image problem. The reasons for this are no doubt varied but it can hardly be an accident that the average Bible college has no philosophy department, and many evangelical seminaries do not offer serious, formal training in philosophy and apologetics beyond a course here and there.

Seventh, the discipline of philosophy is absolutely essential for the task of integration. Since this will be my main topic of discussion, little need be added at this point except to note that the need for integration occurs in at least three ways.

For one thing, the believing community needs to draw from all areas of knowledge in forming an integrated Christian worldview consistent with Scripture. Second, a person grows to maturity to the extent that he or she becomes an integrated, unfragmented self, and one of the ways to become an integrated person is to have the various aspects of one's intellectual life in harmony. If I believe one thing in church and another thing in the lab or office, I will to that extent be a fragmented, dichotomized individual wherein Christ can only dwell in a shrinking, religious compartment of my life. Finally, when the gospel confronts a new culture, then Christian theology must be related to that culture in a way that is at once sensitive to the culture and faithful to Scripture. Such a task will include questions of value, knowledge, thought forms, and so on, and these questions essentially involve philosophical clarification and comment.

These are some of the reasons why the church has always found philosophy to be necessary. C. S. Lewis once remarked that "to be ignorant and simple now—not to be able to meet the enemies on their own ground—would be to throw down our weapons, and to betray our uneducated brethren who have, under God, no defence but us against the intellectual attacks of the heathen. Good philosophy must exist, if for no other reason, because bad philosophy needs to be answered."[12]

The great social critic William Wilberforce (1759–1833) was a man of deep devotion to God and great passion for practical ministry. But Wilberforce saw the value of philosophy and apologetics, even for the training of children in the church! Queried Wilberforce, "In an age in which infidelity abounds, do we observe [believers] carefully instructing their children in the principles of

12. C. S. Lewis, *The Weight of Glory* (Grand Rapids: Eerdmans, 1949), 50.

faith they profess? Or do they furnish their children with arguments for the defense of that faith?"[13] Sources for similar attitudes
could be cited throughout the history of the church: Justin Martyr,
Augustine, Anselm, Aquinas, Calvin, Jonathan Edwards, John
Wesley, Francis Schaeffer, Carl Henry. Nevertheless, there is a general perception among many believers that philosophy is intrinsically hostile to the Christian faith and should not be of concern to
believers. There are at least four reasons frequently cited for such
an attitude.

First, the claim is made that human depravity has made the
mind so darkened that the noetic effects of sin render the human
intellect incapable of knowing truth. However, this claim is an
exaggeration. The fall damaged but did not destroy the image of
God in us. Our reasoning abilities are affected but not eliminated.
This can be seen in the fact that the writers of Scripture often appeal
to the minds of unbelievers by citing evidence on behalf of their
claims, using logical inferences in building their case, and speaking
in the language and thought forms of those outside the faith.

Second, it is sometimes claimed that faith and reason are hostile
to each other, and whatever is of reason cannot be of faith. But
this represents misunderstanding of the biblical concept of faith.
The biblical notion of faith emphasizes personal trust (*fiducia*) or
belief in God and the data/content of his revelation (*noticia*). But
belief **in** rests on belief **that.** One is called to trust in what he or
she has reason to give intellectual assent (*assensus*) to. In Scripture,
faith involves placing trust in what you have reason to believe is
true. Faith is not a blind, irrational leap into the dark. So faith and
reason cooperate on a biblical view of faith. They are not intrinsically hostile.

Third, some cite Colossians 2:8 as evidence against philosophy:
"See to it that no one takes you captive through hollow and decep-
tive philosophy, which depends on human tradition and the basic
principles of this world rather than on Christ." However, upon an
investigation of the structure of the verse, it becomes clear that
philosophy in general was not the focus. Rather, vain and hostile
philosophy was the subject of discussion. In the context of
Colossians, Paul was warning the church not to form and base its
doctrinal views according to a philosophical system hostile to ortho-

13. William Wilberforce, *Real Christianity* (Portland: Multnomah, 1982; based on the 1829
edition), 1–2.

doxy. His remarks were a simple warning not to embrace heresy; they were not meant in context to represent the apostle's views of philosophy as a discipline of study. Those views are not relevant to the context and do not square with the grammar of the passage.

Finally, 1 Corinthians 1–2 are cited as evidence against philosophy. Here Paul argues against the wisdom of the world and reminds his readers that he did not visit them with persuasive words of wisdom. But again, this passage must be understood in context. For one thing, if it is an indictment against argumentation and philosophical reason, then it contradicts Paul's own practices in Acts and his explicit appeal to argument and evidence on behalf of the resurrection in 1 Corinthians 15. It also violates other passages (e.g., 1 Pet. 3:15) as well as the practice of Old Testament prophets and preachers.

The passage is better seen as a condemnation of the false, prideful use of reason, not of reason itself. It is *hubris* that is in view, not *nous*. The passage may also be a condemnation of Greek rhetoric. Greek orators prided themselves in possessing "persuasive words of wisdom," and it was their practice to persuade a crowd of any side of an issue for the right price. They did not base their persuasion on rational considerations, but on speaking ability, thus bypassing issues of substance. Paul is most likely contrasting himself with Greek rhetoricians.

Paul could also be making the claim that the content of the gospel cannot be deduced from some set of first principles by pure reason. Thus, the gospel of salvation could never have been discovered by philosophy, but had to be revealed by the biblical God who acts in history. So the passage may be showing the inadequacy of pure reason to deduce the gospel, not its inability to argue for the truth.

We have seen that there are good reasons why the church has historically valued the role of philosophy in her life and mission, and reasons to the contrary are inadequate. It is time now to turn to the issue of the role of philosophy in the integrative task of a Christian university.

The Role of Philosophy in Integration

It may be helpful to begin this section by listing examples where issues in a field of study naturally suggest philosophical speculation and where someone in that field of study may inadvertently don a philosopher's cap.

Examples of the Need for Philosophy

1. A biblical exegete becomes aware of how much her own cultural background shapes what she can see in the biblical text, and she begins to wonder whether meanings might not reside in the interpretation of a text and not in the text itself. She also wonders if certain methodologies may be inappropriate given the nature of the Bible as revelation.

2. A psychologist reads the literature regarding identical twins who are reared in separate environments. He notes that they usually exhibit similar adult behavior. He then wonders if there is really any such thing as freedom of the will, and if not, he ponders what to make of moral responsibility and punishment.

3. A political science professor reads Rawls's *Theory of Justice* and grapples with the idea that society's primary goods could be distributed in such a way that those on the bottom get the maximum benefit even if people on the top have to be constrained. He wonders how this compares with a meritocracy wherein individual merit is rewarded regardless of social distribution. Several questions run through his mind: What is the state? How should a Christian view the state and the church? What is justice, and what principles of social ordering ought we adopt? Should one seek a Christian state or merely a just state?

4. A neurophysiologist establishes specific correlations between certain brain functions and certain feelings of pain, and she puzzles over the question of whether or not there is a soul or mind distinct from the brain.

5. An anthropologist notes that cultures frequently differ over basic moral principles and goes on to argue that this proves that there are no objectively true moral values that transcend culture.

6. A businessman notices that the government is not adequately caring for the poor. He discusses with a friend the issue of whether or not businesses have corporate moral responsibilities or whether only individuals have moral responsibility.

7. A mathematician teaches Euclidean geometry and some of its alternatives and goes on to ask the class if mathematics is a field that really conveys true knowledge about a subject matter or if it merely offers internally consistent formal languages expressible in symbols. If the former, then what is it that mathematics describes? Do numbers exist and if so, what are they?

8. An education major is asked to state his philosophy of educa-

tion. In order to do this, he must state his views on human nature, the nature of truth, how people learn, what role values play in life, what the purpose of education ought to be and who should be entitled to an education.

9. A physicist ponders Einstein's theory about the relativity of space and time, and she believes that space and time themselves must be distinguished from the empirical, operational space and time utilized in scientific observations and tests. She agrees that the latter are relative, but she does not think that this settles the question of the real nature of actual space and time.

Each example shows how relevant philosophical issues are for all the disciplines of the university. Philosophy asks normative questions (What ought we believe and why? What ought we do and why?), it deals with foundational issues (what is real, what is truth, what can we know and how, what is right and wrong, do right and wrong exist, what are the principles of good reasoning and evidence evaluation?), and it seeks to know what some phenomenon must be in all possible worlds, not what may happen to be the case in this actual world.

Some Philosophical Principles Used in Integration

It should be clear, therefore, that philosophy is central to the task of integration. Nevertheless, that task is a very difficult one, and there is no set of easy steps or principles that exhaustively describes how that task is to be conducted or what role philosophy should play in the quest for integration. With this in mind, the following is a list of principles that I hope will aid someone unfamiliar with philosophy to think more clearly about its role in integration.

1. *Philosophy can point out that an issue thought to be a part of another discipline is really a philosophical issue.* It often happens that scholars, untrained in philosophy, will discuss some issue in their field and, without knowing it, cross over into philosophy. When this happens, the discussion may still be about the original discipline, but it is a discussion within philosophy.

For example, attempts to put limits on a given discipline and attempts to draw a line of demarcation between one field of study and another, say between science and theology, are largely philosophical matters. This is because such attempts assume a vantage point outside and above the discipline in question where one asks second-order questions about that discipline. Philosophy, it will be recalled, focuses on these kinds of second-order questions.

Consider the following six propositions that seek for science to place a limit on theology and vice versa:

(S1) Theological beliefs are reasonable only if science renders them so.

(S2) Theological beliefs are unreasonable if science renders them so.

(S3) Theological beliefs are reasonable only if arrived at by something closely akin to scientific methodology.

(T1) Scientific beliefs are reasonable only if theology renders them so.

(T2) Scientific beliefs are unreasonable if theology renders them so.

(T3) Scientific beliefs are reasonable only if arrived at by theologically appropriate methods.

Contrary to initial appearances, these propositions are not examples of science or theology directly placing limits on the other, for none is a statement of science or theology. Rather, all are philosophical statements about science and theology. Principles about science and theology are not the same as principles of science and theology. These six principles are philosophical attempts to limit science and theology and show their relationship.

Here is a second example of where a discussion crosses over into philosophy almost unnoticed.

Evolutionist: The origin of life from inanimate matter is a well-established scientific fact.

Creationist: But if life arose in the oceans (abiogenesis) as you claim, then dilution factors would have kept the concentration of large, macromolecules to levels so small as to have been negligible.

Evolutionist: Well, so what? I do not think abiogenesis took place in the ocean anyway. Rather, it took place in some isolated pool that had some concentrating mechanism in place.

Creationist: But there is no geological evidence for such pools. Further, the probabilities for such a process are incredibly small, and in any case, evidence appears to be coming in that the early earth's atmosphere was a reducing atmosphere, in which case the relevant reactions could not occur.

Evolutionist: Give us more time, and we will solve these problems. The only alternative, creationism, is too fantastic to
believe, and it involves religious concepts and is not science
at all.

Creationist: Well, neither is evolution science. Science requires
firsthand observation, and since no one was there to observe
the origin of first life, any theory about that origin is not science, strictly speaking.

The discussion starts out as a scientific interaction about chemical reactions, probabilities, geological evidence, and so on. But it
slides over into a second-order philosophical discussion (inadequate though it is) about what science is and how one should
define it. These issues are surely relevant to the debate, but there is
no guarantee that two disputants trained in some first-order scientific discipline have any expertise at all about the second-order
questions of what science is and how it should be practiced. If scientists are going to interact on these issues, then philosophy will be
an essential part of that interaction.[14]

*2. Philosophy undergirds other disciplines at a foundational level by
clarifying, defending, or criticizing the essential presuppositions of that discipline.* Since philosophy operates as a second-order discipline that
investigates other disciplines, and since philosophy examines
broad, foundational axiological, epistemological, logical, and metaphysical issues in its own domain, then philosophy is properly
suited to investigate the presuppositions of other disciplines.[15] In
linguistic studies, issues are discussed regarding the existence, nature,
and knowability of meaning. These issues, as well as questions
about whether and how language accomplishes reference to things
in the world, are the main focus of the philosophy of language.

Again, science assumes there is an external world that is orderly
and knowable, that inductive inferences are legitimate, that the
senses and mind are reliable, that truth exists and can be known,
and so on. Orthodox theology assumes that religious language is
cognitive, that knowledge is possible, that an intelligible sense can
be given to the claim that something exists that is not located in

14. I have tried to show the various ways that philosophy and theology are relevant to
science in *Christianity and the Nature of Science* (Grand Rapids: Baker, 1989).

15. An excellent treatment of the foundational nature of philosophy is John Kekes, *The
Nature of Philosophy* (Totowa, N.J.: Rowman and Littlefield, 1980).

space and time, that the correspondence theory of truth is the essential part of an overall theory of truth, and that linguistic meaning is objective and knowable. These presuppositions, and a host of others besides, have all been challenged. The task of clarifying, defending, or criticizing them is essentially a philosophical task.

3. *Philosophy can aid a discipline by helping to clarify concepts, argument forms, and other cognitive issues internal to a field.* Sometimes the concepts in a discipline appear to be contradictory, vague, unclear, or circularly defined. Philosophers who study a particular discipline can aid that discipline by bringing conceptual clarity to it. An example would be the wave/particle nature of electromagnetic radiation and the wave nature of matter. These concepts appear to be self-contradictory or vague, and attempts have been made to clarify them or to show different ways of understanding them.[16]

Another example concerns some conceptions of the mechanisms involved in evolutionary theory. Some scientists have held that evolution promotes the survival of the fittest. But when asked what the "fittest" were, the answer was that the "fittest" were those that survived. This was a problem of circularity within evolutionary theory, and attempts have been made to redefine the notion of fitness and the goal of evolution (e.g., the selection of those organisms that are reproductively favorable) to avoid circularity.[17] Whether or not these responses have been successful is not the point. The point is, rather, that philosophers have raised problems for a scientific theory regarding issues of conceptual clarity. In these and other examples like them, philosophy can help to clarify issues within a discipline. When philosophy is brought to bear on questions of this sort, the result may be that the theory in question is problematic because it involves an internal contradiction or is somehow self-refuting.

For example, the sociological claim that there is no difference between intellectual history (roughly, the attempt to trace the development of ideas through history by focusing on the rational factors involved in the ideas themselves, including their own inner logic and relationships to ideas coming after them [e.g., the devel-

16. Issues involved in the relationship among physics, philosophy, and theology are discussed in *Physics, Philosophy, and Theology*, ed. Robert John Russell, William R. Stoeger, and George V. Coyne (Notre Dame, Ind.: University of Notre Dame Press, 1988).

17. See Mary Williams, "The Logical Status of Natural Selection and Other Evolutionary Controvrsies," in *Conceptual Issues in Evolutionary Biology,* ed. Elliot Sober (Cambridge, Mass.: MIT Press, 1984), 83–98.

opment of empiricism from John Locke to George Berkeley to David Hume]) and the sociology of knowledge (the attempt to trace the development of ideas as a result of nonrational factors in a given culture, social status, economic conditions, and so on) is sometimes justified by an appeal to conceptual relativism. The claim is made that different cultures have different language games, different views of the world, and so forth, and that all of one's views are determined by nonrational factors and thus are not to be trusted. Such a claim is self-refuting, for presumably this theory itself would be untrustworthy on its own terms.

4. *Philosophy provides a common language or conceptual grid wherein two disciplines can be directly related to one another and integrated.* Sometimes two different disciplines will use a term in a slightly different but not completely unrelated way. When this occurs, philosophy can help to clarify the relationship between the different disciplinary uses of the term in question.

For example, sometimes an operational definition of some notion can be related to an ordinary language definition of that notion or a definition from another field. An operational definition is, roughly, a definition of some concept totally in terms of certain laboratory or experimental operations or test scores. Thus, one could operationally define a number of sociological concepts (minority group, traditional family roles, group leadership) or psychological terms (depression, intelligence) completely in terms of some operation or test score. A person could be said to be depressed if and only if that person scored between such and such a range on some standard psychological test.

Now these operational definitions may be related to our ordinary language notions of the relevant concepts in question; but they may not be clearly related, and in any case, they are certainly not identical to them. So philosophical clarity needs to be given before we can specify the relationship between *depression* as it is understood in ordinary language and *depression* as it is operationally defined in some test.

This type of philosophical elucidation is especially important when the term in question appears to be normative in nature. Thus, if one tries to give an operational, psychological definition of a "mature" or "healthy" adult, then all one can give is a descriptive definition, not a prescriptive one, for psychology is a descriptive field. Philosophy focuses on moral prescriptions and oughts; psychology focuses on factual descriptions. So philosophy becomes relevant in clarifying the relationship between a "mature" adult, psy-chologically defined, and a "mature" adult taken as a normative notion (i.e., as something we ought to try to be like).

Philosophy also helps to clarify and relate the different disci-plinary descriptions of the same phenomenon. For example, biolo-gists describe a human being as a member of the classification *homo sapiens*. Philosophy, theology, law, and political science (to name a few) treat a human being as a living entity called a *person*. It is a philosophical question as to whether the two notions are identical and, if they are not, how they relate to one another.[18]

5. *Philosophy provides external conceptual problems for other disciplines to consider as part of the rational appraisal of theories in those disciplines.* A philosophical external conceptual problem arises for some theory T, in a discipline outside of philosophy, when T conflicts with some doctrine of some philosophical theory P, when P and its doctrines are rationally well-founded. For example, suppose there were a good philosophical argument against the view that history has crossed an actual number of events throughout the past to reach the present moment.[19] If this argument is a reasonable one, then it tends to count against some scientific theory (e.g., an oscillating universe) which postulates that the past was beginningless and actually infinite. If there were a good philosophical argument for the claim that space and time are absolute, then this argument would tend to count against scientific theories to the contrary.

Again, if there are good philosophical arguments for the exis-tence of genuine freedom of the will or arguments for the exis-tence of real moral responsibility and the necessity of full-blown freedom as a presupposition of moral responsibility, then these would tend to count against sociological, economic, or psychologi-cal theories which are deterministic in nature. In cases like these, a rationally defensible position is present within philosophy, and it

18. Philosopher James Rachels seems to identify being a human with falling under the biological classification *homo sapiens*. This identification becomes an important aspect of Rachels's defense of active euthanasia, roughly, the view that it can be morally permissible to intentionally cause the death of an innocent human being who is in certain medical circum-stances or who autonomously and competently requests it. See James Rachels, *The End of Life* (Oxford: Oxford University Press, 1986). For a critique of Rachels's view, see J. P. Moreland, "James Rachels and the Active Euthanasia Debate," *Journal of the Evangelical Theological Society* 31 (March 1988): 81–90; cf. my review of *The End of Life* in *The Thomist* 53 (Oct. 1989): 714–22.

19. For an overview of an argument of this type, see J. P. Moreland, *Scaling the Secular City* (Grand Rapids: Baker, 1987), 15–42.

runs contrary to a theory surfaced in another field. The philosophical external conceptual problem may not be sufficient to require abandonment or suspension of judgment of the theory in the other discipline; it may merely tend to count against it. Even so, these kinds of conceptual problems show that philosophical considerations are relevant to the rationality of theory-assessment in other disciplines.

In sum, we have looked at five different ways that philosophy enters into the task of integration in a Christian university. It is important to realize that the Christian philosopher should adopt the attitude of faith seeking understanding. The Christian philosopher will try to undergird, defend, and clarify the various aspects of a worldview compatible with Scripture. This will involve working not only on broad theological themes, for example, the dignity of being human, but on defending and clarifying specific verses in Scripture. Of course, caution must be exercised. One should not automatically assume that one's particular interpretation of a biblical text is the only option for an evangelical, and one should not automatically assume that the biblical text was intended to speak to the issue at hand. But when due care is given to these warnings, it is nevertheless important that the Christian philosopher tries to forge a worldview that includes the teaching of specific biblical texts, properly interpreted.

We began our discussion with a remark from Saint Augustine to the effect that the Christian intellectual must work on behalf of the church to show that our Scriptures do not conflict with any rationally justified belief from some other discipline. Over seventy-five years ago the great evangelical Presbyterian scholar, J. Gresham Machen, remarked that false ideas were the greatest hindrance to the gospel. According to Machen, we can preach with all the fervor of a reformer and even win a straggler here and there. But if we permit the whole collective thought of the nation or world to be dominated by ideas which, by their very logic, prevent Christianity from being regarded as anything more than a hopeless delusion, then we do damage to our religion.[20]

Members of the Christian university are members of two communities—the community of scholars and of the church. The Chris-

---

20. J. Gresham Machen, *Christianity and Culture* (taken from "The Scientific Preparation of the Minister," an address delivered September 20, 1912, at Princeton Theological Seminary), 5.

tian scholars who populate those universities (and those in secular universities as well) have a responsibility to promote worldwide evangelization, the nurture of the saints, and the penetration of culture with a Christian worldview. This task is important to the very life and health of the church, and when we engage in it, philosophy is now, as it has always been, an essential participant in this great task.

3   Literature

Branson Woodard

Never before has literary scholarship faced a more uncertain future. Since the advent of New Criticism in the 1940s, the academy has strained under the stunningly new hermeneutics of several radical theories. Post-structuralist movements such as deconstruction, Marxism, feminism, and reader response have altered methodology by emphasizing different foci of textual study: from the various ways in which words undermine their own refer-ential function by "deferring" to other words with similar sounds but different meanings (as in deconstruction); to political struggles perceived in plots and in characters' motivations (Marxism); to the implications of a male-dominant literary canon and view of litera-ture (feminism); to the agenda of different communities of readers and how those agenda influence interpretation (reader response). These emphases, moreover, are having a profound impact upon biblical scholarship as well.

At the same time these movements have devastated academe with a disorienting subjectivism that questions the very integrity of authors and their own texts. In its own way, each modern theory has led to an undermining of traditional (i.e., Western) views of literature by emphasizing two basic assumptions: a text has no determinate meaning, and biographical and historical details are irrelevant to the analysis of a literary work. Many theorists attempt, on the one hand, to identify and evaluate the uniquely human aspects of a literary text and, on the other, to disregard the world that God created—the world that is there—and the author's unique background and value as a person. One result of this vain attempt is most ironic—a dehumanization of the humanities, or at least of literature. No wonder the public doubts the value and relevance of literary study in the university curriculum.

According to the prevailing views of criticism, for example, a reader should not perceive a novel as potential commentary upon the author's life or worldview, or even as pertinent social comment upon any world at all. In fact, to many critics texts do not relate in any way to external reality because (among other reasons) nature is chaotic, devoid of either epistemological or ontological coherence. Therefore, texts simply create and present their own realities—verbal structures that are wholly self-referential, without relation even to the author, and objects of comment only because they exist in the mind of a reader.[1]

One need not founder in this mass of confusion. In fact, the time has come to end much of it by reestablishing traditional critical method, as M. H. Abrams has begun to do;[2] not simply because it is traditional, and not merely because twentieth-century pragmatism requires that theory function within some sort of objective reality. Rather, literary criticism must be established upon a bibliocentric worldview, beginning with God and his special and general revelation, then working outward to extrabiblical literature. The following discussion, only a small part of that larger task, will show that

1. Note, for example, Paul de Man's denial of objective meaning, due to the apparently irreconcilable nature of grammar and rhetoric. While readers comprehend a text by decoding its rule-based grammar, he argues, this process becomes muddled by the rhetorical aspect, which undermines the supposed constancy of grammatical rules—hence "an anxiety (or bliss, depending on one's momentary mood or individual temperament) of ignorance, not an anxiety of reference . . . not as an emotive reaction to what language does, but as an emotive reaction to the impossibility of knowing what it might be up to." Therefore, he concludes, "Literature as well as criticism—the difference between them being delusive—is condemned (or privileged) to be forever the most rigorous and, consequently, the most unreliable language in terms of which man names and transforms himself" ("Semiology and Rhetoric" [1979], in *Contemporary Literary Criticism*, ed. Robert Con Davis and Ronald Schleifer [White Plains, N.Y.: Longman, 1989], 259–61).

2. See "The Deconstructive Angel," in *Contemporary Literary Criticism*, 554–63.

divine written revelation is the focal point in literary theory. After all, Scripture is literature; and without it and its Author, other literature would have no absolute basis for its being and function, and critics' judgments would lack the very objectivity that makes literary study credible and meaningful.

Scripture and Literature

To some readers the Bible and extrabiblical literature have no common ground, and therefore should not be associated at all. Throughout this century, the argument goes, Scripture has, like Abel, fallen victim to a fierce worldly spirit and has nothing to say about the philosophy of literature. Or worse, the Bible appears, like Edgar in *King Lear,* as an impoverished beggar, seeking its way back into social acceptance. Besides all that, the Old and New Testaments are theological writings, whereas literature is "secular." What then could be more contradictory than associating the Bible with poetry and prose narrative? On the contrary, what could be more reasonable than such an association? An overview of the literary character of Scripture will show that divine written revelation is essential to an objective, coherent philosophy of literature.

The Author of Authors

God's existence and keen interest in creativity are shown in nature and in the Bible, identified respectively as general and special revelation. Over many centuries following the creation, God and certain humans composed an inerrant, infallible book (2 Tim. 3:16; 2 Pet. 1:21), revealing the Almighty in historically accurate and richly poetic narrative. His omnipotence, for example, appears in the narrator's stance in Genesis 1–3, as Erich Auerbach explained some years ago.[3] Other books, of course, reveal other attributes; the important principle is that the divine Author of Scripture provides the ontological and epistemological basis for literary authorship and the intentionality of literature.

What else do we know about this supreme Author from his own writings? The Old and New Testaments present him as a personal Being; he thinks, feels, and acts. Speaking through Isaiah, for example, God informs Israel that his thoughts and ways (i.e., actions) differ from theirs, and that his "word that goes out from

3. See "Odysseus' Scar" in *Mimesis: The Representation of Reality in Western Literature,* trans. Willard R. Trask (Princeton: Princeton University Press, 1953), 14–15.

[his] mouth" will accomplish his intended purpose (Isa. 55:8–11). God's thoughts and actions are accompanied by feelings, of course. Well known are his anger (Exod. 4:14; Matt. 23), delight (Ps. 147:11; Prov. 12:22), distress (Luke 12:50), grief (Gen. 6:6; Isa. 63:10), and pleasure (1 Kings 3:10; Matt. 3:17)—along with the fundamental attributes of holiness (Lev. 19:2), love (1 John 4:16), wisdom (Isa. 28:29), and excellence (Mark 7:37). Thus the Bible records and reveals the personhood and personality of the Supreme Being, in whose constitutional likeness the first man and woman were created (Gen. 1:27).

The Integrity of Authors, Texts, and Audiences

God is the Originator of the universe and the written Word. These creative acts are indeed miraculous and, in at least one important way, interrelated. Human beings were created to fulfill God's intention to have fellowship with similar, though not divine, beings. This intention was continued through the composition of Scripture, the means of God's written self-revelation to humans. He wanted them to know him intimately, as well as to know about his works.

To explain these truths, he superintended the writing of the Old and New Testaments, using men whom he miraculously kept from making any errors in the biblical text. Of course, divine inspiration does not negate the human dimension: the Bible was not dictated. Accordingly, each book reveals the human author's experiences, viewpoints, literary style, and audience—all of which express his intention in writing. This individuality is crucial to the study of certain books, for example, parallel passages of Israelite history in Kings and Chronicles and the different perspectives of Jesus in the synoptic Gospels.[4] That these passages appear in the canon does not show the Bible to be redundant but, rather, expressive of individual authors' ideas and feelings, that is, of personality. Such personality is found both in God and in human authors, not only in the authors of the Bible but also in authors of noncanonical literature. Because we have the Bible, the inerrant and divinely inspired literature of the supreme Author, and because human authors bear his constitutional likeness, we approach texts in general as expressions of authorial personality and intention.

4. This principle is important in criticism of extrabiblical texts also, for example, in the two eighteenth-century accounts of travels to the Hebridean Islands by James Boswell and Samuel Johnson.

The nature of that approach, moreover, is closely related to the content of Scripture as well. God's revelation of himself in biblical literature legitimizes a human author's self-expression through characters, plots, themes, genres, and other literary features similar to those found in the Old and New Testaments. The many genres in the Bible should convince the most confirmed skeptic of its literary artistry. A few examples include the heroic narratives about Joseph (Gen. 37–50) and Daniel, culminating in the Gospels; the epic of the exodus; the tragedies of Adam and Eve (Gen. 2–3), Samson (Judg. 13–16), and Saul (1 Sam.); the poetic language and rhythms of the Wisdom Books, the Prophets, and the Apocalypse (Rev. 15:3–4; 18:4–8, 21–24); and the persuasive epistles of James, John, Peter, and Paul. To be sure, these forms did not originate in Scripture,[5] but God's use of genres in his own text is reason enough to study both them and those literary forms and structures outside the Bible.[6]

To include extrabiblical as well as biblical literature in the university curriculum, however, calls for stronger evidence than the mere fact that genres appear in Scripture. Such evidence, available in both Testaments, is the biblical authors' citation (however infrequent) of noncanonical works. In the Old Testament Moses refers to a lost manuscript entitled the *Book of the Wars of the Lord* (Num. 21:14–15, 17–18) and to an Amorite taunt song written to chide Moab for suffering defeat in battle (Num. 21:27–30). Other passages (Josh. 10:13; 2 Sam. 1:18) refer to the *Book of Jashar,* a collection of poems apparently written to commemorate Israelite heroes for military, political, and religious achievements. Similar types of citations appear in the New Testament as well. In Acts 17:28 and Titus 1:12 Paul quoted the Cretan poet Epimenides (sixth century B.C.); the apostle also cited the poet Aratus, Cleanthes (author of *Hymn to Zeus*), and the Greek comedy writer Menander (1 Cor. 15:33).

Even without such quotations, believers would find ample support for reading noncanonical works. Christians are commanded, for example, to subject every idea to the lordship of Christ (2 Cor.

5. For comment on extrabiblical literature and the Old Testament, see Umberto Cassuto, "Biblical and Canaanite Literature" in *Biblical and Oriental Studies,* 2 vols. (Jerusalem: Magnes, 1975): 2:16–59; for the New Testament epistles, William G. Doty, *Letters in Primitive Christianity* (Philadelphia: Fortress, 1973).

6. In recent years literary issues have captured the attention of biblical scholars, due in part to the work of Leland Ryken, Northrop Frye, Tremper Longman, and many others who have corrected the misconception that the Bible is only a theology textbook, pure from the supposedly corrupting influences of literature.

10:5), a command that presupposes interaction with unbiblical concepts. But references in Scripture to the *Book of Jashar* and similar writings imply God's approval of the quoted portions of the writings and the biblical authors' knowledge of them. This implication undergirds the Christian university's commitment to the study of all literature, given its diligence to conduct that inquiry from a clear biblical perspective.

Thus far, we have identified the biblical basis for authorship and textuality. What about audience? Literature, in particular the Bible with its message of redemption, is written for an audience, of course; it must be read. How does the Bible establish the integrity of the reader? Could such literary integrity exist apart from divine written revelation?

As with authorship and textuality, Scripture is the foundational document for establishing the audience for literature. To begin with, God was the first Audience for the Bible; as the sovereign Lord, he made it available for his own good pleasure. But he provided it also for humans, the special recipients of his love and the highest beings in the order of creation (Gen. 1:26; Ps. 8:5–8). In addition, the present and future well-being of this audience, possible only through God's forgiveness and grace, motivated him to explain such doctrines as the depravity of humans, the realms of heaven and hell, and the plan of salvation. These explanations are found in biblical literature, written in human language; and as modern scholarship has shown more than once, human language is quite adequate to tell us all we need to know about God.[7] Thus, by revealing himself in the Old and New Testaments, God demonstrated the legitimacy and special worth of his human audience.

Furthermore, Scripture often names, or at least suggests, the audience for a particular discourse. Whereas Luke wrote explicitly to Theophilus and Paul addressed various churches (e.g., in Rome and Galatia) and individuals (Timothy, Titus, and Philemon), Qoheleth (The Preacher) seemed to write for young readers (see Eccles. 12:1, 12); and the poet of the Lamentations directed his

---

7. Jack Barentsen, "The Validity of Human Language: A Vehicle for Divine Truth," *Grace Theological Journal* 9 (1988): 21–43. See also J. I. Packer, "The Adequacy of Human Language," in *Inerrancy*, ed. Norman L. Geisler (Grand Rapids: Zondervan, 1980), 197–226. A more general study of language and truth is Peggy Rosenthal's *Words and Values: Some Leading Words and Where They Lead Us* (New York: Oxford, 1984), which identifies numerous words that imply a theistic worldview and the secularized terms that have displaced them (e.g., soul–self, truth—opinion, love–sex).

verse to the residents of Jerusalem prior to the Babylonian invasion in 586 B.C. (see Lam. 1:1, 4, 7). That the Bible addresses particular persons and groups clearly establishes their importance as individual readers of literature.

Before proceeding to a formal definition of literature, we should notice several implications for reading of divine written revelation. First, the reader has a legitimate place in literary study. In fact, some poems, plays, short stories, and novels defy understanding until one has identified the reader intended by the author.[8] Second, reading is less a creative than a receptive act. Fundamental to communication theory is the fact that the encoder has a message for the decoder. In turn, given the revelatory and declarative nature of the Bible, the rhetorical situation (i.e., writer, text, reader) operates hierarchically, from God and the human authors through their texts to readers. This pattern, the traditional Western approach to literature, is implicit in the Near-Eastern passage Deuteronomy 29:29: "The secret things belong to the LORD our God, but the things revealed belong to us and to our children forever, that we may follow all the words of this law." Though some concepts are known only to God, and will remain so, others have been explained in order to teach obedience, the end of which is godliness in the lives of readers. But this revelation is not bland, preachy, and oppressive; it is poetic, often subtle, lively, and liberating.

A third implication of divine written revelation for the act of reading, had it been voiced seriously in academe a century ago, would have been superfluous because it was commonly assumed. Today, however, the principle contradicts the reader response establishment and may therefore seem revolutionary; perhaps, then, it merits at least passing notice. In short, a reader meets an author in the text and seeks to recover—not to negotiate, much less to create—textual meaning. Whether with Jeremiah or Peter, Dante or Derrida, the reader's primary responsibility is the same: to identify

8. A classic example of misdirected writing, albeit involving the sophisticated and risky technique of irony, is Defoe's *Shortest Way with Dissenters* (1702). The situation is far more humorous now than when it occurred. Himself a dissenter, Defoe assumed a satiric stance, intending through the arrogant voice of a Tory highflier to debunk the Anglican hierarchy. Unfortunately, the dissenters as well as the bishops failed to perceive the irony; the one was horrified, the other delighted, and all was lost—including Defoe's freedom. Shortly after publication of the essay, he was arrested, pilloried, and held to formal church discipline. The outcome involved no calamity, but the biblical principle could hardly be more clear: to speak the truth in love (Eph. 4:15), one must be careful to identify the intended audience, then shape the text accordingly.

the author's intention as it is posited in the text.[9] This process of interpretation, moreover, differs from application, the act of relating the text to the reader's own experience and perspective. Such application is a legitimate, indeed necessary, part of reading; but it does not constitute interpretation, which is the principal task of criticism.

A Definition of Literature

The preceding outline implies a particular set of assumptions about the nature of literature, one that contrasts sharply with modern usage of the term. Today the word *literature* connotes writing of all sorts, with respect to both content and style: research, for example, medical "literature"; tracts and curriculum for Sunday schools, that is, religious "literature"; even the antifeminine pages in so-called adult magazines, that is, pornographic "literature." This last example may be related to the view that steamy stories can display a clever plot, expressed in moist prose, and thus be classified literature. Nothing, literally, could be more false. Unlike stylistic flourishes of narrative, in whatever context, literature ennobles, sharpens the reader's moral vision, and deepens one's awareness of the universal dichotomy between what is and what should be.

Literary theory, then, must be informed by the principles of divine written revelation. The following definition attempts to capture such application: the dramatization of reality through artful writing that brings together plot, theme, language, and characterization so as to instruct and edify a particular reader or group of readers in biblical truths, many of which have earthly as well as transcendent application. Numerous texts by many authors conform to such a definition: the poet of the Gilgamesh epic, the writers of the Old and New Testaments, Homer, Chaucer, Dante, Shakespeare, Milton, Pope, Tennyson, George Eliot, the Brontës, the American Romantics, Twain, Frost, Yeats, Welty, Thurber, and O'Connor. Certainly there are more, but the works of these artists illustrate the varied qualities of literature implicit in the aforementioned definition and therefore occupy a central place in the curriculum of a Christian university.

9. For a fuller treatment of this hermeneutic, see E. D. Hirsch, *The Aims of Interpretation* (London and Chicago: University of Chicago Press, 1976). For issues related to biblical interpretation, consult Walter C. Kaiser, Jr., "Legitimate Hermeneutics," in *Inerrancy*, ed. Norman L. Geisler, 117–50, and Tremper Longman III, *Literary Approaches to Biblical Interpretation* (Grand Rapids: Zondervan, 1987).

If "example is more efficacious than precept,"[10] a biblically integrated literary criticism, while not radically different from traditional Western methodology, must display its own validity, or it has no place in the university. Some evidence of that validity is shown in what follows, in a necessarily brief analysis of several texts. For the sake of variety and dimension, the sketch will include Daniel Defoe's theory of fiction, Samuel Johnson's literary voice, and T. S. Eliot's use of objective knowledge in his own literary criticism.

Literary Purity in an Impure Story

Defoe's preface to *Moll Flanders* (1722) is a telling piece of narrative theory, primarily because it explains how moral and aesthetic considerations shape a story of sin and shame. Moll, a fictional London streetwalker, struggles to survive until, at her lowest point, she becomes a Christian, eventually working with her husband to manage a plantation in Virginia. This lively story, however, has no graphic details or titillating scenes: the author depends upon his own artistry and the reader's imagination to provide the necessary background. "All possible care . . . has been taken to give no lewd ideas, no immodest turns, in the new dressing up this story; no, not to the worst part of her expressions . . . some of the vicious part of her life, which could not be modestly told, is quite left out. . . ."[11]

But Defoe has not spared the arresting power of Moll's sin, and for a particular reason: "To give the history of a wicked life repented of necessarily requires that the wicked part should be made as wicked as the real history of it will bear, to illustrate and give a beauty to the penitent part . . ." (p. vi). The happy ending, to some readers, seems naive, perhaps even incredible; but the literary achievement of *Moll Flanders* is not simply the resolution of the plot but the manner in which the story is told.

Here is no polemical, puritanical zealot dressed in a writer's garb but a gifted craftsman whose method exemplifies biblical principles.[12] The preface makes clear that, first, the dialogue and

10. Samuel Johnson, *Rasselas*, chap. 30.

11. *The Fortunes and Misfortunes of the Famous Moll Flanders* (New York: Signet, 1964), v–vi. All subsequent references are to this edition and page numbers are cited parenthetically in the text.

12. Whether Defoe was a Christian is uncertain; but like Bunyan, whom he read often, Defoe certainly used Scripture for literary purposes, sometimes in conspicuous places such as his title pages and introductions (see John Robert Moore, *Daniel Defoe: Citizen of the Modern World* [Chicago: University of Chicago Press, 1958], 15–16, 41–42, 64). Indeed, as Rodney

commentary are "language fit to be read" (p. v). Defoe recognizes his own responsibility, even in this account of sin and woe, to treat the reader with dignity and respect. The apostle's phrase is speaking the truth "in love," being sure that one's words edify rather than destroy (Eph. 4:15, 29). Second, Defoe writes about sinful acts because, of course, they are factual, the undeniable manifestation of depravity, though even the most pernicious man or woman has value and hope as a person. The author, finally, spares no energy to instruct his readers about the folly of sin and the immense satisfaction of righteous, but not pharisaical, conduct. In fact, the entire book is written to emphasize that each "wicked action" leads to sorrow and misfortune; each "superlative villain" either suffers for his evil or repents; and virtue is praised whereas evil is condemned (p. vii). To be sure, in human experience virtue sometimes goes unrewarded, vice unpunished; but at least in *Moll Flanders*, Defoe presents a clear moral vision that argues for the inherent worth (and accountability) of humans. The Bible, albeit mostly nonfiction rather than fiction, does likewise.

The Prophetic Voice of Samuel Johnson

Defoe's near contemporary Samuel Johnson shared a theory of fiction compatible with orthodox theology. Further, his narrative voice exhorted readers to improve their conduct and to trust the God of Scripture. Throughout his life, Johnson remained troubled about his own eternal well-being; no wonder, then, that critics remain uncertain about the occasion of his conversion to Christ.[13]

Blaine has remarked, Defoe based his writing about the supernatural upon a "sincere belief in the Bible as the supreme and final authority" (*Daniel Defoe and the Supernatural* [Athens: University of Georgia Press, 1969], 74). At the same time, Defoe's theology is often difficult to analyze due to the complexity of his artistic vision, the ways by which he sought to relieve his poverty, and the religious questions raised by the deists. Defoe was responsive to contemporary ideas, Maximilian Novak writes, but remained firm in his commitment to the "infallibility" of Scripture and insisted that repentance and faith are necessary for salvation (*Defoe and the Nature of Man* [London: Oxford University Press, 1963] 8, 12–13). Given such background, surely biblical principles guided his views about narrative theory.

13. From age four, Johnson was taught orthodox Christianity by his mother, though evidence of his conversion has not been found. This uncertainty has sparked a lively debate in recent years about the meaning of a phrase in one of Johnson's prayers (5 Dec. 1784), composed shortly before his death on 13 December: "forgive and accept my late conversion" (*Diaries, Prayers, and Annals,* ed. E. L. McAdam [New Haven: Yale University Press, 1958], 417–18). The scholarly consensus is that the word *conversion* here refers not to sudden, climactic awareness of one's forgiveness, in the evangelical sense of the Methodists and other dissenters, but to full intellectual affirmation of Jesus' propitiatory sacrifice, as taught by Richard Hooker (Chester Chapin, *The Religious Thought of Samuel Johnson* [Ann Arbor:

This anxiety is rooted in Johnson's moral scruples and nagging fear that he was falling short—for instance, his inconsistent reading of the Bible for inspirational help. But his use of it as a basis for his sermons (one written in 1745) raises the possibility that it influenced his literary voice in the late 1740s, only a year or so before his reputation as a moralist was firmly established.

Two early works by Johnson echo the voice of the Old Testament prophet, forthtelling divine truths and warning listeners to heed the heavenly instruction. In *The Vision of Theodore* (1748), for example, the voice of the prophet gives the narrative both continuity and context. This short allegory, set on the lonely island of Tenerife, explains how Theodore, an aging recluse who dreams only of seeing other places, learns to suppress those thoughts and thereby live contently in solitude. He gains this insight through a vision offered by a prophet who has relatively little to say. He speaks, in fact, only four times: first, to identify himself; then to direct Theodore's closest attention to the world before him; later to show the folly of pursuing fanciful thoughts; and finally to reiterate the lesson conveyed through the vision—"Remember . . . and be wise, and let not Habit prevail against thee."[14]

The forcefulness of these speeches flows from the prophet's supernatural character, which is established early in the tale. His sudden and mysterious appearance convinces Theodore to consider him "a being of more than human dignity." Indeed he is, in his own words, "one of the benevolent beings who watch over the children of the dust, to preserve them from those evils which will not ultimately terminate in good and which they do not, by their own faults, bring upon themselves." His heavenly mission, revealed in this solemn introduction, requires keen insight into

---

University of Michigan Press, 1968], 167–68 n. 14; and Charles E. Pierce, *The Religious Life of Samuel Johnson* [Hamden, Conn.: Archon, 1983], 160–63). Part of this ambiguity about Johnson's religious beliefs is due to his insistence that reason is necessary for an understanding of revealed truth; as Maurice Quinlan has argued, Johnson "would be unsympathetic to any form of Christianity that rejected reason, or to any type of conversion based upon justification by faith alone," such as the evangelical doctrine (*Samuel Johnson: A Layman's Religion* [Madison: University of Wisconsin Press, 1964], 187).

This rather lengthy note is intended to illustrate the extreme difficulty facing readers who insist upon biograpical evidence of an author's salvation before they will read his or her work. No author's life has been studied more than Johnson's, but after two hundred years, biographical records leave many questions still unanswered.

14. "The Vision of Theodore" in *Works*, ed. F. P. Walesby (Oxford: Talboys and Wheeler, 1825), 9:164, 167 172, 175. Further references are to this edition and page numbers appear parenthetically in the text.

human affairs. The prophet's vast knowledge of the earthly realm is unmistakable as he urges Theodore, "Look around . . . without fear: observe, contemplate and be instructed; and what thou does not understand I will explain" (p. 164). In this commanding rhetoric one can easily hear the bold voices of the Old Testament prophets whose divine power was expressed in part through practical teaching, whose primary duty was not to foretell the future but to transform the present by urging obedience to revealed truths.

A year later Johnson gained notoriety with the powerful language and images in *The Vanity of Human Wishes*. How best to interpret this imitation of Juvenal's tenth satire remains a scholarly desideratum. The principal point of contention is the extent to which the body of the poem relates to its conclusion (lines 343–68).

A full analysis of the debate is unnecessary, however, to recognize the prophetic voice of the narrator. The weighty tone and manner are evident from the opening charge,

> Let observation with extensive view,
> Survey mankind, from China to Peru;
> Remark each anxious toil, each eager strife,
> And watch the busy scenes of crouded life;
> Then say how hope and fear, desire and hate,
> O'erspread with snares the clouded maze of fate,[15]
>
>   [1–6]

to a subsequent restatement of the trouble and pain that result from selfish motives,

> Unnumber'd suppliants croud Preferment's gate,
> Athirst for wealth, and burning to be great;
> Delusive Fortune hears th' incessant call,
> They mount, they shine, evaporate, and fall.
>
>   [73–65]

to the final exhortation:

> Enquirer, cease, petitions yet remain,
> Which heav'n may hear, nor deem religion vain.

15. *Poems*, ed. E. L. McAdam (New Haven: Yale University Press, 1964), 91–92. Subsequent quotations are taken from this edition and page numbers appear parenthetically in the text.

Still raise for good the supplicating voice,
But leave to heav'n the measure and the choice,
Safe in his pow'r, whose eyes discern afar
The secret ambush of a specious pray'r.
Implore his aid, in his decisions rest,
Secure whate'er he gives, he gives the best.

[349–56]

The entire poem, according to the modern critic Anne Williams, shows this speaker to be the "biblical preacher [who] sees earthly life in the context of heavenly truth—which is one definition of what it is to be a prophet."[16] The context of this distinction is Williams's argument that the concluding lines demonstrate the transcendent power of the gospel to resolve the difficulties of life through hope (p. 81), an approach that Juvenal's perspective, untouched by Christian revelation, never could.

Perhaps so, but how can this figure be a prophet and do little more in the three hundred preceding lines than heap sorrow upon sorrow? The answer is twofold. First, such lamentations are reminiscent of Jeremiah and Isaiah, from whose work Johnson chose the texts for four sermons (2, 7, 14, 18).[17] Second, as Northrop Frye explains (though not in reference to Johnson's poem), the prophet places the realities of pain and sorrow in a larger context, that of God's transcendent plan, and so can raise expectations for the future. This view of things, says Frye, distinguishes a prophet from a sage figure.

> The prophet has a comprehensive view of the human situation . . . [He] incorporates the perspective of wisdom but enlarges it. The wise man thinks of the human situation as a kind of horizontal line, formed by precedent and tradition and extended by prudence: the prophet sees man in a state of alienation caused by his own distractions, at the bottom of a U-shaped curve.[18]

16. *Prophetic Strain: The Greater Lyric in the Eighteenth Century* (Chicago: University of Chicago Press, 1984), 82.

17. Nine incidental references to Isaiah occur in other sermons (6, 9, 10, 14, 20, 22, 23, and 28), though four such references are to a single passage (Isa. 55:6–7). Additional interest in Isaiah is suggested by Johnson's high regard for William Lowth's *Commentary upon the Prophet Isaiah* (1714); see Boswell's *Life of Johnson*, ed. R. W. Chapman, a new ed. corrected by J. D. Fleeman (Oxford: Oxford University Press, 1970), 382; and *Sermons*, Jean Hagstrum and James Gray, eds., (New Haven: Yale University Press, 1978), 39 n. 2.

18. *The Great Code: The Bible and Literature* (New York: Harcourt Brace Jovanovich, 1982), 128.

This distinction, applicable as well to the narrator in *The Vision of Theodore*, provides further evidence that Johnson's narrative voice was influenced by his reading of Scripture.

Eliot's Objective Literary Criticism

In the 1760s and after, Johnson turned his pen more frequently to literary criticism, offering judgments that would command respect from critics even in our own day. He remains, as T. S. Eliot remarked just forty years ago, "a dangerous person to disagree with."[19] So is Eliot, and for two particular reasons. His methodology involves a high view of the Bible and a firm adherence to the concomitant doctrine of objective fact.

Eliot's essay "Religion and Literature," for example, explains the unique role that the Bible must play in one's philosophy of literature. A subtle attack upon the impressionistic tendencies of the Romantics, the essay urges readers to judge texts according to theological as well as literary standards. Eliot argues this thesis, in part, by defining religious literature (i.e., finely crafted language about theology) and citing the Authorized Version as an example. Moreover, the theological distinctiveness of the English Bible, he continues, explains its pervasive influence upon English authors (p. 345). With literature and Scripture so interwoven, we are to conclude, readers simply cannot ignore theology and do justice to many English texts.

Eliot is less subtle in "The Function of Criticism," where he uses the language and ideas of 2 Peter 1 to reject Middleton Murry's belief in a sort of Romantic "inner voice" to guide a critic's judgment if external realities, such as tradition and a sense of history, should somehow fail him. In the final section of the essay, Eliot concludes that valid criticism results not from an "inner light" but from objective knowledge. His satiric introductory sentence in this section is all the more arresting due to its biblical echoes:

> Leaving, then, those whose calling and election are sure and returning to those who shamefully depend upon tradition and the accumulated wisdom of time, and restricting the discussion to those who sympathise with each other in this frailty, we may comment for a moment upon the use of the terms "critical" and "creative" by one

19. *Selected Essays*, rev. ed. (New York: Harcourt, 1950), 250. Further references are taken from this edition and page numbers are cited parenthetically in the text.

[Matthew Arnold]   whose place, on the whole, is with the weaker brethren. (p. 18)

This artful use of the Authorized Version of 2 Peter 1 is dramatic irony at its best. The more obvious borrowing is linguistic (Peter instructs his readers, "give diligence to make your calling and election sure" [1:10]). But Eliot is drawing also upon a Petrine theme in chapter 1, and this technique heightens the irony. Peter asserts that whoever lacks virtue, knowledge, temperance, godliness, and other prescribed qualities is either nearsighted or blind and has lost contact with his own past ("hath forgotten that he was purged from his old sins" [1:9]). Peter's answer to the problem, implicit in verses 9–10, is for one to become more mature by remembering the past; and this is precisely the exhortation that Eliot directs to Murry: to progress as a critic by returning to Classicism and avoiding the introspective tendencies of the Romantics.

The return itself involves a modification of one's theory of interpretation so as to acknowledge the importance of fact. This hermeneutic appears throughout Eliot's essays, in explicit statements about individual works and in his own way of judging authors' prose styles. In "Hamlet and His Problems," for example, the importance of objective knowledge is stated most clearly: "every critic must have a highly developed sense of fact," both to treat the text fairly and to prevent a corruption of taste; such corruption, Eliot adds, results from disregard of theological and ethical norms for making literary judgments and from inattention to fact. In other essays, notably "'Rhetoric' and Poetic Drama" and "Charles Whibley," Eliot mentions how his personal knowledge of authors guides his judgments about their literary styles. These opinions result from comparisons between an author's prose and his manner of speaking.[20] Interestingly, this method of evaluating one's writing according to his speech (and the person that it implies) has been used by one theologian to defend the integrity of the Bible; as John Calvin remarked, the authority of Scripture is

---

20. If an author is to succeed in writing in a conversational style, Eliot argues in "'Rhetoric,'" "he must positively give the effect of himself talking in his own person or in one of his roles" (p. 26). Speech habits as criteria for judging one's writing are used also in "Charles Whibley," an essay commending the long-time contributor to *Blackwood's Magazine*. Whibley's writings, observes Eliot, "have a quality which relates them more closely to his speech than to the writing of anyone else. [W]henever I have known both the man and the work of any writer of what seemed to be good prose, the printed word has always reminded me of the man speaking" (p. 444).

"every where derived from the character of the Divine Speaker."[21]

Principles for a Christian View of Literature

The biblical basis for literature and the suggested definition and examples discussed thus far provide the foundation and context for literary study in the Christian university. To this structure, I would add a few guidelines to remind readers of the importance of integrity, innovation, and diligence. After all, the nature of literary criticism is moral as well as intellectual.

The Study of Author—Not Just Text

The first principle of sound literary criticism is that authors merit study, not only as artists but as persons, created in a divine likeness that extends to the act of writing. When an author composes a poem, a short story, or a novel, that person is imitating God himself, though perhaps unwittingly. Granted, this imitative act involves texts as well as persons, but the crucial point is that the ontological link between God as the Author of Scripture and human authors is personal, not simply textual. To be sure, criticism must emphasize the literary work itself, seeking to identify its author's worldview, which includes a literary personality and a set of assumptions about the nature of creativity, power, politics, and social order. Besides, most authors studied in the university are deceased, some (such as John Webster and Edward Young) without leaving many personal papers. As a result, the literary text itself is our best entrance into the author's literary identity.

But a literary work also expresses a soul, from the perverted Oscar Wilde or Hart Crane to the highly moral Elizabeth Barrett Browning or Christina Rossetti. Each of these gifted writers, when alive, was more important to God than any nonhuman aspect of the universe (Matt. 16:26). This sense of personal worth should remind us that authors, no less than fictional characters, deserve intense study. In fact, if we ever allow the goal of criticism to be textual analysis alone, we have journeyed into a far country and fed ourselves the very husks that have impoverished literary scholarship already. The academy simply does not need another community of readers with its own agenda and pet presuppositions; it

21. *Institutes of the Christian Religion,* trans. John Allen (Philadelphia: Presbyterian Board of Christian Education, 1936), 1:89.

needs a literary theory that, despite the limitations of its proponents, is built upon truth, upon God.

The Importance of History

If criticism necessitates study of the author as well as the text, valid interpretation is impossible without biographical and historical research. How, for instance, could one explore the richness of Boethius' *Consolation of Philosophy* (A.D. 524) without understanding something about the Gothic king Theodoric, who had wrongly accused Boethius of treason, and the Roman senate, who later convicted the author and sentenced him to prison, where eventually he would be executed? *The Consolation,* a splendid dialogue in prose and poetry between a despondent prisoner and the allegorical Lady Philosophy who encourages him to find hope beyond his circumstances, is stimulating even without the historical background. But a reader's impressions alone fail to illuminate the author's life or to anchor his literary intentions in history; therefore, the reader cannot "correctly handle" Boethius' text (see 2 Tim. 2:15)—and after all, on the human level it is first his.

To some literary scholars, the call to historical and biographical research is purely intellectual, quite the proper focus of academic life. No doubt, rigorous study is a part of loving God with all of one's mind (Matt. 22:37), whereas intellectual laziness shames the Lord; but curiosity must not overrule the fact that criticism involves stewardship. Critics must use texts properly and will be held accountable for doing so (2 Cor. 5:10), not only because the critic has been given liberty to examine and respond to the literary work but also because it belong to God (Ps. 50:12) and to its author.

The Twofold Character of Texts

Yet a third principle of criticism is the revelatory and representational nature of literature itself. While *The Scholar Gipsy,* for example, reveals Arnold the academic, worried about the place of classical learning in a rapidly expanding industrial society, the poem also represents a world far removed from the crass materialism of the philistine middle class in Victoria's reign and, by application, any other populace lacking what Arnold called "disinterestedness" (i.e., objectivity and suppression of one's emotions). Likewise, D. H. Lawrence's essay "Why the Novel Matters" expresses his high esteem for art as the reader's guide to ultimate reality, although Lawrence erroneously defines that reality solely within the param-

eters of human experience.[22] In these and other pieces of literature, authors reveal their thoughts and feelings and, at the same
time, fashion a verbal icon. As both expression and image, literature puts us in contact with both the author's world and a fictional
domain that in some sense is recognizable to both author and
reader.

This outline of principles, hardly a complete statement on the
subject, passes over a number of complex hermeneutical problems,
one of which relates specifically to the revelatory and representative nature of texts. The problem appears in the question, To what
extent do authors speak biographically in their fictional characters?
To say "always" or "most of the time" is to risk a serious (and often
embarrassing) mistake, as was done once by a young friend of
mine. He was astonished at *The Screwtape Letters* because he thought
C. S. Lewis considered temptation to be desirable and edifying! On
a more sophisticated level, some critics have argued that the rationalistic Houyhnhnms in *Gulliver's Travels* represented Jonathan Swift's
ideal for men; after all, Swift wrote during the (so-called) Age of
Reason, constantly attacking enthusiasm and other signs of emo-
tionalism. Thankfully, during the 1950s Kathleen Williams corrected this misreading, showing that the Houyhnhnms were in fact
the object of Swift's satire upon deism and rationalistic philosophy.[23] On the other hand, suppose a reader never associates

22. To Lawrence the novel is "the one bright book of life" and includes such works as the
Bible ("a great confused novel"), *The Iliad,* and Shakespeare's plays. These, he argues, are
"supreme old novels" because they "are all things to all men. Which means that in their
wholeness they affect the whole man alive, which is the man himself, beyond any part of
him. They set the whole tree trembling with a new access of life, they do not just stimulate
growth in one direction." Based upon this reasoning, then, Lawrence can assert with some
degree of logic that "there is no absolute good, there is nothing absolutely right. All things
flow and change, and even change is not absolute."

Even if we resist the urge to ask how change can be absolutely relative, constant and
inconstant simultaneously, and how one can even conceive of absolute goodness if such
purity cannot exist in any action or being, we soon notice an even more astonishing claim:
"In all this change, I maintain a certain integrity. But woe betide me if I try to put my finger
on it . . . I shall never know wherein lies my integrity, my individuality, my me. I can never
know it" ("Why the Novel Matters" in *D. H. Lawrence: Selected Literary Criticism,* ed. Anthony
Beal [New York: Viking, 1966], 105–6). By what powers of the imagination can someone
claim to possess a characteristic while being unable to identify it?

All in all, Lawrence's thinking demonstrates the (constant) confusion that results from
denying the moral nature of the universe, a realm created by a moral Being, and the presence of right and wrong in both art and life.

23. *Jonathan Swift and the Age of Compromise* (Lawrence, Kan.: University of Kansas Press,
1958), 177.

authors with their fictional characters. This equally serious mistake eliminates any possibility of understanding the full significance of an author's literary life, in other words, the many potential influences of the author as an author upon his or her society.

How then does one avoid both misreadings? Part of the answer lies in careful attention to literary and historical background. The critic uses documented ideas about the author to guide interpretation and allows interpretation to illuminate ideas about less certain biographical details. History and fiction can be interrelated because an imaginary story is also a factual part of the author's literary experience and of the culture in which the piece was written.

Moreover, each story will have a prescribed, though perhaps an unnamed, audience. Here lies a fourth and final principle for a Christian view of literature: the intended readers for a text are worthy of analysis, both as recipients of the particular work and as persons. Eighteenth-century Londoners, for example, preoccupied with gossip, literature, and social graces, found Addison and Steele's periodical *The Spectator* much to their liking. This audience was attracted also to the eloquence and gentility in Samuel Richardson's *Familiar Letters* (1741).

Who precisely were some of Addison's, Steele's, and Richardson's readers? What were their personal interests, habits, and values not mentioned already? How did they react to the authors' works? Were those reactions appropriate, according to biblical principles? Study of these and related questions is within the province of criticism because the Christian worldview emphasizes audiences in personal, not just literary, roles.

For this reason, the reactions of unintentional readers are important too, this group being anyone for whom the author did not deliberately compose the text. As a case in point, modern American Protestants may dislike the Book of Leviticus, and such is understandable, given the exhaustive detail about a sacrificial system no longer practiced even by descendants of the intended audience. Nevertheless, modern readers, Jew as well as Gentile, have a moral and intellectual responsibility to identify the prescribed audience and analyze them as carefully as possible, in the process of discovering the author's intention in writing the book. This task is complicated, of course, by the modern reader's own cultural identity and feelings about the materials under study; thus, one must be diligent in methodology, carefully distinguishing between interpretation and reaction. Both are worthy of discussion with other readers, but interpretation, not reaction, is the guide to textual meaning. Scripture, as well as extrabiblical literature, means what its author intended; and particularly with the Bible, one's understanding of the text has everlasting consequences.

Implications for the Classroom

The preceding discussion has various practical implications for the teaching of literature in the Christian university. While I have sought to model some of them, perhaps a summarizing comment would be useful. All things considered, the philosophy of literature defended in this chapter has three dynamics, each complementing the others.

The first is the predominance of the text. A student's primary task is to understand what the literature says, through its theme, characters, structure, genre, and other textual features. This work is done through explication and analysis. To explicate is to examine all aspects of the work together; analysis, however, calls attention to one aspect (such as structure or theme or character), then examines the others in relation to it. Both explication and analysis are prerequisite to the discovery of textual meaning.

But studying the work itself is not enough and does not happen in a vacuum. Hence the second dynamic, the necessity of historical context. Students must carefully relate a literary work to its author, intended audience, and contemporary setting. The synthesis of these many textual and historical details, drawing upon the best scholarship available, leads to the identification of textual meaning. Still, the task is not complete. The student's own reaction to the text is important too and deserves consideration, as does the response of other readers for whom the author did not intentionally compose the work under study.

Most important philosophically is the matter of biblical integration. During the process of textual study and historical synthesis, students must consider pertinent illustrations, precepts, and other specifics from the Bible. Often, this application is simple and brief; at other times, more elaborate and time consuming. Whatever the situation, the integration *must* take place. It is integral to the academic and spiritual identity of the Christian university, not in any sense a last-minute addendum to the supposedly "secular" responsibility of studying the text. Literary study that ignores the

Scripture neglects both the ultimate source of literature and the ontological basis for its value and credibility.

Literature and Other Disciplines

This chapter began with a reference to the chaotic state of criticism, and it will end there—with one qualification. While many critics continue to rob literature of its historical and biographical importance as well as its determinate meaning based upon ontological kinship to a higher text (authored by a transcendent Being who has superintended history), the Christian university with its bibliocentric view can transform literary studies, restoring the integrity of the author, authority of the text, and legitimacy of the audience. There is hope.

Literary scholars cannot accomplish the task alone, however. Implementing the ambitious enterprise outlined in this chapter and responding to new models as they arise will require the cooperative expertise of academicians in many disciplines: rhetoric, history, biblical studies, language, hermeneutics, philosophy, theology, and psychology. This need for communal effort becomes all the more important given J. P. Moreland's thesis in *Christianity and the Nature of Science.* His denial that there is one, and only one, scientific method[24] will prompt a literary scholar to rethink Baconian assumptions about the nature of truth as it relates to the development of the informal essay in the seventeenth century. Science and literature are more related than they may appear.

Even with the most diligent effort by the academy, a Christian view of literature will not come easily, and the fragmented worldview that in this century has depersonalized authors and their works will not suddenly disappear.

Nevertheless the same God who empowers his church to evangelize the world can equip scholars within the church to return flesh to the dry bones of modern literary theory. Only then will the Author of authors by properly exalted, ruling the literary domain that has always been rightfully his.

24. (Grand Rapids: Baker, 1989), chap. 2.

4   The Arts

John W. Hugo

A key function of the Christian university is to aid students in translating what is learned into a life of thoughts, words, and deeds that are pleasing to God. The Christian university's task involves the training of mind, body, and spirit to several ends: the attainment of professional competencies, the establishment of a pattern of spiritual growth, and the understanding of how one's profession and one's faith interact in a holy life. In developing a Christian view of the fine arts and exploring its implications for a Christian university, one must recognize that art and Christianity are two separate things: the main business of the fine arts is the objectification of artistic conceptions, while the main business of Christianity is to restore people to a right relationship with God through faith in the atoning work of Jesus Christ as revealed in the Scriptures.

A Christian view of the arts should be an integrative view that relates biblical principles to the experience of Christians active in the fine arts. God has lavishly supplied humanity with both general revelation and divine written revelation of himself, from which it is possible to develop a view of the fine arts that is clearly different from a non-Christian view.

God, Man, and the Fine Arts

When God created the world, he included the human being as the only creature with whom he could have fellowship in kind. He bestowed upon this creature the faculty of reason, and with it the potential to do what none of his other creatures could do. Human beings received the special capacity of representing one thing by using another; no other creature uses metaphor or analogy in expressing itself. And being created in the image of the Creator-God, human beings have the same impulse to create things of all sorts. Of course, even a child knows that something cannot be made from nothing; but in a way, that is what human beings have the ability to do: they can actualize their intangible ideas in things having physical properties, things that did not formerly exist.

It is the nature of the fine arts to exhibit the characteristic human trait of creativity. Being made in the image of God, human beings are creators; perhaps a more accurate term for them would be "synthesizers," because human beings can make things only by bringing preexistent materials together. Human beings make two kinds of things: utilitarian objects, that is, things that are made to serve some necessary physical function; and art works, that is, things that are exclusively expressive in function, using devices other than or in addition to language to express something. Art works are always to some extent symbolic because they express something about the artist's view of reality without actually being that reality. There is the possibility of "artistic decoration" such as carvings on an aqueduct or designs on a fork handle, but those are examples of ornamentation, not art. Art works are special because their purposes are expressive rather than utilitarian. What makes art works different from other made things is that they are always symbolic objectifications of the interior experiences of artists.

The fine arts may be conveniently divided into two main classes: the visual arts, such as painting, sculpture, architecture, pottery, design, photography, and drawing; and the performing arts, such as music, drama, and dance. Within the disciplines of the fine arts, people strive to master the skills necessary to fully express their artistic conceptions. The mastery of these skills enables artists to produce art works that mirror their perceptions of reality with the greatest possible clarity.

Beauty and the Fine Arts

Two great ancient thinkers, one godly and one pagan, have explained that the soul cannot truly know beauty unless it has been purged of all its impurities. Plotinus (c. 205–270) concluded that the human soul, once it has shed the encrusting ugliness of dissolution, unrighteousness, lust, craven fears, envy, and discord, is itself beautiful.[1] He spoke of bodily beauty, but only as a shadow of the real beauty, characterizing it as something spiritual that demands goodness and truth as preconditions for knowing true beauty.[2] Plotinus recognized the futility of the ugly, evil, and false soul seeking the beautiful, the good, and the true in anything.

The apostle Paul in his epistle to the Romans explained the reason for the pitiful human condition.[3] Paul claimed that the truth of God was suppressed by evil in humanity. This truth was made plain to humanity—both God's eternal power and divine nature—in creation itself. Paul claims that humanity knew God, but because humanity was evil, it chose to believe a lie: human beings traded the beauty that God had placed within them (by creating them in his inherently beautiful image) for all that is evil, false, and ugly.

Yet, as Plotinus posited, beneath the encrusting mud of evil, falsity, and ugliness in which humanity has chosen to wallow, the beautiful soul, the very image of God, lies waiting to be cleansed. Jesus said, "No man cometh unto the Father, but by me" (John 14:6 KJV). Without the cleansing of the soul from sin by the shed blood of the Lord Jesus Christ, the soul cannot possibly experience goodness, truth, or beauty. If the Father is good, true, and beautiful, nothing evil, false, or ugly can stand before him.

What then, in view of the supreme aesthetic truth found both in pagan and Christian philosophy, is the artist to do? Is it true that unless artists have not been thoroughly cleansed of wickedness, vice, avarice, lying, and ugliness of soul, that they cannot create beautiful works of art? The answer, in view of the idea that beauty cannot coexist with ugliness, would seem to be yes. Then how can it be that unregenerate humans can produce works of art that are considered beautiful by everyone? And in the arts, what is meant by the idea of beauty?

1. Albert Hofstadter and Richard Kuhns, eds., *Philosophies of Art and Beauty* (New York: Modern Library, 1964), 145–50.
2. Elmer O'Brien, ed., *The Essential Plotinus* (New York: New American Library, 1964), 41–42.
3. Romans 1:18–32.

The Problem of Beauty in the Fine Arts

A problematic term in any discussion of art is the term *beauty.*
Mortimer Adler recognizes two types of beauty: enjoyable beauty,
described as the property of any object that gives one who simply
contemplates or apprehends it a disinterested pleasure; and
admirable beauty, described as intrinsic excellence or perfection of
an object in the estimation of experts.[4] But such a division of
beauty into two types creates a problem for those wishing to know
what beauty actually is: it is possible to fail to appreciate an object
for its intrinsic excellence but to derive disinterested pleasure from
it anyway; it is also possible to appreciate an object for its intrinsic
excellence and yet fail to experience disinterested pleasure from it.
In either case, the object is considered to be beautiful in some way.
Can something be beautiful in one way and yet not in another? Is
it possible for an object to be beautiful and ugly at the same time?
It is difficult to explain by Adler's view the masterworks of French
Impressionists, both in painting and in music, many of which are
considered beautiful by experts today but were scorned by contemporary critics.[5]

It seems necessary to find a theory that views Adler's two types
of beauty as different subspecies of beauty, rather than as different
species in the genus beauty. It has long been observed that beauty
"resides" in works of art, but which of Adler's beauties creates that
impression? Is it remotely possible that the idea of a humanly constructed beauty is fallacious? Has the hazy, illusive, indefinable concept of a divinely inspired beauty in art works been substituted for
the very real, glorious beauty of God? The tower of Babel was constructed in an effort to reach heaven itself, and philosophers from
Plato forward have similarly constructed a tower of impressive theories to help humanity reach a state of inward beauty-conscious-
ness whereby it may know the rapture of divine beauty and thus
know God. While pre-eighteenth-century philosophers focused on
the spiritual nature of beauty and its apprehension, later considerations have centered around the physical, intellectual, and psychological nature of human aesthetic experience. This shift of focus
provided the intellectual basis for a new religion where God's holy

4. Mortimer J. Adler, *Six Great Ideas* (New York: Macmillan, 1981), 39.
5. Nicolas Slonimsky has assembled a *Lexicon of Musical Invective* (New York: Coleman-
Ross, 1965), an amusing collection of critical reviews of musical works, all of which eventually became mainstays in the concert repertoire.

temple became the art museum, his priests and prophets became artists and aestheticians, and worship became a matter of personal aesthetic experience. The fallacy of beauty creates the impression that the beauty in art and the beauty of God are one and the same beauty.

There are two corollary fallacies to the general fallacy that there is a beauty in art. The first is that art objects must be beautiful. If Calvin Seerveld's definition of art is correct, that is, that art is the law-abiding, allusive, symbolical objectification of meaning, then, depending on the meaning, art can even be ugly.[6] Francis Schaeffer also allows for the ugly in art, although he cautions that a Christian artist should not make ugliness a major theme in one's body of works.[7]

The second corollary fallacy is that the pursuit of the beautiful is the sole purpose of art. If this were true, then the Christian artist would be put into the unenviable position of objectifying only a part of the meaning to be found in the reality of existence. Sin, which is an ugly side of reality, is still part of human reality, and its depiction in art can serve to illuminate its nature and its consequences. It is not the purpose of art to obscure the truth by painting (if it might be allowed) too rosy a picture of reality: human experience encompasses more than just the beautiful, and to be true, art must not be entirely one-sided.

In much of their writings, H. R. Rookmaaker, Seerveld, Francis A. Schaeffer, and his son Franky Schaeffer avoid the term *beauty* when discussing art. They seem to agree that art need not be beautiful to be art. Even Adler finds no special kind of beauty in art, but finds that beauty is predicated on admirability and enjoyability: art has no corner on beauty.[8] Rookmaaker denies the validity of the concept of Art, an art disconnected from the normal functions of life, having a beauty seen as an abstract quality unrelated to what is depicted, carrying its own meaning.[9] Seerveld exposes the myth of Beauty by pointing out that thoughts on beauty based in the Platonic tradition misread the divinity of God visible in creation and instead construct out of the observed perfection of nature an abstract idolatrous thing called Beauty, which will supposedly lead

6. Calvin Seerveld, *A Christian Critique of Art and Literature* (Toronto: The Association for the Advancement of Christian Scholarship, 1968), 39.

7. Francis A. Schaeffer, *Art and the Bible* (Downers Grove, Ill.: InterVarsity, 1973), 56–59.

8. Adler, *Six Great Ideas*, 128–29.

9. H. R. Rookmaaker, *Art Needs No Justification* (Downers Grove, Ill.: InterVarsity, 1978), 9–10.

the soul to heaven.[10] Along with this idea, Seerveld denies the idea that God directly inspires artists.

> The Christian poet and architect *Anno Domini* do not receive the divine direction (*tavniyth* Exodus 25:40; *typpon* Acts 7:44) Moses was given at Mt. Sinai for building the tabernacle or Isaiah and Jeremiah were given for the poetry they wrote. Except for our inspired Scriptures called the Bible—this is a confession of faith—literature and art is wholly human, not a whit divine.[11]

Of course, Seerveld recognizes that artistic talents come from God, but states that art works do not. That is why some Christian artists reel when their fellows make claims like: "God gave me this song last night," or "I felt the Holy Spirit guiding every brush-stroke." Rookmaaker states, "We never become passive instruments of God's Spirit. He gave us a personality, gave us freedom and responsibility, so we can never say that our work is directly inspired and therefore his. It would be blasphemous to say that our work is God's work."[12]

If the Holy Spirit did inspire art works directly, then the Bible would require an appendix for art works, preferably after Revelation and before Maps. Perhaps the artistic illustrations sprinkled throughout children's Bibles (Bible-as-storybook) to help them visualize the dramatic events described in the Scriptures plant a false idea about art in the minds of children, the idea that the art-works rank inspirationally with the words they illustrate.

Good Art and Bad Art

A Christian view of the arts sees art for what it is. Art is not less than the allusive symbolical objectification of the interior experience of the artist. The question of the art's being good or bad rests in the success of the artist's technique in externalizing internal experience. Bad art happens when an artist's technique is insufficient to the task. This is true whether or not an artist holds to a Christian worldview. Picasso's *Guernica* is good art: Picasso, despite portraying a view of reality with which Christians must disagree, successfully objectifies his view that God must not be better than a beast if he could allow the slaughter of innocents in war in a world

10. Seerveld, *A Christian Critique,* 32–35.
11. Ibid., 37.
12. Rookmaaker, *Art Needs No Justification,* 61.

supposedly under his control.[13] Picasso's view is wrong, but his art work is more eloquent than many volumes of anti-war, anti-God polemics: good art, bad theology. The vehicle (the art work) should not be confused with the message: when a criminal rides in a fine car, the car does not become less fine, nor does the criminal become more virtuous.

Francis Schaeffer develops the idea that art can be judged on four criteria: (1) technical excellence, (2) validity, (3) intellectual content, that is, the worldview which comes through, and (4) the integration of content and vehicle.[14] With respect to the matter of technical excellence, Schaeffer concludes that a work of art may be praised for its technical excellence even if the worldview represented is not a Christian one. Art works are valid for Schaeffer when artists are true both to themselves and to their worldviews, creating honestly, not for personal gain or acceptance. In Schaeffer's view, the worldview that shows through a body of art works must be seen in the light of a biblical worldview. The fourth criterion is a technical one, judging whether the artistic vehicle has been made to symbolically objectify the subject matter effectively. For Schaeffer good art satisfies these criteria, and bad art does not.

Not one to beat around the bush, Franky Schaeffer boldly states, "There are only two kinds of art, good art and bad art. There is good secular art and bad secular art. There is good art made by Christians and bad art made by Christians. . . ."

There is no such thing as Christian art any more then there are Christian bricks or Christian houses.[15] As a practicing artist, Franky Schaeffer is not concerned with whether or not his art is beautiful, but with whether or not his art is consistent with his worldview.

Beauty, Creation, God, and Art

Another matter that deserves consideration is the relationship between beauty, creation, God, and art. What is the source of artistic beauty? If God is held to be the direct source of artistic beauty, there arise problems of transmission and inspiration: how does God get his beautiful idea into the mind of the artist? Certainly God does not supernaturally guide the hand of the artist; if this were so, art would be a form of divine revelation, which clearly it is not.

13. Seerveld, *A Christian Critique*, 46.
14. Schaeffer, *Art and the Bible*, 41–48.
15. Franky Schaeffer, *Addicted to Mediocrity* (Westchester, Ill.: Good News, 1981), 62.

God does provide people with varying degrees of artistic talent and, by the Word of God and the Holy Spirit, guides the life of the Christian artist. God supplies the artist with talents and guides the artist into situations where these talents may be used and developed. But from where does the artist receive inspiration? Certainly it does not come directly from the Holy Spirit: again there is the problem of transmission. It is more likely that artists form ideas in their minds in response to their environment and experiences, which are then objectified to a greater or lesser extent in art works. But what of beauty? Could it be that because artists are made in the image of God that they have the capacity to recognize beauty (e.g., admirability and enjoyability) in creation and also have conceptions of beauty that to a greater or lesser extent can be actualized (realized) in art works?

And what of ugliness in art? Some people refuse to admit that ugliness has any place in art, and that art should be concerned only with beauty. But did God not create things (slime, ragweed, vultures, and catfish) that people consider repulsive? Yet God declared these things good. Who would dare stand before God and say that catfish and vultures are ugly, when he pronounced them good? It may not be possible to conclude that God approves of ugliness in art works, but any created thing that humans deem ugly, God deems good: Beautiful. If ugliness has a place in God's creation (by human standards of beauty and ugliness), then it follows that ugliness may also have a place in art.

A Christian View of the Arts

Because all artistic activity is human activity and because all human activity has moral implications, artistic activity as human behavior falls within the scope of a Christian view of the arts. Art works themselves fall within the scope of a Christian view because of the worldview they reflect. Non-Christian views of the arts fall within the scope of a Christian view of the arts because they influence artistic activity and express interpretations of the meaning and significance of art works. A Christian view of the arts should reflect the values of its source: the Bible. This is essential in spite of the fact that the Bible is silent on specific issues involving the arts. It is rather specific on the nature of the behavior patterns that ought to characterize the Christian life, yet it leaves the Christian free to make choices within those limits.

A Christian view of the arts should reflect the biblical standards for human activity, but it should be no more limiting than those standards. Such a view should liberate the Christian to engage in artistic activity within the behavioral limitations of a biblically based value system. Among other things, the application of such a view to artistic activity should permit Christians to

incorporate a Christian worldview in their art;

evaluate the propriety of artistic behaviors and the content of artistic creations;

stimulate and promote artistic development;

promote originality and creativity;

participate in a wide range of artistic activities;

consider art works of diverse times and cultures;

allow for the uniqueness of individual expression;

pursue artistic excellence.

The Christian must examine the moral aspects of art works. Certainly for the Christian, the content of an art work is a significant aspect in that content invariably reflects the character of a worldview. But Christians must always be careful not to confuse the artistic vehicle with the message it may be carrying. The engagement of an art work by a Christian becomes a matter for consideration when the experience results in a conflict between the character of the Christian's involvement with an art work and the Christian's beliefs about God and his commandments. A Christian view must consider each art work as a world unto itself *and* as a smaller part of an artist's body of works; then one can decide its acceptability as an expression of the artist's worldview.

Toward a Biblical View of the Arts

The Bible provides many accounts of God's people expressing themselves in artistic ways. The Psalms are replete with musical references and statements exhorting the people of God to sing his praises. All Israel sang and danced in celebration before God on the far side of the Red Sea after he delivered them from the hand of Pharaoh (Exod. 15:1–21). In both the tabernacle and the Solomonic temple, artistic design, metal craft, sculpture, architecture, and textile arts were employed with God's blessing and special inspiration (Exod. 31:3–11; 1 Chron. 28:11–21). These examples show that God has uses for the artistic skills of people and that art works are fit vehicles for serving him, whether in visual or performing media.

The Bible has little to say about nonreligious artistic activity, but it has a great deal to say about art having the form and function of idols. Certainly Aaron's golden calf was an artistic creation, but it was also a symbol of the turning away of Israel (Exod. 32:1–20). God commanded Gideon to destroy his father's Asherah pole and altar of Baal (Judg. 6:25–28). The Philistine god Dagon certainly felt the judgment of God: Samson destroyed Dagon's temple by the power of God (Judg. 16:23–30), and the head and hands of Dagon's image were miraculously cut off by the presence of the ark of the covenant (1 Sam. 5:1–7). Jehu destroyed the sacred stone and temple of Baal (2 Kings 10:25–27).

There are absolutes in God's Word concerning the subject matter of art. Blasphemy is forbidden; therefore Christians should not blaspheme in their art works; art works that contain overt blasphemy should not be encouraged or countenanced by Christians, and the observer-participant should not engage art works that are blasphemous. Idolatry is forbidden; therefore Christians should not create objects to be worshiped nor should art works be worshiped by Christians. God's name is not to be taken in vain; therefore performing artists must not take God's name in vain when performing, Christians should not use the Lord's name in vain in literary efforts, and observer-participants should not engage art works that take God's name in vain. Other examples could be cited, but the point is clear: sin in the guise of art is still sin, and Christians participate in sin at their peril.

There is a great difference, however, between actual sin and the depiction of sin in art. The dramatic arts offer a very clear example of this difference. When a character in a play is "murdered" on stage, the deed is not actual but representational: there is no actual murder, no actual victim, and no actual murderer. However, if one actor actually kills another actor for the sake of realism, that actor has committed an act of murder. Likewise, if actors take God's name in vain, even though they have done so "in character," they have actually sinned, because the act is not pretended, but actual. At the point where symbolized sin becomes indistinguishable from the actual sin, the Christian can no longer take part in good conscience. It follows, then, that Christians should not participate in artistic representations that require of any participant nudity (obscenity), profanity, perversion, vulgarity, lewdness, cursing, blasphemy, or any similar acts. For this reason, a Christian cannot consider some behaviors within some artistic activities acceptable as part of a holy life.[16] Knowingly participating in any activity that is offensive in the eyes of God is not an option for the Christian. Some may ask, "But what if only a tiny part of the work is objectionable?" The Christian response should be, "If the offensive part is so tiny, then why was it included at all? Christians should not wink at sin." Solomon said,

> As dead flies give perfume a bad smell, so a little folly outweighs wisdom and honor. [Eccles. 10:1]

Attendance at dramatic productions or at art exhibitions can be spoiled for the Christian even by "minute" offenses against God, especially when one has paid a price of admission, thereby financially supporting the offense.

Implications of a Biblical View of the Arts for the Christian University

The implications of a Christian view of the arts for the Christian university involve several aspects of artistic activity. A Christian university has the dual obligation of promoting Christian growth and of thoroughly training students in their chosen fields of study. As concerns the arts, it is vital that Christian values be incorporated in the training that students receive, so that students will learn to engage in artistic activities in ways that are pleasing to God. The Christian university should countenance a wide diversity of artistic activities, including all the visual and performing arts, thereby demonstrating that Christians may glorify God in the arts as well as in other disciplines.

The structure of the university, by dividing the pursuit of knowledge among the various academic disciplines, has traditionally

---

16. Some might argue that it is permissible for a person to participate in activities where, while one is not required to act in a manner contrary to one's convictions, others openly violate scriptural principles as a part of the activity. It might be suggested that Christians should consider the effect of their participation in such activities on their Christian testimony and, by association, on the testimony of all other Christians in the eyes of non-Christians.

reflected the tendency of the human mind to classify things. But it seems that no matter how clearly the boundaries between various disciplines are drawn, those encountering them find it necessary to dispute their validity. The mind's analytical abilities tend to resist breaches of established disciplinary boundaries, but this resistance works contrary to the mind's inherent desire for synthesis.

The Christian university is responsible not only for developing analytical thinkers but also for developing minds skilled in the process of synthesis. The arts offer opportunities for engaging the totality of a person in the act of creating or of experiencing works of art. Art works are expressions of the physical and mental discipline of those who create them. Similarly, art works are known primarily through the physical senses and mental resources of the observer-participant. With their engaging structures and their tendency to stimulate the imagination, art works present challenges both to the mind of the artist in the act of artistic creation and of the observer-participant in the act of experiencing the results of the artist's efforts. Art works can speak to the heart as it searches for meaning, significance, and beauty in the world. Finally, art works as embodiments of perceived truth can lead the soul to experience the synthesis of ideas in tangible forms, to find resonances of the beauty that characterizes a "higher reality" (known by Christians as Creator-God).

The fine arts challenge a person's abilities at every level. The painter paints with brush in hand, but the hand is controlled by the mind, and the mind interprets what the artist holds in the heart. The singer sings with the voice, which is controlled by the mind, which is informed by the heart. Artistic activity is integrative by nature and offers opportunities for people to integrate psychomotor, cognitive, emotional, and spiritual activity. People engaging in the arts not only receive the benefit of experiencing the world of art but also receive training in synthesis as an integrative process. This skill can assist people in every field in finding meaning and significance in the activities of daily living, to find significance where they never found it before.

The nature of the relationship between the fine arts and the other disciplines is best described as one of give and take. The arts often provide vehicles of nonartistic expression to other disciplines and, at the same time, receive knowledge and materials that enrich the creative process (see table 4.1).

Table 4.1

Relationships between Fine Arts
and Other Disciplines

Art Gives	Art Gets
Biology	
A way of making models for study; film, recording	Anatomical information for figures
Mathematics	
A way of objectifying theoretical geometric figures	A way to describe proportional relationships in art works
Literature	
Media for literary expression: music, dance, song, theater	Performing materials Programmatic subjects
Chemistry	
A stimulus to invent new materials for painting, sculpture, architecture	Materials that can be provided only through chemical engineering
Languages	
Practice in the use of language in music and drama and in performance and research	Translation, pronunciation, cultural enrichment
Biblical Studies	
Models for discussing beauty	Subjects for art works
History	
Artifacts providing insight into past cultures	A record of artistic development
Physics	
Media for illustrating physical laws	A science of sound, description of motion, optics

Characteristics of a Christian View of the Arts

A Christian view of the arts may be effectively summarized in the following statements:

1. God is the source of all things, including human beings, who have the potential to freely express their worldviews in works of art.
2. Although the Bible is silent on many specific artistic issues, the spiritual principles it contains apply strongly to the activities of artists and observer-participants and to the worldviews presented in works of art.
3. All who choose to engage in artistic activity are ultimately responsible to their Creator for their actions.
4. The beauty of God cannot be achieved by the craft of human beings, but because they are created in his image, human beings can make things that are admirable and enjoyable.

In light of this view, the Christian university's posture regarding the arts could be summarized in the following statements:

1. The Christian university should encourage artists to create in the spirit of a Christian worldview.
2. The Christian university should clearly articulate a Christian view of the arts.
3. The Christian university should promote the artistic development of students and should encourage the expression of God-given human creativity.

It is evident that the Christian university needs to nurture and support the arts. The current national debate concerning federal funding for the arts may cause some in the Christian community to recoil from all art forms, detecting sin in the shadows of every gallery, theater, and concert hall. Instead, the emergence of this debate should provoke a constructive response from Christians, one which demonstrates that the arts are worth supporting and that presents alternatives to the art with which they disagree. God gives each artist a creative potential and it is the duty of the Christian university to develop that potential and to educate artists in fulfilling that potential to the glory of God.

5   Social Sciences

David Miller

Social science seeks to discover, explain, and illuminate human life in a social context. Social scientists are those who formulate and carry out methods of analyzing the human behavior of individuals and groups. Social science, unlike art, is a system of derivative ideas filtered through centuries of human experience. It is probably unavoidable that people studying people have been prone to interpret human activity according to their personal philosophies of life.

A Christian university confronts the unique challenge of fairly and accurately analyzing and interpreting human life while retaining its biblical base. First and foremost, a Christian university is called on to teach and pursue knowledge within the framework of a Christian perspective. Likewise, Christian social scientists must be aware of personal presuppositions and assumptions and scrutinize them in light of Scripture before they interpret social science to a particular generation of students. Thus, the hope is that a social science department at a Christian university would be able to develop a binocular view of humanity, in the sense that the social scientist would put the knowledge gained through study and observation in focus with God's revelation, thereby reaching a truly integrated body of knowledge to pass along to students.

Such a binocular perspective ideally would treat biblical revelation and general revelation with an equal degree of fairness and reason. With such a mindset, a working social scientist would interpret reality naturally and congruently within a Christian framework.

Thus, a Christian student training to become a psychologist or sociologist at a Christian university would be taught in such a manner that integration of biblical data with current research and theory would become a natural part of it. The student automatically would learn to integrate current data with Scripture. When certain information appears to conflict with biblical principles and teachings, the student would accept, naturally and consistently, the biblical viewpoint. As Harry Blamires correctly points out, the Christian worldview sets earthly issues within the context of the eternal and relates all human problems—social, cultural, political—to the doctrinal foundations of the Christian faith[1]

In addition, the Christian social scientist must avoid the pitfalls encountered when ignoring or denying his or her own philosophical underpinnings. The challenge is to avoid the temptation to change the facts of biblical revelation to fit the archaeological or evolutionary finding of the day. Herman Dooyeweerd holds that "everyone engaged in scientific research proceeds from definite presuppositions, from certain basic convictions, and is tied to all kinds of conceptions and insights in his inner being. And the less a social scientist is conscious of this inescapable attachment to certain presuppositions, the more he is chained to them and the more strongly he is dominated by them."[2]

University professors who teach and conduct research in the social sciences have, then, a responsibility to be aware of their own belief base, to state those beliefs to their students, and to interpret their own and other's findings in light of an awareness of such personal presuppositions. Honesty and academic integrity demand that personal biases of interpretation be acknowledged.

1. *The Christian Mind* (Ann Arbor, Mich.: Servant, 1963).
2. *The Search for Wisdom in the Concept of Law* (Amsterdam: 1936).

Foundational Points

Once the Christian social scientist has accepted the need to be aware of personal foundational beliefs, identification and definition of such beliefs becomes the next step. What follows is not exhaustive but rather is a reflection of important considerations relevant to discussing the social sciences.

1.There is but one unifying truth, grounded in the supernatural character of God. This truth is objectively available through natural revelation. General revelation through nature and specific revelation through God's Word provide professors of social science with ample evidence of the reality of God.

2. The historical reality of Christ and his redemptive power must be accepted, internalized, and integrated into the data of social science. In Christ we find our hope and our strength; though subjectively felt by believers, the objective and historical reality of Jesus Christ overwhelms all other realities.

3. Our world consists of natural laws supernaturally formulated. Social scientists are in fact seeking the face of God when they do their work. As human beings are studied individually and in groups, as psychologists, sociologists, anthropologists, archaeologists and others labor after the truth, they ultimately and inevitably find the mind of God behind all social realities. As Elton Trueblood stated, "In the theistic conception, God is not only the creator, without whom the world as we know it would not be, but also the One who is constantly sustaining the world and is involved in every step. The order of nature, far from limiting God's action in the present world, is dependent upon His purpose and subservient to it."[3]

4. The God-likeness of human beings is found throughout Scripture. Social scientists learn about God through learning about the people of his creation. Many passages in the Bible declare the reality of humanity's creation in the image of the Creator. Genesis 1:26–27, 5:1, 9:6, and 1 Corinthians 11:7 provide just a sample of the emphasis God has placed on telling us about our creation in his image.

Though different in many important respects, humans and animals share the same Creator and thus share many characteristics. Natural scientists can learn something about the circulatory system of humans by studying that function in laboratory rats. Experiments with chimpanzees and other animals have led to cures for many diseases that once afflicted humans. Social scien-

3. *The New Man for Our Times* (New York: Harper and Row, 1970).

tists, too, can learn something about humans by studying animals. All creation shares but one Creator, and social scientists have been given the opportunity to put that reality to valuable scientific and social use.

5. *Evil is a reality and assaults our senses every conscious moment.* Viewed from a Christian perspective, behavior is either good or evil, and it matters which. Christians accept the objectivity of morality and expect that perfection in Christ will reestablish that morality on earth one day. But until that time, sociologists must continue to research the effects of crowding on people, psychologists will still try to explain how a human brain is capable of such evil as is perpetrated every day in our cities, anthropologists will offer new explanations of how we got into this condition so quickly, and all Christian social scientists will accept the fact that only by including biblical data can reality be understood and dealt with appropriately.

Social Science and the Christian University

Social science is a term encompassing several subject areas, including psychology, sociology, anthropology, economics, political science, archaeology, and others. The original purpose of a social science curriculum within education was to equip young people with practical knowledge and ideals that could improve society and better the quality of life.

A Christian university must accept the role of social science as an indispensable element in the curriculum and accept as well the need to update and adapt course content to a changing world. New historical, archaeological, anthropological, psychological, and sociological findings must be welcomed, not feared, by Christian higher education. To truly be of the mind that all truth *is* God's truth implies that the Christian university is afraid of nothing. Keeping God's inerrant Word a ready resource, the Christian social scientist accepts all challenges as new opportunities to see the hand of God working among people.

Jesus Christ: A Social Science Perspective

Christians acknowledge Jesus as the greatest Teacher ever to have ministered to people. Christians recognize the Savior as a perfect judge of the character of people, a perceptive psychologist, a criminologist who understood the criminal mind as no other could, a sociologist who knew why people treat one another as they do, a historian who always had his facts right, and one who acknowledged those with business sense and marketing skills.

A person wanting to know the Savior better could take advantage of the social sciences to facilitate that learning. What were the social influences on Jesus as he grew? Social, economic, and cultural practices unique to middle-eastern life most certainly became part of his education. The knowledge that Jesus was educated, though whether formally or informally we do not know, comes from Luke 2:52: "Jesus grew in wisdom and stature," a statement confirming the need for learning by Jesus.

We can learn about Jesus as well by studying his home environment, the parenting practices common to that day, the political and military influences in the area, and his education as a Jewish boy. To what extent was Joseph an influence on Jesus as a child? What other family members were influential? How did growing up in an occupied land influence his education and outlook on others?

In other words, what did God arrange in the life of Jesus so that his Son would be able to know what it was to be truly human? And what can we learn from this that will help us understand the value of social science? From 2 Timothy 3:14–17 we know that biblical revelation is given specifically to enable us to live the kind of life we were designed to live. Since everything is created by God, everything can be studied to learn more about him.

Psychology: The Controversial Social Science

Psychology has become a focus of criticism within Christian higher education. The critics are generally other Christians with a different perspective on the need to learn about the world. While not everything done in the name of Christian psychology can be justified, truly biblical psychology is able to deal with assaults on morally legitimate investigation and not succumb to such pressure or criticism.

The humanistic roots of psychology in the theories of Sigmund Freud, C. G. Jung, and others has led some to believe that no usefulness remains for psychology among Christians. Psychology has traditionally been known as "the science of the soul"[4] and as such has earned a great deal of negative attention from Christians. Yet the task before Christian psychologists remains that of advancing

4. Malcolm A. Jeeves, *Psychology and Christianity: The View Both Ways* (Downers Grove, Ill.: InterVarsity, 1976).

the cause of Christ through their profession while providing a strong biblical basis for their efforts.

Psychology in the University

Little more than a century ago, psychology was a relatively minor branch of philosophy. The first university courses in psychology began during the 1870s and the first laboratories in psychology were established in the United States and Germany. By the turn of the century psychological laboratories, still primarily in the United States and Germany, numbered more than one hundred. Psychology was well on its way to becoming a major social science.

Though Sigmund Freud is recognized as the father of psychology, his studies applied more to the philosophical and sociological than to the inner workings of the mind. The father of American psychology was William James (1842–1910). Educated at Harvard and interested primarily in physiology, James became the first to write a major textbook on psychology (1890). Although not a biblical Christian, James was a deeply religious man concerned (as are many today) with applying his new-found psychological insights to the field of religious experience.

James attempted to deal with subjective mental experiences and thus created a backlash, leading eventually to the establishment of behavioral psychology under James B. Watson. Watson is remembered as the psychologist who argued that scientific theory cannot be built on the soft and subjective foundation of introspection, religious or otherwise.

The Mind-Soul Issue

A physician recently lectured to a group of Christian psychologists and counselors about the functioning of the limbic system. Among the many points he made to this audience was that rather than say "I love you with all my heart," one could more accurately say "I love you with all my limbic lobe." After the laughter subsided, the speaker went on to explain at great length and in convincing detail the accuracy of his point. The limbic system is the mediator of our feelings in many cases, he explained, and if this portion of the brain is diseased or stressed by tumor or accident, emotional control and expression can cease to function. The discussion leads to a serious consideration for Christian psychologists. Is there a similar misunderstanding about the relative role of mind and soul?

William Wilson, professor of psychiatry at Duke University, believes there is such a misunderstanding. Wilson argues that both psychological data and theological thinking speak to the issue of mind versus soul, whereas he contends that mind and soul are one and the same.[5]

Students of psychology know that the mind serves several crucial functions in human beings. The significance of the following comments is accentuated by the traditional view that psychologists and psychiatrists are "mind doctors" while theologians and pastors are "soul doctors." The reality is that the distrust expressed by many Christians stems from the belief that psychologists, psychiatrists, and counselors are stepping over into the territory of pastors. If mind and soul are really the same, as Wilson proposes, then the integration of psychology and theology is not only possible but necessary!

What do psychologists know about the human mind? First, the mind contains consciousness, an awareness of self and environment, and an awareness of one's past, present, and anticipated future. Consciousness is related to the concept of "brain life" as compared to the medical determination of "brain death." To be brain dead is to be mind dead, and to be mind dead is to be "soul transported." One is physically dead when awareness is permanently removed from the physical body and cannot be restored by natural means.

Psychologists know as well that the mind controls the majority of passive reflexes (functional behaviors often present before birth that enable the person or animal to survive until the active mind can take over). Theologians have long proposed that reflexes are God's gift to his struggling creation, put in place genetically and diminishing in importance as the person grows and develops.

Psychologists also know that the mind contains instincts, that is, biological drives related to survival needs. We have instincts to parent, protect, and reproduce, instincts to eat and sleep, to act aggressively or passively, to struggle to live or accept the inevitability of impending death. Humans have instincts leading toward logic and hypothetical thinking, end-times driving all thinking human beings toward some form of relationship with or understanding of God.

Psychologists know, too, that the mind performs mental manipulations of symbols, ideas, concepts, and patterns that normally

5. W. P. Wilson, *"The Mind, God's Word, and Psychotherapy,"* unpublished paper, Duke University, 1977.

lead to adaptive living. Human beings are the only part of God's creation capable of becoming aware of their own future and inevitable death. Only human beings know they are going to die. Only human beings are able to think about thinking, that is, to reflect on and analyze the content of thoughts in such a way as to refine and change those thoughts as necessary or expedient.

Only humans think about death and only humans think about thinking. Thinking is central to human nature, but where is it that thinking occurs? When small children are asked to point to that part of their body where they "live," most point to that part of the head directly behind the eyes.

Perhaps there is truth in the mouths of such small children. Perhaps in some sense our conscious life is focused in a particular part of the body. Perhaps the historical hostility between theology and psychology is not as justified as it seemed initially.

The Mind in the Bible

1. The mind contains awareness: "And the LORD God formed man of the dust of the ground, and breathed into his nostrils the breath of life; and man became a living soul" (Gen. 2:7 KJV). To be alive is to be potentially aware of one's environment. To live is to possess the potential to know that which is outside one's own environment, God the Creator. To be alive and aware is to have the power to make choices to accept the forgiveness and grace of God. To become a living soul is to have the potential to know God and accept his Son as Savior.

2. The mind is a part of the "flesh": "Now the works of the flesh are manifest, which are these, adultery, fornication, uncleanness, lasciviousness, idolatry, witchcraft, hatred, variance, emulations, wrath, strife, seditions, heresies, envyings, murders, drunkenness, revellings, and such like" (Gal. 5:19–21 KJV). It is the mind that moves the body, and the works of the body are controlled by the works of the mind. To have a soul far from God is to have a mind steeped in the environment of sin. What the body does, the mind first imagines. A boy wanting to climb a tree must first imagine grasping a lower limb so that he can reach one a little higher, then see himself pulling himself up a little, and then a little more, and so on. What confounds small children who are prone to predicaments such as getting stuck in the treetop is that they did not imagine how to get back down once they had attained their goal. What the body does, the mind first imagines. The mind is intimately involved in what the Bible calls the "flesh."

Among whom also we all had our conversation in times past in the lusts of our flesh, fulfilling the desires of the *flesh* and of the *mind;* and were by nature the children of wrath, even as others. [Eph. 2:3 KJV, emphasis added]

As the body desires, hungers for, needs, or feels, the mind serves as the enabler of these actions. If the mind (brain) is damaged or diseased, the desires of the flesh are changed. If portions of the brain that control emotion are damaged by tumor or accident, the desire to eat leads to either uncontrolled eating or self-starvation. If the limbic area is damaged, emotions can run wild, leading a once peaceful person to commit terrible acts. The mind is indeed a part of one's "flesh."

3. *The mind is Spirit-influenced:* "Create in me a clean heart, O God; and renew a right spirit within me" (Ps. 51:10 KJV). What becomes contaminated by sin is the heart, which in reality involves the mind. Those actions often attributed to the heart really reside in the mind. As heart transplant recipients experience a changing of the physical heart, so Christians can experience a changing, a renewing, of the mind. However, we can undergo a "change of heart" in the hospital operating room with no corresponding change of heart in our core character or personality. Not so with the mind; when it changes, so, in some respect, does the character.

The mind with which we think can be influenced by the indwelling Holy Spirit. Christians can ask for a change of heart, knowing that what must change is in fact the mind.

4. *The mind parallels the soul in function.* From a human stand-point, the mind, and from a theological standpoint, the soul, have common functions: for example, memory (Ps. 119:167), love (Song of Sol. 1:7), anger (Isa. 1:14), confusion (Ps. 6:3), and awe (Ps. 139:14). It may prove profitable to examine each of these briefly.

Memory: "My soul hath kept thy testimonies; and I love them exceedingly" (Ps. 119:167 KJV). What we "keep" of past experiences depends on the functioning of memory, at least while we are in these physical bodies. To be able to remember, at will, what God promised is a function of mind, the storehouse of memories. Does mind mean the same thing as soul here? Or are we to understand that mind and soul function interchangeably in this context?

Love: "Tell me, O thou whom my soul loveth. . ."(Song of Sol. 1:7 KJV). The capacity to love is uniquely human, and the capacity to love God is universal in his human creation. The functioning of the mind can lead a person to spiritual and intellectual decisions to reject God. The person then becomes a reprobate (Rom. 1:28). A renewed mind can lead to a refreshed soul.

Anger: "Your new moons and your appointed feasts my soul hateth; they are a trouble unto me; I am weary to bear them" (Isa. 1:14 KJV). Anger and hate are emotional entities. Human beings have the unusual ability to become angry and feel hate without being conscious of the motivations behind these emotions. Believers know that our spirit can be angry even when the mind is cautioning against becoming too upset. Humans have the potential to be angry yet not sin in that anger, as long as their anger and hatred are congruent with what God hates.

Anger and hate must have targets. The selecting of targets for these emotions is generally a mental process based on facts and memories as perceived by the one who is feeling anger or hatred. The soul and the mind are serving the same function here.

Confusion: "My soul is also sore vexed; but thou, O LORD, how long?" (Ps. 6:3 KJV). Trying to sort out the different functions of mind and soul when considering the state of confusion is difficult and perhaps impossible. When believers find themselves in a state of "spiritual" confusion regarding the correctness of some action or thought, is it the soul that seeks clarity from God or the mind that seeks information and insight from God? Or is it both? When resolution of that confusion takes place, does it occur in the residence of the soul or in that part of the body above the neck and behind the eyes?

Human beings alone have a rational soul, and human beings alone have the capacity to experience spiritual confusion. Spiritual confusion is healed through a changing of the mind and a healing of the soul. Mind and soul occupy common ground.

Awe: "I will praise thee; for I am fearfully and wonderfully made; marvelous are thy works; and that my soul knoweth right well" (Ps. 139:14 KJV). Here again we find "soul" capable of gathering, internalizing, and interpreting information, functions ordinarily assigned to man's mind.

Where does worship originate? Where does the sense of awe develop and grow in a believer? Is "worshipful reverence" based on the *knowledge* that one has acquired about God or is it based on a felt need in every human being to worship a creator? The functions of mind and soul so often overlap in the Bible that Christian psychologists should not assume that mind and soul serve totally different functions for the believer. The practice of psychology carried out by Christians is not fundamentally different from the work of pastors, teachers, and evangelists. Mind doctors and soul doctors are doing the same basic work. The challenge is to accept this reality and move from building competitive, often antagonistic systems for helping people toward constructing cooperative networks wherein pastor and Christian psychologist work together for the common good of those they serve.

Integration of Psychology and Theology

Two related but separate issues lie at the heart of the tension between psychology and theology. There is significant semantic ambiguity in the concept of *psyche* and its derivative *psychology* fostered by the historical transformation of our understanding of the functioning of the brain.

The battle between psychologists and theologians has a long history and deep philosophical roots. For those who seek a resolution of the partition between these fields, four positions deserve consideration.

The "Against" Model

Psychology and theology are viewed by many as destined to remain mortal enemies, each intent on the destruction or relegation to a place of irrelevance of the other. The fields are mutually exclusive and mutually antagonistic in most instances. Revelationists such as Jay Adams and Larry Crabb reject the theories of empiricists such as Sigmund Freud and B. F. Skinner. Neither believes he has anything substantial to gain from studying the other or considering their viewpoints. From an educational standpoint, the camps would be secular humanists on one side, totally rejecting anything outside the reality of the senses, and religious isolationists on the other, choosing against the teaching of psychology unless forced to do so by accrediting agencies.

The "Of" Model

This approach seeks to find the psychology inherent in other entities. In this pursuit we find academic coursework in psychology of religion and psychology of mass conversion. Human beings are described as being neutral/active in their nature, born neither good nor bad but developing as they interact with their environment. What becomes of a person is the responsibility of the environment one experiences early in life.

Psychology becomes the missing answer for all questions. If religion is not enough to satisfy need to know or if the answers religion provides are not satisfying, simply develop a course called "Psychology of Religion" that will go that extra step and explain (using psychology rather than the Bible as a base) what religion failed to explain satisfactorily.

The Parallel Model

The parallel model perceives psychology and theology as being separate but equal. The two fields seek the same answers by traveling different routes. The parallel model ultimately develops into an unsatisfactory form of educational "apartheid," wherein theology always finds itself in minority status and academically disenfranchised.

The Integrated Model

Psychology and theology do not exist to supplant each other or to explain each other into irrelevance; rather, they exist to serve one another as mutual partners in pursuit of knowledge. Integration means that the rigidity of educational disciplines becomes secondary in importance to the Christian student. All truth is God's truth, and though there are many ways to perceive God's revelation (i.e., nature/Scripture), all academic disciplines handled honestly lead to the Creator.

Criteria for Integration of Psychology and Theology

At least five essential criteria exist for the attainment of true integration of psychology and theology. These are suggested in the hope that they will serve to assist the Christian student in any field of study but in particular those studying psychology or theology.

1. Integration is essential rather than dependent. If an honest integration is achieved, it will occur only on the basis of equality. Students in either field must see the other discipline as central to their own and an indispensable part of the whole. Rather than viewing the world with the eye of psychology *or* the eye of theology, the Christian student will look through both eyes to enhance the total worldview.

2. God is central to any complete understanding of the Bible or humankind. The concept that "all truth is God's truth" is incomplete in itself. Of course all truth emanates from God, but the goal of that truth is to lead us back to him. It is not sufficient for social scientists simply to legitimize their educational endeavors with such a rationale without taking the next step and using these studies to lead people to Christ. God is the Author and Finisher, the One who is the ultimate reality and the final goal of life. No science can be truly scientific without recognizing the Creator as well as the creation.

3. *Jesus Christ must be acknowledged as dynamically involved in both scriptural and natural revelation.* Social scientists seek laws by which to understand and predict the activities of humankind. Jesus Christ, as revelation, serves the function of explaining humanity to human beings. The purpose of the incarnation was in part to convince us that we could know both ourselves and our Creator by examining revelation.

4. *Integration must be practical.* As Christians, our concern with "other-worldly" issues cannot distract us from making the gospel and Christian living both useful and practical to the unbelieving world. Though interested in the distant future and knowing that there is no limitation on that future for any believer, Christian psychologists must be careful to stay in the "here and now," continually focused on the cares and concerns of the people we seek to serve.

5. *Integration must be comprehensive.* Integration is an important and necessary component in the life of every believer. Jesus Christ should be integrated into family experience, vocation and avocation, that is, into every aspect of living. In the academic community, integration must characterize every discipline, every scholarly field, and sports and extracurricular activities.

A Christian social scientist is directed to the creation of the universe and the making of the human species in God's own image all the way through the fall and the corruption of that creation and back again, full circle, to restoration. Other philosophies do not give an adequate explanation or philosophical structure to the nature of the universe, the personhood of human beings, and the work of redemption.

A Christian perspective on the utility of social science gives not only an adequate basis for the value of human life and the relationship of those lives to the Creator, but builds a realistic structure as well. Christianity resolves the philosophical inadequacies of humanly inspired theories and constructs out of their chaos a uniform, knowable, and cogent rationale for humanity's place in the universe.

As E. J. Carnell points out,

The enigmatic situation in the modern world is that the scientist rejects the Christian worldview because it involves certain non-empirical, metaphysical hypotheses, while assuming for himself a truckload, each of which goes as much beyond sensory observation as does the Christian's postulate of the God who has revealed Himself in Scripture. The Christian questions the sport of this game. Fair rules in the context of hypothesis-making ought to dictate that the winner be he who can produce the best set of assumptions to account for the totality of reality. The Christian finds his system of philosophy in the Bible, to be sure, but he accepts this, not simply because it is in the Bible, but because when tested, it makes better sense out of life than any other system of philosophy.[6]

The Christian social scientist assumes that God exists and is the source of all truth. They also assume that the people God created are able to come to know the truth, even though God has not chosen to reveal everything to us, and even though the truth revealed cannot be known without some degree of human distortion.

A Christian perspective on the utility of social science, and psychology in particular, calls for an expanded level of empiricism, a renewed emphasis on biblical absolutism, a Christian supernaturalism, and a biblical anthropology.[7]

The Christian social scientist has within reach an objective, historical, humanly feasible hope for the problem of living in a sinful world. Scripture elucidates the promise of God's forgiveness, faithfulness, protection, guidance, love, and mercy. Social science built on a Christian foundation gives no place to the naive and incorrect view that we are naturally good and will inevitably (if only the environment would leave us alone!) progress up the evolutionary ladder, nor does it opt for existential despair and future self-destruction.

A Christian perspective on life as practiced by Christian social scientists provides believers with an understanding of our personhood, our place in creation, and the illumination of past error and sin. Such a perspective also provides a realistic hope through the God who took on humanity and lived among us, experiencing all we experience, and yet did not sin. A Christian perspective on social science answers questions that ought to be answered, and such answers themselves are dependent upon the light of biblical truth.

6. E. J. Carnell, *An Introduction to Christian Apologetics* (Grand Rapids: Eerdmans, 1948).

7. Gary R. Collins, *The Rebuilding of Psychology: An Integration of Psychology and Christianity* (Wheaton: Tyndale, 1977).

6   History

Paul R. Waibel

The Christian historian, like Christian colleagues in other disciplines, begins with this basic presupposition: that a personal, infinite God exists; that he is not silent; and that he has spoken in a way that is understood.[1] Divine communication is found in Scripture (the Word written) and in the earthly ministry of Jesus Christ (the Word incarnate) as recorded in Scripture. There follows from this basic presupposition, or axiom, a number of characteristics of a Christian view of history that distinguishes it from other approaches to history.

The Christian historian brings a Christian worldview to the study of history. It is the Christian worldview that sets the Christian historian apart from non-Christian colleagues. The Christian worldview gives the Christian historian an insight into the meaning of history and of individual historical events that is not available to the non-Christian historian. Whereas the non-Christian historian must find meaning in the historical process itself, or conclude that history is

---

1. Francis A. Schaeffer, *The God Who Is There* (Downers Grove: InterVarsity, 1968), and *He Is There and He Is Not Silent* (Wheaton: Tyndale, 1972).

meaningless, the Christian historian finds the meaning of history in divine revelation. Since that revelation has been given in Scripture, acceptance of the inerrancy and infallibility of the Bible, and therefore its authority, is crucial to formulating a Christian view of history.

Along with Christian colleagues in other disciplines, the Christian historian accepts the historic orthodox position with respect to the divine inspiration of Scripture. The Bible is the very Word of God (2 Tim. 3:16), "inspired in the sense of being word-for-word God-given."[2] Therefore, what the Bible communicates is absolute truth, not relative truth, both with respect to the historical events recorded in the Bible and to the meaning of history itself. The Christian worldview, then, grows out of a fundamental difference between Christian historians and their secular counterparts: their differing views regarding the nature of the Bible.

Non-Christian historians are compelled by the presuppositions, or axioms, of their own worldview to reject the Christian view of history because of its reliance upon revelation. Although one may intellectually understand the Christian view and perhaps even acknowledge its logic, to accept a view of history that recognizes the personal, infinite God of the Bible as the One who created and exercises lordship over the historical process is an insurmountable obstacle to anyone who is not a Christian.

Christopher Dawson (1889–1970), for many years a distinguished professor of medieval and Renaissance history at Harvard University, summed it up well: "It is very difficult, perhaps impossible, to explain the Christian view of history to a non-Christian, since it is necessary to accept the Christian faith in order to understand the Christian view of history. . . ." He went on to note that those who reject the idea of divine revelation "are obliged to reject the Christian view of history as well." Even those who are willing to accept "revelation" in the form of a possible religious truth beyond human reason will, of necessity, reject the Christian view of history because of the "enormous paradoxes of Christianity."[3] From the perspective of a non-Christian worldview, the Christian view of history, derived from biblical revelation, will seem absurd.

From biblical revelation, then, the Christian historian derives the

2. J. I. Packer, *"Fundamentalism" and the Word of God* (Grand Rapids: Eerdmans, 1958), 47.
3. Christopher Dawson, "The Christian View of History," in *God, History, and the Historians: Modern Christian Views of History,* ed. C. T. McIntire (New York: Oxford University Press, 1977), 30.

insights that account for the distinctive characteristics, or guiding principles, of the Christian view of history. These include the fact that history has a definite beginning and end; that there is a divine plan to history; that history has both temporal and supernatural sides; that although there is technological progress over time, there is no moral progress in history; that history is not "value free"; and finally, that within history, people exercise free will under the sovereignty of God.

Basic to a Christian view of history is the understanding that history has a definite beginning and a definite end, with God, who exists outside history, as both the Initiator of history and the One who will bring it to its preordained conclusion. In short, there is a flow to history.

When we speak of history having a "definite beginning" and a "definite end," or of God existing "outside history," we simply acknowledge that history is part of the created order. It is another way of speaking of time. Outside this created order there is only eternity. Hence, when we speak of "history," for all practical purposes, we are referring to human history. Although events occurred prior to the six days of creation described in Genesis 1, and events will continue to occur after the eternal kingdom is established, it would be misleading to refer to them as "historical." Where there is no beginning or end, there is no history.

History came into being when God created time. In Genesis 1:3–5 we are told of the beginning of history:

> And God said, "Let there be light," and there was light. God saw that the light was good, and he separated the light from the darkness. God called the light "day," and the darkness he called "night." And there was evening, and there was morning—the first day.

The conclusion of verse 5, "And there was evening, and there was morning—the first day" tells us that God measured out a period of time, consisting of day and night, and that that period of time became the first day. Since then, time (and therefore history) has moved down to the present as a continuous succession of days and nights. And history will continue until after the millennium when the new Jerusalem comes. Then the succession of days and nights will end, and with it, history also (Rev. 21).[4]

4. Some Christians believe that Revelation 21 describes the millennial kingdom. It seems clear to this writer, however, that the New Jerusalem is the eternal kingdom. Verse 4 speaks of there being "no more death," and of the "old order" having "passed away." In verse 23,

The Bible teaches that God is the One who not only began and will conclude the historical drama but also controls the flow of history. This means simply that there is a divine plan to history that gives it purpose and meaning. History is not, as Henry Ford was fond of saying, one darn thing after another. Rather, history is going somewhere.

Scripture records various historical events, both those which have occurred and those which are yet to occur, which provide the Christian historian with a key to understanding the whole historical drama. In the early chapters of Genesis we are told of the fall of humanity, not as a kind of moral fable but as an actual historical event. Galatians 4:4 teaches that "when the time had fully come, God sent his Son. . . ." We are also told in Revelation and elsewhere that a day and an hour has been appointed when the Lord Jesus Christ will return and bring down the curtain on history. Hence the Christian historian knows that history is not a meaningless repetition of cycles, or an endless cause-and-effect progression to some earthly utopia or dystopia. Instead, the biblical view is of history as a linear development under the sovereign lordship of Jesus Christ. From the fall, all history looks forward to the birth of Jesus Christ. From the crucifixion and resurrection, all history looks forward to his return. Romans 8:22–23 says the whole creation is groaning, waiting for the Lord's return.

The fall as recorded in Genesis provides the Christian historian with a number of insights, which in turn can guide him in seeking to understand the flow of history since then. From the record of the fall we learn that history is not one-dimensional. There is a supernatural aspect to history. To study history as if historical events had only a temporal significance would be incomplete.

History since the fall may be viewed as a "conspiracy within a conspiracy." Satan has a plan, or goal, in his continuing rebellion against God. But Satan's conspiracy is operative only within the limits set by God's sovereignty. That is, God's "conspiracy," or plan for history, is superior to Satan's. There are two forces in history, but God is the Lord of history. History is not out of control.

Although as a result of the fall humanity was drawn into Satan's rebellion, we are not a helpless pawn of deterministic forces, spiritual or otherwise. Although fallen, we remain created in the image

the sun and moon are no longer present, and in verse 25, it is said that "there will be no night there." Clearly, what is being described is the eternal kingdom, where time, and therefore history as we understand it, is no more.

of God (Gen. 9:6; James 3:9). The biblical account of the fall, and the whole of Scripture, provides the Christian historian with insight into human nature, which in turn helps us understand our actions in history.

Although Adam and Eve were created without sin, their disobedience and fall left them and all subsequent humanity with an inclination to sin, to do evil. To say that we have an inclination to sin, and will sin (Rom. 3:10, 23) is not the same as saying we were created evil. Not at all. Our sinful nature is a byproduct of the fall, not of creation. Even when individuals accept God's saving grace through Jesus Christ's finished work on the cross, they remain sinners—sinners saved by grace, but still sinners (1 John 1:8).

The fact of the fall and its consequences does not excuse our evil deeds, for we remain morally responsible agents. Our choices have significance not only for the flow of temporal history but also for the war Satan is waging against God's sovereignty (see the Book of Job). Hence, the Christian historian understands that historical events are a product of both human action and the actions of supernatural beings, both good and evil.

The Christian historian rejects the humanistic notion that we are progressing, or evolving, morally over time. Rather, the Christian historian knows from the testimony of Scripture that fallen, corrupt human nature does not change, except as individuals accept God's redeeming grace through Jesus Christ's finished work on the cross. Even then, total redemption awaits the Lord's return. The Christian historian can agree that there has been technological progress in history but must reject the secular notion of moral progress.

Because his insights are gained from Scripture, only the Christian historian can provide an adequate explanation for the existence of evil. The non-Christian historian is at a loss to explain how human beings can be capable of acts of great nobility, and at the same time, of unbelievable cruelty. How could the same men who drafted the United States Constitution condone slavery? How can their descendants, who have fought wars to defend freedom, condone the abortion holocaust? How does one explain the destruction of European Jewry under the Nazi tyranny, or the killing fields of Cambodia?

The Christian historian likewise rejects the secular notion that history should be written void of value judgments. Virtually all modern historians of whatever philosophical bent acknowledge the "myth of objectivity" in studying history. A value element enters in when the historian selects which data, or facts, are important. Likewise, a value judgment enters in when those facts are interpreted or evaluated. The same historical facts may provide evidence for vastly different interpretations, depending on whether the historian is a Marxist, humanist, or Christian. It is the historian's worldview that determines how he interprets and records history. The historian's particular interpretive framework (worldview) by necessity imposes a certain value system upon history. Hence, to claim that any history is value-free is inaccurate.[5]

Having in Scripture an absolute moral standard by which to judge history, the Christian historian will openly apply that standard. History written by a Christian historian is rich in meaning, for it is by its nature interpretive history. Like all competent historians, the Christian historian strives for factual objectivity, but history is never merely a record of facts or a meaningless exercise in academic footnoting.

Perhaps one of the most significant insights that the Christian historian derives from Scripture is the knowledge that fallen humanity retains freedom of choice under the sovereignty of God. How God can be in control of the course of history, while we are free to make choices that influence the course of history, is an apparent paradox that is understandable only in light of the Bible's account of the fall and subsequent history recorded in the Bible.

God is sovereign over all history. But there are opposing forces in history. Scripture testifies that God ordains certain specific historical events. Many are recorded in the Bible, both as history and prophecy. Other events are specifically attributed to Satan and his followers. Indeed, we read in 1 John 5:19 "that the whole world is under the control of the evil one." Whether a historical event falls under God's active or passive will, one fact remains: God is sovereign and nothing occurs apart from his will.

The Christian historian, therefore, distinguishes between God as the ultimate causal factor, and "the immediate, proximate causal factors through which God works."[6] Referring to historical events recorded in Scripture, the Christian historian may boldly speak of God's hand being evident in those events. However, once one

5. Because it is part of divine revelation, history as recorded in the Bible is objective. God is the only objective historian.

6. Donald C. Masters, *The Christian Idea of History* (Waterloo, Ontario: Waterloo Lutheran University, 1962), 15.

moves beyond the period of biblical history, one should only with great humility attempt to see God's hand in specific historical events. This does not mean that one should cease writing providential history. On the contrary, one may, for example, wish to see God's hand in the sixteenth-century Reformation, or the fulfillment of prophecy in the establishment of the state of Israel in 1948, but here and elsewhere such pronouncements should be made with caution and humility. Only the Bible is infallible. How individuals apply it will always be subject to error.[7]

In summary, then, the Christian historian derives guiding principles from Scripture, which may then be applied to the study of extrabiblical history. The goal is a greater understanding of the historical record. Certainty about God's role in specific extrabiblical events is beyond grasp. For now, all one can really say with certainty is that there is no "chance happening" in history. God is sovereign. Jesus Christ is the Lord of history.

Views of History

The uniqueness of the Christian view of history and our understanding of it, is enhanced by contrasting it with other views of history.

The Cyclical View

With the notable exception of the Hebrews, ancient historians viewed time, and therefore history, in terms of an endless recurrence of cycles. This meant that ultimately history was meaningless, since there was no escape from the cycles. No matter how far into the future one might project the cycles, there was only endless repetition. In the end, history was going nowhere.

Cyclical views of history are not limited to the ancient Near East and Greco-Roman worlds but are also characteristic of non-Western cultures. Traditionally, the Chinese divided history into a succession of dynastic cycles. The Indian Brahmans viewed history in terms of vast cosmic cycles, each of which lasted some twelve thousand years. The Mayan and Aztec Indians of Central and South America also viewed history as a series of cosmic cycles.[8]

7. Many Christians believe that the fulfillment of prophecy will be recognized as the events occur. Thus Isaiah 11:11 may be used as evidence for suggesting that the founding of the modern state of Israel in 1948 was the fulfillment of prophecy.

8. David W. Bebbington, *Patterns in History: A Christian Veiw* (Downers Grove, Ill.: Inter-Varsity, 1980), 18; Earle E. Cairns, *God and Man in Time: A Christian Approach to Historiography* (Grand Rapids: Baker, 1979), 112.

Neither are cyclical views of history limited to ancient and non-Western historians. Since the Renaissance, such views have resurfaced from time to time in the West, usually during periods of crisis. Whether ancient or modern, they have tended to be characterized by pessimism, determinism, and humanism. They are pessimistic because history is seen as a degenerative cycle, moving from some golden age in the past toward inevitable decay and death before starting all over again.[9] They are deterministic because human beings are helpless to alter the course of events. They are humanistic because there is no room for a divine role in history. Also, cyclical views of history tend to concentrate upon recording the deeds of great individuals, even though those deeds do not influence the inevitable course of the historical cycle.

The Judeo-Christian View

By the fifth century A.D., the cyclical histories were out of vogue in the Christian West and were displaced by the Judeo-Christian, or Christian, view of history. This change was due in no small part to the prestige of the works of Augustine (354–430), Bishop of Hippo in North Africa. The Christian view of history was firmly established in the West by the appearance of Augustine's monumental work, *The City of God,* written between 413 and 427. It was the first systematic philosophy of history written from a clearly Christian perspective.

All the elements of a Christian view of history are present in *The City of God.* For Augustine, history could never be either deterministic or meaningless. He rejected all cyclical views of history in favor of the biblical view of history as a linear development from creation to the return of Jesus Christ and judgment. Augustine believed history was under the providential direction of the God who acts in history for the redemption of the lost. Since the temptation and fall of Adam and Eve, history, wrote Augustine, is marked by a spiritual struggle between the City of God, those who love God first, and the City of the Earth, those who love self. Man is fallen, but free to serve either God or Satan. Thus history has both temporal and supernatural aspects, intertwined with one another.[10]

Historians writing during the medieval period, roughly the sixth

9. More recently there are exceptions to the traditional pessimism. These are found in the cyclical views of history common to the New Age movement.
10. Cairns, *God and Man,* 136–38; 146–47.

Figure 4.1
Medieval (Christian) View of History

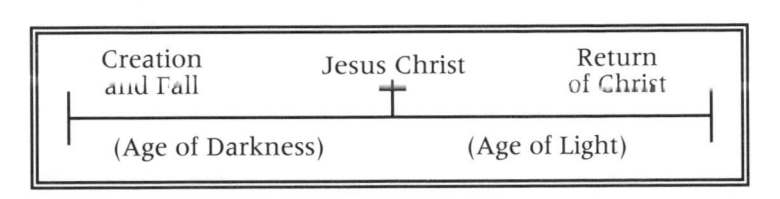

through the fourteenth centuries, were much influenced by Augustine's views. Their approach to the study of history was distinctly Christian. History was meaningful and instructive for their own age, because it was under divine control. Hence, theirs was a providential view of history. They did not shy away from including supernatural explanations for temporal events.[11]

The medieval historians viewed history as consisting of two ages (see fig. 6.1). The first, an age of darkness, extended from the fall of Adam and Eve to the life of Christ. The second, an age of light, extended from the death and resurrection of Jesus Christ to his future return. It was a medieval scholar-monk in Rome, Dionysius Exiguus (c. 500–560), who in 525 began the practice of numbering the years forward from the birth of Christ.[12] The Christian historians of the Middle Ages adopted Exiguus's view that history is centered on Jesus Christ.

By 1350, Renaissance scholars were largely preoccupied with a renewed interest in the study of the languages and culture of the Greco-Roman period. They felt an intellectual affinity with the secular, humanistic worldview of the classical writers. The revival of interest in classical studies was accompanied by a rejection of the immediate past. The Middle Ages became the "Dark Ages." The medieval "Age of Faith" was viewed by the Renaissance as a period of intellectual ignorance and superstition.

The shift in worldview was paralleled by a shift in how historians of the Renaissance and their descendants viewed history. The two-apart division of history characteristic of the Middle Ages was abandoned in favor of a tri-part division (see fig. 6.2). The classical

11. Ibid., 73.

12. James Montgomery Boice, *God and History,* vol. 4 of *Foundations of the Christian Faith* (Downers Grove, Ill.: InterVarsity, 1981), 45. Interestingly, it was not until the eighteenth century that it also became common practice to number backwards from the birth of Christ.

Figure 4.2
Renaissance (Modern) View of History

period of Greco-Roman civilization was viewed as an "age of light."
The period from the fall of Rome in 476 to the mid-fourteenth century was viewed as an age of darkness. The third period, contemporary with their own lifetime, was seen as a rebirth of the age of
light, or a modern age. The "new" periodization reflected a growing
secularization of worldview. It was humanistic. It reflected a shift in
the perceived focal point of history from Jesus Christ to man.[13]

The Modern-Secular View

The beginning of the Renaissance in Italy in the fourteenth century to the eighteenth-century Enlightenment was a period of
transition from the Christian-based worldview of the Middle Ages
to the thoroughly secular worldview of the modern age. It was
with the Enlightenment that the transition was complete.
Revelation in Scripture was abandoned in favor of the light of reason. Neither nature nor humanity was fallen; both were intrinsically good. With reason as a guide, both technological and moral
progress were not only possible but inevitable. There was a great
sense of optimism about the future, since both the perfectibility of
man and some future earthly utopia were awaiting humanity.

The Enlightenment historians retained the linear view of the
Christian historians but ignored its biblical basis. The individual,
not God, was the lord of history, and an earthly utopia, not the

13. For a discussion in popular language of the shift away from the Christian worldview
of the Middle Ages to an increasingly more secular and humanistic worldview during the
fourteenth century and following, see the works of Francis A. Schaeffer, especially *Escape
from Reason* (Downers Grove, Ill.: InterVarsity, 1968) and *How Should We Then Live?* (Old
Tappan, N.J.: Revell, 1976), and G. I. Williamson, *Understanding the Times* (Phillipsburg, N.J.:
Presbyterian and Reformed, 1979). Although they are not without problems, these works
remain good introductions for the average reader. For a more scholarly, bu highly readable,
approach, see Jacob Burckhardt, *Civilization of the Renaissance in Italy,* 2 vols. (New York:
Harper, 1958).

kingdom of God, the goal of history.[14] They retained the Christian belief that history was going somewhere and was, therefore, meaningful. But beginning with different presuppositions, they produced a secular, rather than a providential, view of history.

Although this "idea of progress" school of historiography did not go unchallenged, even as it was taking shape during the eighteenth century, it did remain in vogue throughout the nineteenth century. The achievements in science and industry, the triumph of Western imperialism, and the popularity of Darwinian evolution all seemed to confirm the Enlightenment's faith in inevitable progress. It took the twentieth century with its world wars and holocausts to cause secular historians to question the belief that human beings are intrinsically good and therefore pefectible.

Historians during the nineteenth century were influenced by both the Romantic reaction to the Enlightenment's emphasis on reason and the growth of scientism during the second half of the century. Beginning in Germany, where the reaction to the Enlightenment was strongest, the historicists emphasized intuition, rather than reason, as the guide to understanding history. They rejected the linear view of history in favor of the study of individual cultures and/or nation-states.

It was German historians, most notably Barthold G. Niebuhr (1776–1831) and Leopold von Ranke (1795–1886), who led the way in establishing the scientific approach to history. Basic to the scientific approach was the belief that historical truths, what Ranke called history "as it actually happened," could be obtained by reconstructing the past from the historical documents (e.g., diplomatic archives) alone. The "facts of history" were to be presented without any moral judgment. In short, these historians sought to be objective.

With the advent of scientific history, the practice of history became professionalized. The university seminar became the training ground and natural habitat of the professional historian. Monographs and articles for professional journals came to characterize the "scholarly" history of the professional (i.e., academic) historians, as opposed to the "popular" history of the amateur, armchair historians. Often extremely limited in scope, copiously documented and unenlightened by any particular philosophy of

14. Dawson, "The Christian View" 40–42; Masters, *Christian Idea*, 18–19; Bebbington, *Patterns*, 68–91; Cairns, *God and Man*, 78–80.

history, academic works tended to be lacking in didactic value and unable to arouse interest among laymen.

By the end of the nineteenth century the scientific approach triumphed in America also. But by the turn of the century a new school of "relativistic" history appeared in Europe, spreading to America after the First World War. The relativists rejected the "cult of objectivity," insisting, in the words of the Italian philosopher and historian Benedetto Croce (1866–1952), that "history is only contemporary thought upon the past."[15] They retained the scientific method in their research, but insisted upon including a subjective element in their interpretation of the facts. Contemporary professional historians tend to combine the scientific and relativistic schools.

Contemporary Christian Historiography

Having surveyed very briefly the history of the practice of history, we may now wonder what has become of the Christian view of history? Do historians still write history from an openly Christian perspective? Where, if anywhere, does the Christian approach to the study and writing of history as practiced by Augustine and the medieval historians survive today? Here a distinction must be made between a Christian view of history and Christians who are historians. Many, perhaps most, Christian historians write history that is indistinguishable from that written by non-Christian historians. The point is, a Christian view of history grows out of a specific worldview (i.e., biblical), just as does a Marxist, or other non-Christian, view of history.

Why do most Christian historians, especially in the academic community, mimic non-Christian historians? Like their secular colleagues, they too earned their doctorates in the graduate schools of secular universities, for the most part under professors themselves not Christians. Hence, like their non-Christian counterparts, most Christian historians tend to write monographs and articles for journals in the mode of scientific-relativist history. What rare attempts have been made to write history that takes into consideration the supernatural, or attempts a providential view of history, have been undertaken by nonprofessional generalists (e.g., Francis A. Schaeffer), as part of a more comprehensive Christian apologetic.

15. Cairns, *God and Man*, 92.

Such attempts at a Christian interpretation of history have met with silence or hostility from professional historians.

The plight of Christian history has to be understood in terms of the plight of Christian higher education itself. That, of course, is a topic beyond the scope of this essay. It was the subject of a three-year study by a University of Virginia sociologist, James Davison Hunter, whose findings were published in *Evangelicalism, the Coming Generation* (1988). Hunter's book was the subject of discussion at the forty-seventh annual convention of the National Association of Evangelicals.[16] According to Hunter's findings, much of the problem lies in the desire of Christian educators, historians included, to be accepted and respected by their colleagues. Christian historians who wish to be taken seriously by their professional colleagues must learn not to allow their Christian faith to influence their writing of history. To allow it to do so is to commit professional suicide, that is, to experience what Harry Blamires calls "the loneliness of the thinking Christian."[17]

How might the Christian historian who wishes to allow a biblical worldview to inform the practice of history be helped? The problem needs to be addressed from at least two directions. First we need to create a Christian presence in the world of professional historians. Secondly, we need to create a natural habitat, or environment, in the Christian university where the Christian historian can thrive, and from which the outside world, both Christian and non-Christian, can be addressed.

The former need has been alleviated to some extent by the existence of an association of professional historians who are also professing Christians. Known as the Conference on Faith and History (CFH) and recognized by the American Historical Association (AHA), the association publishes a quarterly scholarly journal entitled *Fides et Historia (Faith and History)*, hosts professional conferences, and conducts a session at the annual meeting of the AHA.

The membership of the CFH is diverse. Many members are Christian professors, from both secular and Christian colleges and universities. Others have no formal connection with academia. They represent all the various theological and doctrinal positions

16. See "Passing It On: Will Our Kids Recognize Our Faith?" and related news coverage in *World*, 11 March 1989, 5–7.

17. Harry Blamires, *The Christian Mind: How Should a Christian Think?* (Ann Arbor, Mich.: Servant, 1978), 13–14.

within the body of Christ. Most, no doubt, would not identify with the definition of a Christian view of history presented here. The all-important function that the CFH serves, however, is to provide Christian historians a point of contact with the wider community of professional historians. Thus is avoided the separation and isolation of Christian historians in an ideological ghetto, a situation that is unbiblical and hinders the advance of the cause of Christ.

Equally important is the constructing of Christian colleges and universities where a biblical worldview not only underwrites the doctrinal statements at the front of academic catalogs but also governs the content of individual courses and the integration of faith and learning across the curriculum. Such institutions provide an environment in which the individual Christian historian can pursue the practice of history in both teaching and scholarship without fear of harassment or ridicule. Those who enjoy such a privileged position, and they are few, should seek to encourage, not criticize, their Christian colleagues at colleges where they must contend daily with an indifferent and often hostile environment.

The Role of History in Christian Universities

We come now to the role of history in the curriculum of a Christian university. Like most departments, the history department has a dual function. It must contribute to the core curriculum of the university, and it must train history majors who will move on to graduate studies in history, eventually becoming professional historians themselves or branching off into a related field such as education, law, or archaeology. The former is achieved traditionally through a survey course in world history or in the history of Western civilization. The latter is achieved through a variety of specialized courses, including historiography and research seminars for majors.

The survey courses at the Christian university likewise must serve a dual function. As is true at any institution, survey courses must introduce students to the practice of history, thus contributing to the liberal arts ideal of exposing students to all, or at least a majority, of the disciplines. In this capacity, the course must provide a survey of history, while illustrating how historians have variously interpreted the past. However, at a Christian university, the survey course has an added apologetic function.

A primary function of the Christian university is to help its students develop a Christian worldview. The history teacher works together with colleagues in other disciplines to achieve that goal. The survey course in history plays a key role, perhaps second only to the basic Bible courses (e.g., Old and New Testament surveys). To achieve this goal, the history survey course is openly apologetic, that is, it provides the student with a specifically Christian view of history. Although this may sound revolutionary, it is not. Survey history courses at non-Christian institutions serve the same dual function, only there the "apologetic" is not openly pursued. Rather, it is hidden behind the myth of historical objectivity.[18]

How does a course in world history or in the history of Western civilization become apologetic? The Christian view of history is characterized by an awareness, derived from the Bible, that God, not the human mind or any material forces external to the human mind, is the initiating force in history. Furthermore, the Christian historian knows that God acts in the historical drama. History is meaningful because God began it, and he continues to guide it to its preordained fulfillment. But human acts are also meaningful. Therefore, there is a distinction between God as the ultimate causal factor, and "the immediate proximate causal factors through which God works."[19]

It is in noting and applying this distinction that we distinguish between the interpretive framework of a course (its philosophy, or worldview) and the narration of specific historical facts or events. Having a Christian view means, for example, seeing history providentially. This presents an immediate problem, or challenge, for the Christian history professor. Although there are numerous world history and Western civilization textbooks on the market, not a single one is written from a Christian perspective. Nor are there any readers or interpretive histories from a Christian perspective that can be used to supplement a traditional textbook.[20]

18. The hidden agenda is often not even evident to the professor, who, trained to be "scientific," sincerely believes that he or she is being objective. Nevertheless, a specific worldview is being communicated, whether it is through the particular interpretive slant of the textbook or the particular presuppositions (worldview) of the professor. One thing is certain: history cannot be written or taught without some interpretive framework (worldview).

19. Masters, *Christian Idea*, 15.

20. There are several texts written by Christian historians for use in Christian secondary schools (e.g., *Streams of Civilization*, 2 vols. [San Diego: CLP, 1978] and *The History of the World in Christian Perspective*, 2 vols. [Pensacola, Fla.: Beka Book Publications, 1979]), but none for college and university courses. Ronald A. Wells of Calvin College recently published *History through the Eyes of Faith* (New York: Harper and Row, 1989). Sponsored by the Christian College Coalition, Wells's volume is intended for use as supplemental reading in survey his-

The basis for the providential view of history in a survey course can be provided by discussing the historical events of the Bible and how they provide insight into the nature of history. God's role in history as the ultimate causal factor is evident in Old Testament history, especially the early chapters of Genesis. Here the history survey course will complement the survey courses in the Bible and science departments. Students should be able to see the relevance for history of what they are learning in their other courses, especially those identified as core courses. It should be unthinkable, for example, for students to find that what is taught about biblical history in a Bible course is contradicted or challenged by what is taught in a history or a science course. The various disciplines must complement one another if a Christian worldview is to be communicated.

In developing a Christian approach to a survey course, the professor will be guided by the fact that the Bible deals with historical events in two ways. First, "it records certain historical events, but only through the end of the first century A.D."[21] Second, it speaks prophetically of historical events that are yet to happen. The latter might be termed "history future," for they will happen "in the fullness of time." From these, a Christian philosophy of history may be derived, which in turn can be used to interpret history since the end of the first century. This is essentially what Augustine and other Christian historians since him have done.

One might see the hand of God, for example, in the sixteenth-century Reformation. However, the secondary causal factors (e.g., the rise of the nation-state, the commercial revolution) must not be neglected. Here, valuable insights can be gained from other dis-

tory courses at Christian colleges. Although his text is meant to provide a Christian view of history, Wells specifically rejects the characteristics of the Christian view as outlined in this essay (e.g., providential history). Wells does not believe the historian can discern the hand of God in history. His neo-orthodox approach to the Bible leads him to apply this principle to biblical history also. Whether or not the resurrection of Christ was a historical reality is, according to Wells, unknowable. Historical reality, like reality per se, is only subjective, existing in the mind of the observer. "The 'past' is what happened," writes Wells, "whereas 'history' is our engagement with the past." Rather than provide the student with a Christian view of history, *History through the Eyes of Faith* is more likely to reinforce the secular view of the traditional textbook. A good model for developing a providential approach for a survey course may be found in the works of Francis A. Schaeffer, especially *How Should We Then Live? The Rise and Decline of Western Thought and Culture* (Old Tappan, N.J.: Revell, 1976) and the film series by the same title. Also helpful is Renald E. Showers, *What on Earth Is God Doing? Satan's Conflict with God* (Neptune, N.J.: Loizeaux, 1973).

21. Renald E. Showers, *What on Earth*, 10.

ciplines. A Christian view of psychology, for example, can help enrich the student's understanding of such key figures as Martin Luther,[22] John Calvin, and Charles V.

In conclusion, the Christian worldview upon which a Christian view of history is based distinguishes it from a non-Christian view of history. Since developing a Christian worldview is the primary goal of a Christian university, by harmonizing with the other academic disciplines also taught from a Christian perspective, history contributes to a wholistic approach to education. Non-Christians, without a biblical basis for understanding who they are or the true nature of the world, are paralyzed by a fragmented view of reality. It is the goal of Christian education, of which the study of history is but one part, to provide the individual with a biblical basis for a view of reality.

22. Non-Christian historians have often used the presuppositions of nonbiblical schools of psychology to avoid confronting, or to explain away, the possibility of providence in history. Erik H. Erikson in *Young Man Luther: A Study in Psycholoanalysis and History* (New York: Norton, 1958) attempts to use psychoanalytical theories to explain the Reformation as a result of Luther's alleged personality disorders.

7   Economics

Bert Wheeler

It is difficult to define "Christian economics."[1] Some philosophers and theologians believe that even to think of Christian economics is misguided, as Ronald H. Nash says: "There is no such thing as revealed economics. There is no such thing as positive Christian economics. The distinction that counts is that between good and bad economics. I make no attempt to deduce a system of economics from the Bible. Such an activity strikes me as muddle-headed as an attempt to deduce a theory of the solar system from the Bible."[2] However, Nash explains that he does not mean that one's thoughts on economics should be isolated from Scripture or detached from a Christian worldview. If an economic theory is true, it will be congruous with Scripture and a worldview based on biblical revelation.

By contrast, Gary North states that "the Decalogue itself is the

---

1. Some authors have tried to formulate an explicitly Christian economics. The results have been variable and wholly inconsistent.
2. *Poverty and Wealth: The Christian Debate over Capitalism* (Westchester, Ill.: Crossway, 1986), 12.

master plan, the *blueprint* for biblical social order. These laws have very definite economic implications. This sort of thinking is foreign to virtually all modern Christian social and economic thinkers, whether conservative or liberal, Protestant or Catholic."[3]

In my opinion, the Bible does not contain an explicit blueprint for economics. Economics is as old as humanity, but it has existed as a discipline for just over two hundred years.[4] Economics traces its birth as a "science" to the publication in 1776 of Adam Smith's *Inquiry into the Nature and Causes of the Wealth of Nations*. It was around that time that capitalism developed both in North America and on the European continent. To insist that capitalism existed at the time of the writing of the Bible is both erroneous and irrelevant. Ancient economies were motivated by reciprocity and redistribution and consequently were stagnant. Individuals performed economic duties for one another in return for a reciprocal task. A certain portion of one's produce was brought to a central storage facility to protect against unforeseen contingencies. This is not to say that markets did not exist, but rather that there was no market economy. Individuals did meet to buy and sell, but few were totally dependent upon commerce for their survival.

The encumbrance of capitalism on ancient economies points to the need to avoid the "deductive impulse"[5] when ascertaining the proper relationship between the Bible and economics. The deductive impulse occurs when one takes specific historical situations in operation at the time of the writing of Scripture and treats them as if they were God-ordained for all time. Giving in to the deductive impulse in relation to the command in 2 Timothy 4:13 would involve packing one's bags and setting sail for Troas! If one were to follow the deductive impulse it would be possible to deduce that the Book of Acts endorses socialism. Acts 2:44–47 and 4:32–35 clearly indicate that there was a sharing of goods. Does one conclude that socialism is the economic system the New Testament supports? No, the second and fourth chapters of Acts detail a spe-

---

3. *The Sinai Strategy: Economics and the Ten Commandments* (Tyler, Tex.: The Institute for Christian Economics, 1986), 7. North takes several pages of his introduction to attack Nash as a "conservative protestant economic antinomian."

4. Economics is as old as fallen man. Before the fall, there was no need to make economic decisions in the same way we do today.

5. Taken from a lecture by Ronald Nash delivered April 7, 1989, at a Conference on Christian Economics sponsored by the Center for Business and Government at Liberty University and the Contemporary Economics and Business Association (CEBA).

cific historical situation confronted by God's people according to his will. The community of goods in Acts does not encourage socialism as a system.[6] Another example of the deductive impulse is to say that the Bible favors a return to a metallic-based currency simply because Scripture speaks in terms of weights and measures when referring to money. A return to currency backed by precious metals may very well be consistent with a Christian worldview,[7] but not because the Bible speaks in terms of precious metals. Scripture describes monetary transactions in terms of precious metal because precious metals were the commodity that functioned as money at the time of the writing of the Old Testament.

One should avoid searching for a simple economic blueprint in Scripture and refrain from the urge to follow the deductive impulse. At the same time, one should seek to start from an explicitly Christian worldview. In the field of economics it is extremely difficult to know truth apart from the absolute standard of the Bible; individuals have arrived at opposite conclusions when identifying a "good" and "true" system of political economy. Proponents of a Marxist solution believe just as strongly as those who favor an allocation of resources by a free market that their system is the only system. This difference of opinion over the best economic system is not limited to secular scholars. Well-meaning Christians have proposed different versions of economic "truth" as supposedly revealed in the Bible.[8] It is correct that God is the author of all truth, and that all truth is God's truth; but with economics, the actual determination of truth is in itself an insurmountable task without the aid of an objective standard explaining the foundations of social reality. One's economics is unquestionably effected by the way one views the world, by how one thinks the world works. The

6. This was a specific example where the sharing of goods was voluntary.

7. There is a movement among conservative Christians for a return to a metallic-backed currency or even a free market in money. This is due to a desire to eradicate the immoral redistributive effects (theft) that result from inflation inherent in our current monetary system. Removal of inflation would be commensurate with price level stability or "honest money." In actuality it is not necessary to have a currency backed by gold or silver to achieve price level stability. Stability could be achieved by stripping the Federal Reserve of all discretionary policymaking power. The Fed should proceed according to a precise *monetary rule*. Specifically, the rate of growth of the money supply should be equal to the rate of growth of output adjusted for changes in the velocity of money. This would lead to honest money.

8. Witness the chasm between the liberation theologians (Marxists) and theonomists or reconstructionists (free market). Both of these groups claim to be Christian and believe the Bible supports their position. Obviously, either one or both of them must be wrong.

Bible alone has God's special revelation of the true human condition and environment. Hence, Christians should be able to develop economic theory based on the way the world actually does work.

To be truly biblical, one's worldview must by necessity explicitly refer to Scripture. One should start from Scripture, not reasoning deductively, but inductively. To start from specific historical circumstances and attempt to define economic reality on the basis of what was done in the past is to open the door to any interpretation that happens to strike one's imagination. One must garner specific principles from the Bible that deal with economic matters and then apply those principles to today's historical situation. One must build economic theory from what the Bible says about human nature and the human condition.

Economic theory that is based on a solidly biblical worldview will not be applicable exclusively to Christians.[9] It will be equally apropos to individuals of any religious or ethnic group. A biblically based economics will transcend the labels *liberal* or *conservative*. It will not necessarily be "capitalistic" or "socialistic." Economic theory derived from a biblical understanding will simply be correct.

The Biblical Basis for a Christian View of Economics

The Bible makes certain assertions that are directly pertinent to economics. In turn, we can use these data to formulate some basic principles of political economy.

Individual Responsibility

According to Udo Middelmann, "the Bible says remarkably little about business practice and systems for the distribution of wealth."[10] Most of the references to economics in Scripture refer to individuals and their relationship to wealth, not to specific economic systems. "The Bible enters its concern on persons."[11] Proverbs indicates that one source of poverty is the actions of individuals. Idleness (Prov. 6:10–11), parsimoniousness (Prov. 11:24),

9. This does not imply that Christians have no greater responsibility to the poor than non-Christians. If fact, Christians do have a unique responsibility and right to share material things with those in need, particularly those of the household of God (Gal. 6:10).

10. "Personal Effort, Contribution, and Merit as the Primary Biblical Grounds for Distributing Wealth," in *Biblical Principles and Business: The Foundations,* vol. 1 of *Christians in the Marketplace,* 4 vols., ed. Richard C. Chewning (Colorado Springs, Colo.: Navpress, 1989), 186.

11. Ibid.

hedonism (Prov. 21:17), drunkenness and gluttony (Prov. 23:21), and foolish endeavors (Prov. 28:19) are given as reasons for poverty. These verses do not imply that individuals are always responsible for their own poverty or that everyone who practices bad habits will be poor.

Other causes of poverty include calamity, exploitation, and personal sacrifice.[12] Calamity is beyond the control of the individual and may reduce not only individuals but also entire societies to poverty. Exploitation involves governments, businesses, or individuals taking unfair advantage of people under their control. Personal sacrifice might be referred to as voluntary poverty and include full-time volunteers or people who give away large portions of their income.

One implication of the verses from Proverbs is that most people in a free democratic society should not attribute their individual wealth or their poverty to other people. People are responsible for their economic situation. In some situations (e.g., theft, slavery, or totalitarian control), one individual may very well be responsible for another's poverty. Individuals in a society where political and economic freedoms are curtailed may well find themselves shackled by tyranny and unable to pull themselves out of their economic situation. One economic system is more conducive to economic growth than another economic system. Capitalism is the only organizational pattern that allows and is instrumental in the accumulation of economic wealth and hence the eradication of poverty. What is important in the current socioeconomic situation in the United States (i.e., interventionist welfare state) is that individuals assume responsibility for their situation. The economic infrastructure in the United States does allow for resource mobility. People who are dissatisfied with their economic situation may choose to move to a different city or state in search of monetary success.

Another lesson that one must glean from Scripture's emphasis on individuals is that economics should focus on the behavior of the individual and how an individual might change the economic system. One cannot hope to formulate an economic system that will provide a utopian environment because the ultimate problem lies with individual sin. To attempt to change individuals through a

12. E. Calvin Beisner, *Prosperity and Poverty: The Compassionate Use of Resources in a World of Scarcity* (Westchester, Ill.: Crossway, 1988), 194–98.

specific economic system is to commit the "enlightenment error.[13] Any economic theory that reflects a Christian worldview must realize that there is no salvation in a particular system.

Scarcity and Insatiability of Wants

The basis for the discipline of economics is the scarcity of resources coupled with the innate propensity of human beings to want more. If resources were not scarce, there would be no economics because needs and wants would be readily fulfilled. Scarcity and the insatiability of desires ultimately originate in the fall, and so any correct economic theory must conform to the biblical account of man's fall.

> To Adam he said, "Because you listened to your wife and ate from the tree about which I commanded you, 'You must not eat of it,' Cursed is the ground because of you; through painful toil you will eat of it all the days of your life. It will produce thorns and thistles for you, and you will eat the plants of the field. By the sweat of your brow you will eat your food until you return to the ground, since from it you were taken; for dust you are, and to dust you will return." [Gen. 3:17–19]

At least two results of the fall directly influence the discipline of economics. The first is the fact that humanity is destined to "toil" for its livelihood. The fall imposed constraints such that we cannot easily provide for our material needs and wants. This lack of usable resources is known as scarcity.[14] The second result of the fall that directly effects economics relates to the effect of original sin on desires. Post-fall desires are effectively insatiable. When people achieve goals set for themselves, they can find no satisfaction. The relationship that Adam and Eve had with God in the Garden of Eden is lost. Until one's relationship with God is set right, people will not find complete, permanent gratification of their inmost desires. They will attempt to fill the void caused by the absence of a

---

13. Herbert Schlossberg, *Idols for Destruction: Christian Faith and Its Confrontation with American Society* (Nashville: Thomas Nelson, 1983). This is a theme running throughout the book.

14. "An item is a scarce good if the amount available (offered to users) is less than the amount people would want if it were given away free of charge." See Roy J. Ruffin and Paul R. Gregory, *Principles of Economics*, 5th ed. (Glenview, Ill.: Scott, Foresman, and Company, 1988), 32.

right relationship with God with material possessions or some other object that is not God.[15]

Economics itself derives from the fall. If there had been no fall there would be no economics. When Adam and Eve were in the garden ". . . they could do as they pleased . . . [they] refus[ed] to worry about time, [and] it is possible that they had no concept of scarcity."[16] With no concept of scarcity there would be no need to economize; economic decision would be virtually nonexistent. Even if one recognizes that time was not infinite for Adam and Eve (and hence scarce), they had communion with God. He met both their needs and wants. Economics had its birth with the fall of man.

Humanity's Sinful Nature

"Political economy," writes Michael Novak, "must deal with humans as they are."[17] For an economic theory to be correct it must recognize the fact of universal sin, the essence of which is selfishness. It must also be recognized that our sinful nature leads us to abuse power; as Lord Acton observed, "Power corrupts, and absolute power corrupts absolutely." For these reasons, an economic system that treats humanity as perfectible is destined to fail. (This view of humanity was held by Karl Marx, who believed that human nature was determined by the economic environment. When one eradicated capitalism, humans would be free to pursue noble goals.[18] Fixation with an economic system, however, rather than concentration on individuals in the system, leads to tyrannical control and callousness about human life,[19] as the murderous escapades of communist regimes show.)

15. In *Idols,* chap. 3, Schlossberg presents an excellent discussion of the idolatry of mammon. See also Beisner, *Prosperity,* chap. 1.

16. Gary North, *The Dominion Covenant: Genesis* (Tyler, Tex.: Institute for Christian Economics, 1982), 111–12.

17. Michael Novak, "The Ideal of Democratic Capitalism," in *Is Capitalism Christian?* ed. Franky Schaeffer (Westchester, Ill.: Crossway, 1985), 52.

18. The best summary of Marxist thought is by Thomas Sowell in *Marxism: Philosophy and Economics* (New York: Morrow, 1985).

19. This is an extreme example of what Schlossberg calls the "Enlightenment mistake" (*Idols,* 105). The Enlightenment error occurs when one attributes problems, and hence suggests solutions, to elements of one's environment, including the economic system. The particular quote is taken from a section of *Idols* in which Schlossberg is criticizing the Austrian School of economic thought. The Austrian School is perhaps the most free-market oriented of any school of economic thought and is hence espoused by many conservative Christians. However, members of the Austrian School do believe that solution to economic problems may be found by changing the economic system, not by changing the person.

By contrast, Jesus was the perfect opposite of selfishness. He did acknowledge that there is a proper love of self, which, in the words of Henry C. Thiessen, "constitutes the basis of self-respect, self-preservation, self-improvement, and of a proper regard for others. None of this is inherently sinful."[20] Economists have long recognized that a certain self-interest, as opposed to selfishness, is both natural and healthy. Correct economics must first deal with individual behavior and then work to restrain the totalitarianism that will emerge if individuals are given too much power. Economic theory based on a Christian worldview must reflect the individual's self-interest without promoting selfishness. It must devise a system of checks and balances to avoid concentration of power.

Justice

Good economics must conform to biblical concepts of justice. If an economic system is not just, it will not long remain a workable system. The inhabitants of the country will eventually rebel.[21] There are two images of justice in the Bible.[22] One deals with conformity to a right standard and implies that it is necessary to have truthfulness in all economic transactions. All behavior is judged by the same standards, ". . . the same standards apply equally to all people in all relationships."[23] The second image of justice in the Bible says that one must give to each according to what is due. Compensation is rendered according to what an individual has produced. In labor transactions (i.e., wages or salaries) this entails paying each person according to his marginal productivity.[24]

Classical and Christian traditions lead one to similar results about what is just for individuals and hence what is just for a society composed of those individuals. Classical tradition relies heavily on natural law for its basis, while Christian tradition is based on the

20. Henry C. Thiessen, *Lectures in Systematic Theology,* rev. Vernon C. Doerksen (Grand Rapids: Eerdmans, 1981), 174–75.

21. There are many examples of revolt and rebellion against communist dictatorships. Perhaps the clearest example in the minds of many Westerners is the protests in China during April and May 1989. Via satellite one was able to see daily the students demonstrating for freedom—and the inevitable crackdown by the Chinese government.

22. Beisner, *Prosperity,* 43.

23. Ibid., 44.

24. Marginal productivity is the "increase in output per period that results from increasing the factor by one unit, holding all other inputs and the level of technology fixed." Ruffin and Gregory, *Principles,* 748. See James Gwartney and Richard Stroup, *Microeconomics: Private and Public Choice,* 5th ed. (San Diego: Harcourt Brace Jovanovich, 1987), 268–70, for a discussion pertaining to the difficulties of applying this criterion in a modern economy.

Torah as well as natural law. Romans 2:14–15 declares that the Gentiles "do by nature things required by the law" and that the "requirements of the law are written on their hearts." "Thus Christian thought widely recognizes that the fundamental requirements of God's law are recognized by all men everywhere."[25] While the "natural man" does not accept spiritual matters (1 Cor. 2:14), he can and does recognize righteousness. Hence, biblical law and natural law are in harmony. If natural law conflicts with the clear revelation of Scripture, natural man has distorted the general revelation of God, and the distorted "natural law" is not truth or law. By developing an economic theory consistent with correctly interpreted natural law one will provide the ethical basis necessary to conduct business in a pluralistic society.[26]

Creation in the Image of God

We are created in the image of God. Because of this creative endowment, we are rational, moral, and able to execute volitional judgments.[27] Correct economic theory must be consonant with that rationality, morality, and free agency. We are also imbued with a certain amount of creativity. An economic system that encourages creativity will encourage the creation of wealth. An economic system that stifles creativity will also suppress the creation of wealth and will by its very nature fail to eradicate poverty to the extent which a system that promotes creativity will eradicate poverty.

"The God of the Bible is a Person who thinks, feels, and acts. . . . Man made in the image of this God, is defined by God's intentions and actions. The emphasis on the human being as a choice-maker in the image of the Creator is central to the Bible."[28] Because we are able to make rational judgments, the incentive structure is all-important. An incentive structure that sanctions thrift, hard work, and honesty will lead beings created in the image of their Maker to produce the maximum possible wealth given the constraints they face. An economic system that fails to induce individuals to labor to their potential will not be consistent with individuals who are

25. Beisner, *Prosperity*, 45.

26. Norman L. Geisler, "Natural Law and Business Ethics," in *Biblical Principles and Business: The Foundations*, vol. 1 of *Christians in the Marketplace*, 4 vols., ed. Richard C. Chewning (Colorado Springs, Colo.: Navpress, 1989), 162.

27. Charles Hodge, *Systematic Theology* 2:96–97, cited by Thiessen, *Lectures in Systematic Theology*, 155.

28. Middelmann, "Personal Effort," 187.

made in the image of God. It would encourage idleness, stinginess, pleasure seeking, and dishonesty. These behaviors are at the root of the poverty people want to eliminate. Perverse incentive structures obviously lead to poor economic performance.

The Nature of a Christian View of Economics

A Christian view of economics should be consistent with a biblical explanation for the condition and environment of humanity. It must be based on scarcity and the insatiability of wants. A Christian view of economics requires an anthropological perspective that encompasses both the fact of sin and the fact that we are created in the image of our Maker. A correct economic system will deal in terms of justice as delineated in the Bible and shown in natural law not as the product of *ressentiment* generated by a distorted view of social justice. The five principles of the sociological condition of man are not meant to be exclusive of other postulates derived from Scripture that will affect political economy. They will, however, serve as a starting point for the development of an economic theory consistent with a Christian worldview.

Christians should endeavor to live their lives in a manner that is pleasing to God. As much as it is possible we should be at peace with all men. The elect need to shine as lights in a world shrouded in darkness. The unfortunate truth is that God's children are in the minority, and the number of Christians who live in such a way as to glorify God is small indeed. It is unrealistic in a pluralistic society to expect individuals to act as though they were born from above and to live in conformity to the image of Christ. It is unrealistic to assume that unregenerate individuals will behave with altruistic motives and treat each other as they would have others treat themselves. A Christian view of economics is not primarily to teach believers how to behave in this world. Right behavior is of great importance, but a Christian view of economics goes beyond individual behavior. To be of greatest service to humanity, a Christian view of economics must deal with the world as it is, not as the way one would like it to be.

Principles of a Christian View of Economics

Economics is a way of thinking; it is a specific methodology. To derive principles of a Christian view of economics one begins with basic postulates of a Christian worldview and builds a system of political economy from those axioms. One's way of approaching the economic problem of scarcity coupled with insatiability of wants (which itself derives from the fall) is tempered by one's worldview. Economics gives one a set of tools to use in making economic decisions. A Christian view of economic theory provides a correct and well-honed instrument for understanding economic reality and making consistent decisions.

Scarcity is at the heart of all economic systems. Poverty is a direct result of the fall and of the consequences subsequently incurred. The entire creation longs for release from the constraints imposed at the fall (Rom. 8:20). How one answers the question of how best to allocate scarce resources[29] is what economics is all about. In fact, the standard definition given in economics textbooks of economics is consistent with a Christian worldview.[30]

While the secular world defines the central tenet of economics correctly, the manner in which the problem is dealt with is frequently faulty. The individual is pushed to the rear of the bus and does not reemerge until most of the pertinent economic questions have been answered. A proper emphasis is not placed on individuals and how they respond and react in the context of the economic system.[31] A Christian view of the economic problem will place emphasis on the individual as a decisionmaker created in the image of God. The primacy of an individual's decisions will then be applied to developing an economic model[32] that describes how the

29. Resources are also called factors of production and are defined as "the resources used to produce goods and services; they can be divided into three categories—land, labor, and capital." Ruffin and Gregory, *Principles*, 33.

30. A leading textbook defines economics as "the study of how a society chooses to use its limited resources (land, labor, and capital goods) to produce, exchange and consume goods and services." "Economics is the study of how scarce resources are allocated among competing ends." Ruffin and Gregory, *Principles*, 3, 31.

31. Socialism is the greatest example of how individuals are relegated to the dustbins of economic importance, but the same error is made in capitalistic analysis. Most standard textbooks begin their analysis with macroeconomics (which looks at economics from the perspective of the entire economy) without a full understandig of microeconomics (which purports to explain the behavior of the individual). Hence, an effort is made to understand the whole without first understanding the parts. The whole may not always be the sum of its parts, but it is ludicrous to expect one to fully understand an economic system composed of individual economic agents without first understandig the agents themselves. The reason for this structure is that the standard economic dogma denigrates the place of the individual.

32. Economic models are necessary because of the complexity of the economic environment. Humans do not have the ability to simultaneously process all the data in any given economic situation. Therefore one abstracts from economic reality by choosing what one believes are the most important economic variables. One then studies the chosen variables in an attempt to understand the complex economic environment.

world works. An economic model that places proper emphasis on the individual will suggest a market allocation of resources. However, a fundamentally free market does not imply libertarian anarchy.[33] A limited civil government does play a key role in an economic system based on a Christian worldview.

Because the individual is central to a Christian understanding of economics, the incentive structure of the economic system will also be of central concern. Humans are rational beings and respond in more or less predictable ways.[34] The manner in which individuals are motivated must reflect the fact of indwelling sin. There are essentially two types of external incentives.[35] Individuals may be motivated positively or negatively. Positive motivations occur when individuals are given reward for their efforts. Reward in the economic realm entails allowing economic agents to partake in the fruits of their labors. One is remunerated according to the net additions to the economy. If one is productive, one receives the benefits from that productivity. If one fails to produce, no reward is forthcoming.

Negative motivation occurs when punishment is meted out when a specific object is not obtained. There is little reward for exceeding the set objective, only punishment for failure and the consequential fear that is generated. Negative motivation gives rational beings little incentive to excel. It is rational simply to attempt to survive. Capitalism, for example, rewards in a positive fashion; a planned economy rewards in a negative way.

To have a properly functioning incentive structure, the society must be free. Economic agents must be free to succeed or fail based on their use of resources in a competitive environment. When the incentive structure of an economic system is bound by regulation and government control, individuals cannot economize efficiently. They are unable to receive the full benefits of their work and hence

33. What one does not want to do is to assume that market allocation of resources is not compassionate and hence cannot be consistent with a Christian worldview. If an economic system restrains economic growth, the system itself will lead to further poverty or will stand in the way of elimination of poverty. Good intentions about the redistribution (the economist's word for theft) of income do not lead to the desired result. See Charles Murray, *Losing Ground: American Social Policy 1950–1980* (New York: Basic, 1984).

34. Some are more or some less rational than others! What is important is that on average individuals perform in a predictable manner.

35. This does not deny that there are internal incentives which may motivate individuals to make certain economic decisions. However, material incentives are the strongest motivating factors in the economic realm. See E. Calvin Beisner, "Christian Economics: A System Whose Time Has Come?" a lecture delivered at the conference on Christian Perspectives on the Free Enterprise System, April 7, 1989, at Liberty University.

are not able to adequately judge costs and benefits. Without economic freedom it is likely that the cost for inefficient use of resources will be lower than if the producers were competing against each other. This leads to waste. Goods that could be produced are left unproduced. Wealth is created only as goods are produced. If goods are not produced, wealth is not created, and the world is poorer as a corollary. Poverty is extended.

A free society with a limited civil government is favorable to making the most from the limited resources available. A free market not only allows individuals to work to the glory of God, but also best restrains the corruption that results when political and economic power is concentrated in a few hands. In a free market, as economic profit[36] accrues to an individual, other entrepreneurs are attracted to the industry. As these newcomers in the market begin to compete, they take demand away from the original producer. In this way economic power is restrained.

A free market is the best system for harnessing the sinful nature of individuals to work for the good of society as a whole. By pursuing their own self-interest individuals in a free-market economy are more likely to further the needs of society as a whole. Perhaps the most eloquent statement of this fact was made by Adam Smith over two hundred years ago:

> Every individual is continually exerting himself to find out the most advantageous employment for whatever capital he can command. It is his own advantage, indeed, and not that of society which he has in view. But the study of his own advantage naturally, or rather necessarily, leads him to prefer that employment which is most advantageous to society. . . . He intends his own gain, and he is in this, as in many other cases, led by an invisible hand to promote an end which was not part of his intention. By pursuing his own interest he frequently promotes that of society more effectually than when he really intends to promote it.[37]

The now-famous "invisible hand" was simply an elucidation of economics built from a Christian worldview.[38] Society is best

36. Economic profit refers to a return over and above that necessary to induce an entrepreneur to remain in the business. It represents an "icing on the cake."

37. Adam Smith, *An Inquiry into the Nature and Causes of the Wealth of Nations* (New York: Modern Library, 1937), 423.

38. Adam Smith was not an evangelical Christian as the term is understood today. He was knowledgeable, however, about Scripture, and his worldview was formed to some extent by the Bible. See my unpublished monograph "The Epistemology of Adam Smith."

served through the free market because individuals must compete in the marketplace for the business of their customers. If producers cannot serve the public with as low a price (and therefore with fewer resources) as their competitors they will be driven from the industry. The "loser" in the economic battle is then free to produce any type of good for which a demand exists. In this way maximum output is derived from the resources available. The more output is produced, the more wealth is created and hence the less poverty.[39] In a free-market economy the fact of innate sinfulness is taken and used to promote the elimination of poverty.

The appropriate question to ask when one is attempting to determine why one nation has more wealth than another nation is not What made the destitute nation poor? The proper question is why more successful nations have material prosperity. This is analogous to the unregenerate asking how a loving God could allow an eternity in hell. The person who has met God through Christ Jesus asks, "How can a holy God save someone like me?" Part of the depraved nature is that one has a tendency toward envy. The natural economic condition is poverty. The history of the world is fraught with the story of how poverty has held humanity in its grasp. The anomaly is not that there are less-developed countries today, but that there are developed countries. A free-market economy has allowed the majority of individuals to partake in the prosperity that has come through the rational economy practiced by application of free-market principles. While capitalism has led and will continue to lead to some concentration of wealth, it has led to the eradication of poverty when its principles have been allowed to work. The wealth that is concentrated is wealth that did not exist before the market was allowed to function.

Capitalism not only has placed wealth in the hands of workers, but also has ensured that the goods that are produced are those they desired. To be competitive in the marketplace each entrepreneur must be able to sell the good that is produced. Economic agents that buy the goods are those with purchasing power. Because a free market distributes the wealth generated

39. This may not be the case if there is monopolization of a specific industry. By virtue of its control over price the monopolist is able to restrict quantity and raise price. This may lead to economic profits in the long run and concentration of wealth to the monopolist. If the monopolist has gained the market position through innovation and success in the competitive arena, it would be unjust to take the results of hard work and "redistribute" it to another party.

among those who have had a hand in its creation, the workers are able to demand the goods they desire and hence dictate what is produced.[40]

A free market is consistent with a Christian view of economic justice. There is a certain congruence between ". . . biblical justice and economic efficiency. These two standards always yield the same results because God made spiritual and material reality consistent with each other."[41] A redistributive system takes the produce of one individual and "assigns" it to another. A Christian concept of economic justice is to render to each according to his due. Each individual must be treated equally. There should be no partiality in economic transactions. A free market distributes wealth according to one's contribution. Individuals may sometimes "feel" they are not receiving their "fair" share. They envy what others have and desire it for themselves. This will induce the economic agents in question to take measures to see that more wealth comes their way, that their slice of the economic pie is larger. It is quite possible that they will now receive more than what they produce. Economic justice has been violated because of envy. Covetousness is at the heart of economic redistribution.

A free-market system for resource allocation is the economic system most consistent with a Christian worldview. However, one must keep in mind that the economic problem will not be solved by a system. There are no magic solutions to the problem of scarcity. The core of the problem is sin. No economic system will change human depravity. Even with conversion, the sinful nature remains; hence the individual must live under the leadership of the Holy Spirit to overcome the innate propensity to sin. A free market best deals with the fact of sinfulness, but it will not change it. Proponents of the Austrian School of economic thought are perhaps the greatest advocates of the free market. Yet, they ". . . make the same Enlightenment mistake, supposing that a technical solution, such as the return to the gold standard, will eliminate the evils they have identified."[42] The same rudimentary flaw is inherent in the logic of those who advocate Statism. "The basic assumption justifying the extension of government power over economic

---

40. Obviously the laborer will not be the only one who has an effective demand. A free market will ensure that all who have means will be able to purchase the goods they value most highly.

41. Beisner, *Prosperity*, xiii.

42. Schlossberg, *Idols*, 105.

life is the Enlightenment conviction that the people have the goodness and wisdom to control other people."[43] Individuals are sinful and will abuse power. No economic system will remove scarcity. It is inherent in all of human existence. Neither capitalism nor socialism will change the results of the fall. The utopian solution all humanity dreams of will not be attainable until the eschatological climax of the age.

An Example of a Christian View of Economics

Minimum-wage legislation was enacted in 1938 with the passage of the Fair Labor Standards Act. The legislation requires that all workers in specified industries be paid at least the stated minimum hourly rate of pay. The motive for passage of the act was humanitarian. The intention was to provide for the working poor. Some individuals certainly gained from the legislation. Those who retained their jobs after the passage of minimum-wage legislation were paid a higher wage. Economic theory suggests that as the wage rate increases, fewer workers will be hired. In human terms, that means more unemployment than would be the case if the market were allowed to determine the level of employment. Many individuals gained, but only at the expense of those who lost their jobs. The amount of wealth produced fell as output dropped because of higher input costs. Minimum-wage legislation is a negative sum game in the short run.

The long-run consequences of minimum-wage legislation have failed to receive adequate analysis. The secondary effects of the law have proved to be more detrimental than the initial effects. As years have passed not only have the redistributive effects of the law taken wealth from one individual and given it to another, but as a group, low-skilled individuals who were the initial beneficiaries have been harmed.[44] Entry-level jobs that might be used as "stepping stones" have been eliminated. Workers with low skills are priced out of the labor market. Hence, the door of opportunity is slammed in the faces of people without marketable skills. They are relegated to employment with very little possibility for advancement. It then becomes difficult to attain job experience. Certain work habits necessary for successful employment are best learned through simple experience. Because of minimum-wage

43. Ibid., 126.
44. Gwartney and Stroup, *Microeconomics*, 291–95.

legislation unemployment of low-skilled workers has been increased.

A free-market perspective on the minimum wage might seem uncharitable to the uninitiated who make only a cursory analysis. If the market determines that wages are below what certain special-interest groups, or even the general populace, believe is sufficient, then wages simply *appear* too low. The basis for this appearance is envy and covetousness. Failure to enact minimum-wage laws will not take income from the least productive members of society and distribute it to individuals with more skills. Total output will not fall if the laws are not enacted. The true basis for wealth is the output of a nation. Income is generated when output is produced. Therefore it follows that if output is not generated, wealth will not be created. If minimum-wage laws do not pass the Congress, low-skilled workers will not be priced out of the market. They will be able to gain access to entry-level jobs and gain work experience, thus making them productive members of society. If the market is allowed to determine wage rates, the most equitable result possible will emerge. The good intentions of legislators result in harmful consequences that fall upon the very individuals the laws were designed to help. A free market remains the most just economic system. A Christian worldview is consistent with a free market and in fact demands a free market.

8   Natural Sciences

Robert Chasnov

As believers in Christ, we must begin our discussion of any subject with the acknowledgment that God is the Author of all things (Col. 1:16). As Creator, he has the only authoritative interpretation of the "natural" world. He alone knows with certainty why, how, and when the universe was born. What we know about the universe comes from his revelation, both in Scripture and in nature.

God has two great revelations of himself: a general revelation and a special revelation. His general revelation is seen not only in human nature (Rom. 2:12–14) but also in physical nature. "For since the creation of the world His invisible attributes are clearly seen, being understood by the things that are made, even His eternal power and Godhead, so that they [unbelievers] are without excuse" (Rom. 1:20 NKJV). Paul told the heathen at Lystra that they should turn to the living God "who made the heaven, the earth, the sea, and all things that are in them" (Acts 14:15 NKJV). He also rebuked the Greek philosophers on Mars Hill because they were not worshiping "God, who made the world and everything in it"

(Acts 17:24 NKJV). Indeed, the psalmist spoke of God's revelation in nature, proclaiming: "The heavens declare the glory of God; / And the firmament shows His handiwork" (Ps. 19:1 NKJV).

While God's revelation in nature reveals his greatness, his revelation in Scripture declares his redemptive grace. Only Scripture is a divinely authoritative written revelation. In view of this, we must, first of all, be submissive to his authority before we can expect to receive wisdom and knowledge. Secondly, we must be aided by the Holy Spirit to receive truths from the written Word (1 Cor. 2:14). Finally, we must recognize that our human nature, being made in the image of God, includes an ability to understand the physical world as a reflection of its Creator (Ps. 19:1). All three aspects of our relationship to God and his creation are important to a Christian view of the natural sciences.

The Nature of a Christian View of Natural Science

Historically science has undergone tremendous changes both in philosophy and methodology. Astronomy was perhaps the earliest of the modern sciences. Ptolemy (A.D. 150) devised a complex mathematical model that roughly portrayed the motions of the sun and the then-known planets in our solar system.[1] Even the sun was shown moving about the earth along a fixed circular orbit. In 1543, however, a conflict arose between the religious and scientific communities. The heliocentric model of our solar system presented by Copernicus stirred the waters and prompted the debate between Galileo and the Catholic church. Briefly, Galileo defended the Copernican model as being "more pleasing to the mind."[2] In other words, the same predictions made by applying Ptolemy's complex mathematics could be achieved much more simply were the sun placed at the center of the system with the planets revolving about it. The Roman Catholic Church brought Galileo before the Inquisition for holding and teaching this opinion.[3]

Alfred North Whitehead, in his famous book on the philosophy of science, recognized the Judeo-Christian conviction that God is a rational being and thus created a rationally knowable world to be one of the inspirations for the emergence of modern science. He put it this way:

1. Max Born, *Einstein's Theory of Relativity* (New York: Dover, 1965).
2. M. M. Payne, O.S.B., *The Physics Teacher* (Feb. 1987): 86.
3. George De Santillana, *The Crime of Galileo* (Chicago: University of Chicago, 1955).

The greatest contribution of medievalism to the formation of the scientific movement . . . [was] the inexpungable belief that every detailed occurrence can be correlated with its antecedents in a perfectly definite manner. . . . How has this conviction been so vividly implanted in the European mind? . . . It must come from the medieval insistence on the rationality of God.[4]

M. B. Foster, in the prestigious English journal *Mind,* spoke specifically to the relationship of Christianity and the rise of modern science when he wrote,

What is the source of the un-Greek elements which were imported into philosophy by the post-Reformation philosophers, and which constitute the modernity of modern philosophy? And . . . what is the source of those un-Greek elements in the modern theory of nature by which the peculiar character of the modern science of nature was to be determined? The answer to the first question is: The Christian revelation, and the answer to the second: The Christian doctrine of creation.[5]

Whitehead also pointed to the emergence of a second factor. He noted that

the final ingredient necessary for the rise of science . . . was the rise of interest in natural objects and in natural occurrences, for their own sakes. . . . It is unnecessary to tell in detail the various incidents which marked the rise of science: the growth of wealth and leisure; the expansion of universities; the inventing of printing; the taking of Constantinople; Copernicus; Vasco da Gama; Columbus; the telescope.[6]

The Copernican revolution and Galileo's development of experimental science were the crucial factors that gave birth to modern science. As Max Born states, "This new doctrine [the Copernican model] was destined to be victorious. For it drew its power from the burning desire of all thinking minds to comprehend all things in the material world—be they ever so unimportant for human existence—by simple, unambiguous, abstract concepts."[7]

4. *Science and the Modern World* (New York: Macmillan, 1967), 12.
5. "The Christian Doctrine of Creation and the Rise of Modern Natural Science," *Mind* (1934): 448.
6. *Science,* 15.
7. *Einstein's Theory,* 11.

The key to defining a Christian view of the natural sciences is, first of all, to understand what science is and, second, how it interacts with one's biblical perspective. Modern science is done according to principles accepted by the community of scientists. The following statements summarize how most scientists would describe their discipline: There simply is no fixed set of steps that scientists follow, no one path that leads them unerringly to scientific knowledge. There are, however, certain features of science that give it a distinctive character as a mode of inquiry.[8]

These "distinctive features" are commonly combined into what has come to be called the scientific method of induction. Simply stated, one needs first to conceive of a problem to be solved. This may be as shallow as the dream that fathered the invention of the paper clip, or as detailed as the yet unobserved quarks that may compose subnuclear structures. The next step is to perform experiments and make observations that lead to a hypothesis. Continued and more detailed experimentation is then used to refute the hypothesis or to refine it into a viable theory. If such a theory is consistently supported by further experimental testing, it may be elevated to a scientific law. Sometimes, however, these experiments lead to new problems to solve, and the cycle begins anew. Note that this entire process may lead to a false conclusion. Because the error is not one of mathematical logic (which makes use of deductive methods), there is no harm done.

A good example of the failure of inductive reasoning to reach a correct conclusion is found in the work of Sir Isaac Newton in the field of optics. He believed that light was particulate in nature. His hypothesis led to experiments in reflection and refraction of light, which yielded data strongly supportive of this belief. Then along came Christian Huygens with the wave theory of light that predicted not only the observations already seen by Newton but additional behavior that could not be explained by Newton's theory—namely, diffraction and interference phenomena. Does that mean we must discard the old as useless? On the contrary, any optometrist worth his salt relies on the ray diagrams of Newtonian optics for generating corrective lenses.

Now that we have a working understanding of science, let us attempt to incorporate science into our biblical perspective. The

8. American Association for the Advancement of Science, *Science for All Americans* (Washington, D.C.: AAAS, 1989), 26.

Christian does not "do science" to bring honor and glory to himself, but to honor and glorify God (1 Cor. 10:31). The scientist is not attempting to disrobe God of his authority but to discover his beauty, simplicity, and creativity by learning of his mighty works. A father is honored when his child comes of age and finally understands the reason for his father's discipline and how disciplines his own children likewise. So too, our heavenly Father is honored when we discover the means of power generation by the burning of coal or by the decay of radioactive isotopes.

The Principles of a Christian View of Natural Science

For the Christian, the Bible is our only authoritative basis for truths about God's creation. And Scripture reveals that our greatest duty is to love God and our neighbor (Matt. 22:37–39).

The Christian Motivation to Do Science

In view of the great commandment, the basic motivations for Christians to "do science" can be broken into three categories: a love for God, a love for God's physical creation, and a love for other human beings. Taken together, this imperative should help give guidance to all believers in their quest for rightly describing scientific behavior in search of truth.

A Love for God

Deuteronomy 6:4–9 (the Shema) is probably the most sacred of all Jewish writings.[9] Christians claim it as support for educating their children according to God's Word and not by man's secular and naturalistic philosophies. The foremost statement of the passage reads as if it were an amendment to the Ten Commandments; it orders God's people to love him (v. 5). Jesus explains in John 14:21–24 just how important this command to love God is. Our life in Christ is the cornerstone of knowledge; to obtain blessings from God we must love him and obey him. Even the Preacher, who had lived life to the fullest, obtained all wisdom from God, and felt "all is vanity" wrote, 'Let us hear the conclusion of the whole matter: Fear God, and keep his commandments, for this is the whole duty of man' (Eccles. 12:13 KJV).

Just as a young married couple desires to know each other, the

9. The Shema was considered the basis of the Law by the Jews of old (as declared by Christ in Matthew 22:36–37) and by modern Jews alike.

goal of the Christian should be to know God. Love drives the wheels of science in the heart of the believer because "to know God is to love God." Just as the character of God is found in his written revelation, so it also is found in his created world (Ps. 19:1; Rom. 1:20). We show our love for God, therefore, by learning of his might, power, and creativity as revealed in creation itself. Science has a methodology for unraveling some of the mysteries of God that he has hidden in his creation.

A Love for God's Creation

Parents know the joy of having a child come running to them with a "work of art," only to find it difficult to express praise for something they cannot identify. We are motivated by love of that creative piece of art and may even press it into an album as a memento. How much more ought we to cherish the marvelous works of God by determining how best to be stewards over his creation? Adam was given strict orders in the Garden of Eden to take care of God's beautiful creation (Gen. 2:15).

Too often Christians are criticized for being so interested in the next life that they neglect this one. They are more concerned about the theology of heaven than the ecology of earth. The criticism is often valid. Some seem willing to sacrifice our natural resources for an opportunity to bring the gospel to our own generation. What is forgotten, however, is that the next generation will have the same responsibility and must have those same resources available to it. Conservation, the greenhouse effect, and the ozone layer are not non-Christian issues that biblical Christians should avoid. On the contrary, the most avid environmentalists should be Christians who have a proper understanding of the stewardship of God's creation.[10] Science provides an avenue for learning how best to care for the environment and thus preserve the beauty so graciously given to us by God.

A Love for Other Humans

In Matthew 22:34–40, Jesus spelled out the importance of our love for one another as second only to our love for God. It makes sense that, if we are God's ultimate creation, we should have the highest respect for mankind. This is no doubt the reason for the harsh penalty for murder found in Genesis 9:6.

10. Francis A. Schaeffer, *Pollution and the Death of Man* (Downers Grove, Ill.: InterVarsity, 1970).

Science provides many wondrous ways to benefit the human creature. From pure biology and chemistry, we attain the field of medicine. From pure physics and mathematics, we develop engineering and computer science. The technologies that have provided so much of the leisure time we now experience have permitted us to communicate the gospel to the world. From the printing press to the typewriter to the photocopying machine to the fax machine, we have advanced our abilities not only to bring people the gospel but also to put it into their own languages. Agricultural advances have allowed us to produce more food of better quality than ever thought imaginable. Observing the Christian motivation for doing science in the light of the commandment to "love one another" should be easy.

A more direct approach to fulfilling the Great Commission is seen as scientists win scientists to Christ. Who but a scientist can effectively gain the respect of another scientist? A Christian who practices science well will be permitted a forum within the scientific community. Local or national meetings of a given scientific society provide opportunities for the Christian to express excitement about the results of one's work and then to give honor to God as the Author of wisdom and knowledge. The greatest testimony of our love for each other will be the fruit we bear as the "branches" of the Savior (John 15:1–8).

Our obligation as Christians in science, however, is more than personal; it is also intellectual. We are to love God with our minds as well as our thoughts. We must bring every thought captive to Christ (2 Cor. 10:5). Thus, we must struggle with the intellectual difficulties generated by the divergent understandings of God's Word and his world.

Reconciling Conflicts of Science and Scripture

Since God is self-consistent, it follows that his two great revelations do not contradict each other. His Word and his world represent a unified expression of himself. Whatever conflicts exist must arise from either a misunderstanding of science or a misinterpretation of Scripture.

As the Word of God, the Bible speaks unerringly on every topic. Although its message is primarily redemptive it does speak to matters within the domain of science. However, while the Bible is scientifically accurate on whatever topic it addresses in that area, it is not really a scientific textbook as such.[11] While the Bible is infallible, our interpretations are not. Thus, Scripture may not appear, in specific instances, to be scientifically accurate because of our poor interpretation of the passage or our inaccurate assessment of the scientific data.

Are Miracles Scientific?

Much of modern scientific thinking rejects miracles outright. Logically, this would mean the rejection of God too, but not all are willing to go this far. Most, however, repeat the argument of David Hume against belief in miracles. If valid, this argument would not only eliminate the miracles of Jesus, but also rule out creation as a scientific event. Let us consider the argument as Hume formulated it:

1. Natural law is by nature regular and repeatable.
2. A miracle is by nature irregular and irrepeatable.
3. The evidence for the regular and repeatable is always greater [than for the irregular and irrepeatable].
4. The scientific mind should always accept what is based on greater evidence.
5. Therefore, the scientific mind should never accept miracles.

Since the first and second premises are true by definition, and rejecting the third is tantamount to rejecting science, there seems to be no room for a scientist to accept miracles. For many scientists today, to accept a miraculous creation of the universe and of life would be to reject science.

Christians have no quarrel with the first two premises of Hume's argument. Rather, they challenge the third premise. It is simply untrue that modern science does not accept singularities.[12] Scientists believe sufficient evidence exists for many unrepeated events. First of all, paleontologists know that the fossil record is filled with past singularities that are not being repeated today. Likewise, archaeologists unearth evidence of past singularities. Also, many astronomers believe in the "Big Bang" origin of the universe, a phenomenon that has not been repeated since. Then too, macroevolutionists believe in the one-time spontaneous gen-

11. For contrast see Kenny Barfield, *Why the Bible Is Number One* (Grand Rapids: Baker, 1988).

12. The term *Singularity* is used differently in mathematics.

eration of life in the universe and the unique unrepeated transitions in their evolutionary ladder. For that matter, everyone believes in a past that is unique. As C. S. Lewis noted, "Since it happened only once, it is by Hume's standards infinitely improbable. But then the whole history of the Earth has also happened only once, is it therefore incredible?"[13] So Hume's antisupernaturalism fails. A belief cannot be ruled out of the realm of science simply because it is supernatural and hence nonrepeatable.

Creation versus Evolution

Of course, accepting the possibility of miracles does not, in the minds of some, place miracles within the realm of science. As we saw, natural science has its own set of rules that involve a study of the physical world by the "scientific method." But this method is based on the observation of regularly occurring events in the world. Therefore, many scientists insist, there is no room for creation as "science," for, by nature, science involves *observation* and *repetition* of events in the *present*. Creation, by nature, deals with *unobserved* and *unrepeated* events in the *past*. While past miracles, like creation, are not out of the realm of possibility, they are out of the realm of scientific scrutiny—by definition.

The creationist has no problem with this conclusion, provided that it is applied equally to macroevolution. For if science is defined in the narrow sense of dealing only with present regularities, then it follows that macroevolution is not science either, since it also involves unobserved past events that are not being repeated in the present. Evolutionists freely acknowledge that life is not spontaneously springing into existence today as they believe it did at one time in the past. Neither can we observe the great macroevolutionary transitions occurring between fish and reptiles or between reptiles and birds, such as they believe happened in the past. So, if the term *science* is limited to presently observed regularities, then neither creation nor evolution is science.

Most evolutionists, however, are not willing to exclude macroevolution from the realm of science. To describe their discipline as science, they must have a more inclusive use of the term. Science, in this sense, must be able to handle events that cannot be repeated in the present. Science, then, when dealing with origins must be more like a forensic science than an empirical science.

13. *Miracles* (New York: Macmillan, 1947), 112.

These two types of science have been called, respectively, *origin science* and *operation science*.[14]

So is "creation science really science"?[15] The answer must be a resounding no if we adhere to the definition of empirical or operation science. However, under these strict guidelines, neither are the studies of paleontology, astrophysics, and evolution truly science. In his excellent book on this subject, Michael Denton puts it this way: "However attractive the extrapolation, it does not necessarily follow that, because a certain degree of evolution has been shown to occur, therefore any degree of evolution is possible."[16]

For some, including myself, both creation and evolution are more a philosophy of origins than a science of origins. But then again, it all depends on how one is willing to use the word *science*. One thing is clear: a "scientific" approach to past unobserved events of origins is not the same as a scientific understanding of the present operation of the world. At best, a "science" of origins, like forensic science, is simply a speculative reconstruction of the past based on analogies with observed evidence and events in the present. Unlike an empirical science, its speculations cannot be tested by measuring them against some repeatable pattern of events in the present. One philosopher of science writes,

> The creation/evolution debate of the nineteenth century was not simply about scientific evidence or facts. More importantly, it was a philosophical debate between two epistemologies regarding the issue of what science was and how it should be practiced. . . . Thus, the . . . debate . . . has been a largely philosophical [one] about how to view science, theology, man, morality, and the cosmos.[17]

Did the Sun Stand Still?

One of the most disputed statements in the Bible is that of Joshua 10:13: "So the sun stood still, and the moon stopped" (NKJV). It is inferred by some that this supports the outmoded Ptolemaic view of the world rotating around the sun. Even Martin Luther is quoted as saying of Copernicus, "He must do something of his own. This is what the fellow does who wishes to turn the

14. See Norman L. Geisler and J. Kerby Anderson, *Origin Science* (Grand Rapids: Baker, 1987), chaps. 1 and 6.

15. M. Ruse, *Journal of College Science Teachers* (Sept./Oct. 1984): 14; C. K. Svensson, *The Scientist* 1, 5 (1987): 12; S. Dutch, *Physics Today* (April 1983): 12.

16. *Evolution: A Theory in Crisis* (Bethesda, Md.: Adler and Adler, 1986), 86.

17. J. P. Moreland, *Christianity and the Nature of Science* (Grand Rapids: Baker, 1989), 217.

whole of astronomy upside down. . . . I believe the Holy Scriptures, for Joshua commanded the sun to stand still and not the earth."[18]

Does the Bible, as Luther's quote would indicate, teach a geocentric (earth-centered) view of our solar system? If not, how then can we hold that it is scientifically accurate? The answer lies in the use of observational language. It must be remembered that the Bible is not addressed to astronomers, but to the common person. Its statements about the heavens are made from the perspective of an observer on the face of the earth. Thus, it speaks, as even scientists do to this day, of the "sunrise" (Josh. 1:15). But to speak of the sun "standing still" is no more unscientific than to speak of sunrise and sunset, as meteorologists do. It is literally true from the point of view of an observer on the face of the earth that the sun sets and rises. Likewise, saying that the "sun stood still" is not less true. Neither statement is a commitment by Scripture to a geocentric view.

As to just how God made the sun stand still, the Bible does not say. But this is no problem for a God who can and did create the sun, moon, and the whole universe. Once we admit the Creator, miracles follow. As Lewis noted: "But if we admit God, must we admit Miracle? Indeed, you have no security against it. That is the bargain."[19]

The Mustard Seed

Christ described the mustard seed as "smaller than all seeds on earth" (Mark 4:31 NKJV). This seems to many to be scientifically inaccurate, since there are other seeds, such as the lily, that are smaller. However, if the biblical statement is taken in context, the problem disappears. In the discourse, Jesus is speaking about seeds that are "sown on the ground" (Mark 4:31 NKJV), that is to say, seeds that a first-century Palestinian farmer would sow. And, as Gleason L. Archer points out, the black mustard seed was most likely the smallest seed sown by the Palestinian farmers of the day.[20] Jesus, then, was speaking a scientific truth in terms understood by the general public. He was not making a statement about all seeds in the world, and, therefore, his statement should not be taken as such.

18. *Table Talk*, June 4, 1539.
19. *Miracles*, 109.
20. *Encyclopedia of Bible Difficulties* (Grand Rapids: Zondervan, 1982).

Is the Bat a Bird?

Another example can be found in Leviticus 11:13–19, where the list of unclean birds is given. The final "bird" on the list is a bat. Is the Bible making an incorrect scientific statement, calling a bat a bird? No! It is merely classifying warm-blooded, flying animals together. The present taxonomic classification system separates the egg-layers from the live-birthers. This does not make a different system of classification scientifically inaccurate. Even one of the recognized authorities on mammals finds it useful to reorganize the accepted scheme, commenting that "the following is not the recognized scientific classification of bats, but it represents groups arranged according to their feeding habits and physiology."[21]

In short, the Christian who is a scientist must perform within the framework of each discipline. The notion that the Christian is not able to perform quality work because of bias is ludicrous. Francis Bacon said, "Only let the human race recover that right over nature which belongs to it by divine bequest, and let power be given it; the exercise thereof will be governed by sound reason and true religion."[22]

We were created to have dominion over nature (Gen. 1:28; Ps. 8:6). Science is a means of doing just that.

Examples of a Christian View of Natural Science

We will look at three examples of how Christians ought to perform their work as scientists. Obviously, we will want to exemplify the principles already stated. We will look at models from astronomy (Johannes Kepler), biology (Carolus Linnaeus), and technology (Robert Stirling).

Johannes Kepler

The German astronomer Johannes Kepler was born in 1571. His astronomical views were bedded deeply in his biblical beliefs about creation and the Creator. Kepler revealed his Christian roots in an early letter:

> May God make it come to pass that my delightful speculation [the *Mysterium Cosmographicum*] have everywhere among reasonable

---

21. E. P. Walker, et al., *Mammals of the World,* 2d ed. (Baltimore: Johns Hopkins Press, 1968), 182.
22. *The New Organon,* ed. F. H. Anderson (New York: Bobbs-Merrill, 1960), 119.

men fully the effect which I strove to obtain in the publication; namely, that the belief in the creation of the world be fortified through this external support, that thought of the creator be recognized in its nature, and that his inexhaustible wisdom shine forth daily more brightly. Then man will at last measure the power of his mind on the true scale, and will realize that *God, who founded everything in the world according to the norm of quantity, also has endowed man with a mind which can comprehend these norms.*[23]

Kepler believed that God created the world to operate in a regular and orderly (mathematical) way so that we may, by observing natural laws, think God's thoughts after him. For "those laws [which govern the material world] lie within the power of understanding of the human mind; God wanted us to perceive them when He created us in His image in order that we may take part of His own thoughts. . . ." And "our knowledge [of numbers and quantities] is of the same kind as God's at least insofar as we can understand something of it in this moral life."[24] So for Kepler, to study nature is to study the mind of God.

As a Christian, Kepler saw the universe as a great mathematical machine created by God. He wrote,

My aim in this is to show that the celestial machine is to be likened not to a divine organism but rather to a clockwork . . . , insofar as nearly all the manifold movements are carried out by means of a single, quite simple magnetic force, as in the case of a clockwork all motions [are caused] by a simple weight. Moreover I show how this physical conception is to be presented through calculation and geometry.[25]

Because of the mathematical regularity of the universe, Kepler believed one could study the universe in a scientific way. However, the Greeks (particularly Pythagoras) believed this as well, at least for heavenly bodies beyond the moon. Although Kepler obviously was inclined toward the mathematics of Pythagoras, he was not a Pythagorean; rather he was a Christian using mathematics as a means to express his Christian belief that the universe performed like a great machine, which God, the great Mathematician, had

23. Quoted by Gerald Holton, *Thematic Origins of Scientific Thought* (Cambridge: Harvard University Press, 1973), 84.
24. Ibid., 85.
25. Ibid., 72.

created. Kepler's convictions led him to the conclusion that we can discover something about ultimate reality by observing the physical world. For Kepler the physical world was not only real but observation of it was the basis on which to correct any *a priori* mathematical speculation about it. He wrote,

> My aim is to assume only those things of which I do not doubt they are real and consequently physical, where one must refer to the nature of the heavens, not the elements. When I dismiss the perfect eccentric and the epicycle, I do so because they are purely geometrical assumptions, for which a corresponding body in the heavens does not exist.[26]

It was because of this conviction that Kepler rejected his own theory that disagreed with Tycho Brahe's's data regarding eight minutes of arc in the orbit of Mars. In brief, Kepler's scientific approach to the world can be stated as follows: "The physically real world, which defines the nature of things, is the world of phenomena explainable by mechanical principles."[27] He claimed that "from these magnetic [gravitational] forces, by other propositions which are also mathematical, I deduce the motions of the planets, the comets, the moon, and the sea." He also desired to "derive the rest of the phenomena of nature by the same kind of reasoning from mechanical principles. . . ."[28]

Kepler wrote to the German astronomer Fabricius: "The difference consists only in this, that you use circles, I use bodily forces."[29] Even Kepler's former teacher, Michael Mastlin, tried to dissuade him from this radical new departure in scientific procedure, saying, "I think rather that here [concerning the motion of the moon] one should leave physical causes out of account, and should explain astronomical matters only according to astronomical method with the aid of astronomical, not physical, causes and hypotheses. That is, the calculation demands astronomical bases in the field of geometry and arithmetic. . . ."[30]

The genius of Kepler's view was not that God was the solution to some scientific problem but that without a Creator of the physical

26. Ibid., 78.
27. Ibid.
28. Ibid., 77.
29. Ibid.
30. Ibld., 76.

world there could not be true science. So to leave the Creator out, as the Greeks did, is to deify nature and frustrate the efforts to have a viable science of nature. Kepler was convinced that the Creator had left his imprint on his physical creation in such a distinct way that it was worth his while giving up the Christian ministry for which he had prepared. He wrote, "I wanted to become a theologian; for a long time I was restless: Now, however, observe how through my efforts God is being celebrated in astronomy."[31]

Kepler's revolutionary discoveries in science were grounded in his belief that the universe is a finite, contingent creation of God. His theistic beliefs were a strong influence on forming his approach to nature and made his scientific views characteristically modern. Like Bacon, he believed in a primary cause, who worked in his creation in an orderly way. This belief formed the basis of his study of the secondary causes in the world of nature.

Carolus Linnaeus

Another practicing scientist who acknowledged that a Creator was the Author of the universe was Karl von Linne, better known as Carolus Linnaeus. His extraordinary work, *Systema Naturae*, is regarded by biologists as having begun modern taxonomy.[32] He developed the binomial nomenclature for plants and animals by genus and species. His appreciation for God's creation led him to group animals according to similarities of structure. He attributed these similarities to his belief that God created certain animals to have similarities, much the same way an artist's body of work can be identified by similarities. Unlike the evolutionary model of common ancestry, Linnaeus attributed the similarities to the planning of a single Creator at the time each plant or animal was individually created.

Robert Stirling

Our final example is a relatively unknown scientist, Robert Stirling. As a matter of fact, he is not even listed in *World Who's Who in Science*, possibly because he was a minister of the Church of Scotland.[33] In 1816, this man of God received a patent for design-

31. Ibid., 86.
32. Willis H. Johnson, L. E. Delanney, E. C. Williams, and T. A. Cole, *Principles of Zoology*, 2d ed. (New York: Holt, Rinehart, and Winston, 1977).
33. M. W. Zemansky and R. H. Dittman, *Heat and Thermodynamics* (New York: McGraw-Hill, 1981).

ing an external combustion engine. By 1818 he had completed a working model of the engine, which was used to pump water. This invention predated the formal theory of thermodynamics by about twenty years. Although we have only a sketchy biography of Stirling, one might suppose that this preacher of the gospel had intended to make life a little simpler and better for the average worker, as the compassion of Jesus for the physical needs of people led to the feeding of the five thousand described in the Gospel accounts. Robert Stirling's ability to identify and fulfill a need was a God-given gift. He relied upon this inspiration, and combined it with what he had observed, to develop a time-saving device, the Stirling engine. His basic design would later be used (and is still used today) in reverse as a refrigerator.

Although we could give a host of other examples of God-fearing individuals who worked in the pure and applied fields of science, the intention here is to cite historical precedent for today's Christian to engage actively in scientific endeavor. Whether one has a gift for physics, biology, chemistry, or one of a number of other natural and applied sciences, there is no need to worry that one's Christian beliefs will reduce the value of one's scientific work. Quite the contrary, we have shown that a genuine belief in a Creator is an inspiration to do great things for him.

The Relationship of Natural Science to Other Disciplines

We will concentrate now on a few of the major arenas where science has either formed a friendly relationship with another discipline or has clashed and caused a rift between those of opposing viewpoints.

Mathematics: A Friendly Partnership

Galileo was probably the first of the modern scientists to adopt the philosophy that rigorous science could not be accomplished without rigorous mathematics. Even before the development of calculus, Galileo discovered the relationship between a freely falling object's distance of fall (d) and its time of fall (t) to be $d=1/2gt^2$ (the value of g represents the constant gravitational acceleration).

As one looks down the list of the great mathematicians, one cannot help but notice how many of them were considered great scientists as well: Galileo, Newton, Gauss, Pascal, Maxwell, Dirac, Landau, and Boltzman, to name a few. The deep involvement of mathematics in the formulation of scientific theories is obvious. As a group of scientists stated, "Mathematics provides the grammar of science—the rules for analyzing scientific ideas and data rigorously."[34]

It is the unerring logic of mathematical proof that glues together the data accumulated by the inductive method of science. It provides a check on the fallible human scientist. The relationship has so developed between science and mathematics that the latter is called by some "the Queen of the Sciences."[35]

Biblical Studies: A Misunderstood Relationship

Just as our selection of mathematics as it relates to science may have been an obvious choice, so too is the following firestorm of controversy. At the outset let me say that most of the problem between biblical studies and science lies with poor interpretation of Scripture by both the staunch theist who attacks science as evil and by the atheistic scientist who attacks religion as useless to the scientific endeavor.

As for the atheist's view, Paul teaches us in 1 Corinthians 2:14 that the unregenerate mind does not accept the things of God. Scripture itself is foolishness to the atheist, who therefore believes that those who abide by its principles must be fools (1 Cor. 1:18). The atheist's own bias clearly shines through the attempt to be religiously neutral. Human beings do science, and human beings have biases and are fallible. The atheistic scientist's concept of science is more like a religion with a set of doctrines aimed at winning people over to a perspective.[36] Thus, atheistic scientists must come to grips with their own anti-Christian commitments.

The unbeliever, however, is not the only one at fault in the conflict between science and Scripture. Many theists have a wrong view of science. As we have seen, some theologians reviled science for its development of the heliocentric theory of our solar system, only to be found wrong centuries later. Others claimed that the

34. AAAS, *Science*, 34.
35. Kappa Mu Epsilon, *Initiation and Installation Ceremonies* (KME, 1970), 2.
36. Howard J. Van Till, D. A. Young, and C. Menninga, *Science Held Hostage: What's Wrong with Creation Science and Evolutionism* (Downers Grove, Ill.: InterVarsity, 1988).

Bible pointed to such a system all along, discrediting themselves further.[37]

Others praise the second law of thermodynamics because of its supposed contradiction of evolutionary theory, without understanding its principles. Yet few take the time to learn the difference between "micro" and "macro" evolution or between entropy and disorder. Little wonder that they are unable to gain the support of the scientific community in the educational process.

Some have even gone so far as to claim that Einstein's theory of relativity has become the springboard for modern hedonism. They simply do not understand its principles and confuse the word *relativity* with *relativism*. They blame science for the present state of our society instead of turning to the church as the most likely source of spiritual deficiency (1 Pet. 4:17). Understood properly, Einstein's theory implies the reverse of relativism.

> According to special relativity, when we pass from one reference frame to another, some properties change (. . . length, and mass) and some do not (. . . the velocity of light and the "Einstein interval") . . . what came to be labeled Einstein's "relativity theory" might just as well (and perhaps more accurately) have been called "invariance theory." And this in turn would have given rise to very different "inferences" about morals. . . .[38]

True scholarship can lead only to a united growth in knowledge about our Creator. He does not lie, either in his revelation in Scripture or in his revelation in nature.

Ethics: A Strained Relationship

The professional scientist has played Dr. Jekyll and Mr. Hyde for a long time. The give-and-take between the pure satisfaction from gaining knowledge and the pillaging of society for gain has not been absent from the scientific endeavor. The most obvious example of this problem is the relationship between science and warfare. Whether one is a biologist working on genetically engineered hybrids, or a physicist working on nuclear power, or a chemist working on fertilizers, the fact remains that in the hands of an evil mind or society, any advancement of knowledge for good can be used for bad. In addition to accidental casualties that may occur during the

---

37. Barfield, *Why the Bible,* 110–12.
38. J. L. Hammond, *American Journal of Physics* 53 (1985): 873.

research or development of new technologies, new scientific developments may become lethal if used immorally. In the hands of terrorists, scientifically developed materials could lead to the destruction of a neighborhood, a city, a country, or even a continent.

How does society check the advances of science? In this country the President has a science advisor who has access to a large number of professional organizations throughout the country and the world. When questions regarding the nature or ethics of new scientific developments arise, input can be collected from a large number of sources, a practice that is suggested in Scripture (Prov. 11:14). Scientists hold conferences on ethics and proper practice within their fields. American society applies pressure on its elected leaders and on those who gain financially from a particular scientific breakthrough. Threats of economic boycott have proven to be useful in turning the tide of a rising technology, as seen in the recent furor over the French-made abortion pill (RU 486). Many in our society decry the work of scientists whose research leads to the development of destructive forces. Yet those same critics enjoy the comforts of automobiles, air conditioners, and computers, all resulting from the same basic research that produced tanks, mustard gas, and radar-tracking for missiles.

As God's creation we are able to praise him, love him, serve him, and know him. Science avails us of a methodology whereby we can learn some of the most marvelous characteristics of the Creator through direct interaction with the created work. The psalmist cried out:

O LORD, our Lord,
How excellent is Your name in all the earth,
You who set your glory above the heavens!" (Ps. 8:1 NKJV).

Those who recognize their position as submissive to God will rely on his written as well as his general revelation for guidance. They will base their scientific theories on the assumption that God exists and interacts with us through the witness of the Holy Spirit within the believer. All supposed conflicts between Scripture and science, therefore, can be attributed to poor analysis, either of Scripture or of science.

Those who refuse to acknowledge God's authority may yet be able to solve some of the mysteries of the universe. However, their conscious effort to deny God what is due him can only lead them to further affirm their basic and incorrect assumption that he does not exist. It is a credit to God's patience that he permits such folly. The psalmist wrote, "The fool has said in his heart, 'There is no God'" (Ps. 14:1 NKJV). May God have mercy on those scientists who, after clearly seeing the works of God, have denied his glory (Rom. 1:20–21).

9   Mathematics

Glyn Wooldridge

> The universe cannot be read until we have learnt the language and become familiar with the characters in which it is written. It is written in mathematical language.
> —Galileo Galilei (1564–1643)

> God made the whole numbers, all the rest is the work of man.
> —Leopold Kronecker (1823–1891)

A book that appeared a few years ago was entitled *Mathematics, The Man-Made World*. The title reflects a modern view that holds that the applications of mathematics come about by fiat. The mathematician creates a variety of patterns or structures and then tries to force the various physical and social aspects of the universe into these patterns. This view is related to the assumption that theories of applied mathematics are merely "mathematical models" that mimic or predict the behavior of the universe. If a model is found to be inadequate in some respect, one looks for another or for an improved version. It is becoming increasingly popular in universities today to offer courses in mathematical modeling.

In contrast, virtually all of classical mathematics derived from the universe itself. Early mathematicians believed that nature imposed the mathematics upon mankind. A piece of mathematics was valid to the extent that it agreed with nature. The truths of geometry had as subject matter those ideal forms whose existence was evident to the mind. To question their existence would have been a sign of ignorance or even insanity. Thus, the study of mathematics was considered the study of God and creation.

Jacob Bronowski proposes that the reason astronomy as a science developed ahead of the other sciences was that the observed motions of the stars turned out to be calculable and (from perhaps as early as 3000 B.C. in Babylon) lent themselves to mathematics.[1] The well-known quote from Plato that "God ever geometrizes" reflects the reverence with which the ancients approached the science of mathematics. The Bible asserts that "the heavens declare the glory of God; the skies proclaim the work of his hands" (Ps. 19:1), so it is natural that science and mathematics had many of their roots in astronomy.

Mathematics in an earlier view is the science of space and number. In a later view it is the science of patterns and deductive structure. Since the time of the Greeks it has also dealt with the infinite. Herman Weyl states that

> purely mathematical inquiry in itself, according to the conviction of many great thinkers, by its special character, its certainty and stringency, lifts the human mind into closer proximity with the divine than is attainable through any other medium. Mathematics is the science of the infinite, its goal the symbolic comprehension of the infinite with human, that is finite, means.[2]

The process of developing a Christian view of mathematics will require that we give attention to several aspects of mathematics, both classical and modern. We must address two important ques-

1. "The Music of the Spheres," in *Mathematics: People, Problems, Results*, vol. 1, Douglas M. Campbell and John C. Higgins, eds. (Belmont, Calif.: Wadsworth International, 1984).
2. Philip J. Davis and Reuben Hersh, *The Mathematical Experience* (Boston: Birkhäuser, 1981), 108.

tions: Is mathematics a purely human endeavor, or is it imposed upon us by nature? Is new mathematics discovered or invented?

We shall need to give attention to some of the current philosophies of mathematics. We shall then turn our attention to the development of a view of mathematics that honors God, that is consistent with a Christian worldview, and that complements today's scholarship in the mathematical sciences.

A Biblical Basis for a Christian View of Mathematics

The Bible is not a mathematics text. The intricacies of mathematical theories are not spelled out in Scripture. However, some areas of mathematics (geometry for example) were well-developed at the time the Scriptures were written.

Historians believe that the beginning of mathematics predates the earliest civilizations. Carl B. Boyer and Uta C. Merzbach state that it is hazardous to make statements about the origins of mathematics, whether geometry or arithmetic, for the beginnings of both are older than the art of writing.[3] Howard Eves places those beginnings at approximately 3000 B.C. among the Egyptians and Babylonians.[4]

It is likely that the writers of the Scriptures knew some, perhaps a lot, of mathematics. But there was no need to describe complicated mathematics in the Bible. Therefore, the mathematical sciences have been and continue to be a part of God's general revelation to humanity and a part of his charge to "subdue" the earth (Gen. 1:27).

Indeed, the history of mathematics reflects a gradual revelation of mathematical truth that is more cumulatively progressive than is the development of other branches of learning. Herman Hankel stated, "In most sciences one generation tears down what another has built, and what one has established another undoes. In mathematics alone each generation builds a new story to the old structure."[5] In our time new mathematics has been and is being discovered (invented?) at a rate never seen before. We will pursue this further in the next section.

Mathematics is used in Scripture in various ways. God's people were "numbered" (i.e., counted) on several occasions. They were

3. *A History of Mathematics*, 2d ed. (New York: Wiley and Sons, 1989).
4. *An Introduction to the History of Mathematics*, 5th ed. (New York: Saunders, 1983).
5. Boyer and Merzbach, *History*, 619.

numbered by Moses (Num. 1:18; 26:1–4), and by David (2 Sam. 24:1–4). In Genesis 15:5, God told Abraham to "look at the heavens and count the stars." In Psalm 139:17–18, David wrote,

> How precious to me are your thoughts, O God!
> How vast is the sum of them!
> Were I to count them, they would outnumber the grains of sand.

Further references to very large finite, even infinite, numbers are made. Eliphaz, in beseeching Job to lay his cause before God, says that "He performs wonders that cannot be fathomed, / miracles that cannot be counted" (5:9), and this is acknowledged and reiterated by Job (9:10).

The mathematics in Scripture occurs in a natural way in the form of numerical references to how many, to weights and measures, or to specific order. Few fractions occur; most numerical quantities are given in round numbers.

Some elementary probability also occurs in Scripture. The modern science of probability involves the making of decisions in the face of uncertainty. There are several instances in Scripture where "casting lots" was used to make a decision. Aaron was instructed by God (through Moses) to choose by lot which of two goats would be chosen for the sacrifice and which would be set free (Lev. 16:10). Further, the Lord instructed Moses to distribute the land by lot to the Israelites (Num. 26:55). The Roman soldiers divided up Jesus' clothes by lot (Matt. 27:35).

Because he is omniscient, God knew the outcome before the lot was cast. He could have told his people what the outcome was going to be, but instead he instructed them to cast lots. Why? There are two verses in Proverbs that shed some light here. Proverbs 18:18 reads, "Casting the lot settles disputes and keeps strong opponents apart," so that the decision appears to be an objective one. But God knows the outcome because "the lot is cast into the lap, but its every decision is from the LORD" (Prov. 16:33).

Most of the decisions with which the Christian (or anyone else) is confronted are made in the face of uncertainty. God asks us to use the tools he has given us, and many of those tools are mathematical, and he will do the rest.

In summary, a Christian view of mathematics acknowledges that God is the source of all truth, that he is omniscient (he even knows mathematics), and that his charge to subdue the earth includes the development of all the mathematical tools that our finite minds are able to comprehend. We will consider the continuing revelation that is mathematics in the following section.

The Nature of a Christian View of Mathematics

If one does mathematics every day it seems to be the most natural thing in the world. But if one stops to think about what one is doing, it becomes mysterious. Developing a Christian view of mathematics requires that one reflect on the nature of mathematics. What is mathematics? How do we know that what we are doing has meaning? These are philosophical questions.

Philosophies of Mathematics

In any discussion of the philosophy of mathematics one encounters three major schools of thought. They are referred to by various titles, but perhaps the most descriptive ones for our purposes are Platonism, formalism, and constructivism.[6]

Platonism

According to Platonism, mathematical objects are real. Their existence is an objective fact independent of our knowledge of them. To a Platonist a mathematician is an empirical scientist. One cannot *invent* anything because it is already there. All one can do is observe or discover what is there. René Thom, a whole-hearted Platonist, writes that ". . . mathematical forms indeed have an existence that is independent of the mind considering them."[7]

A Platonic view of mathematics has a special appeal for the Christian mathematician whose belief in an all-wise Creator and Sustainer of the universe carries over into one's profession. Each discovery is but a further revelation of God's truth about his creation.

The Platonic view has been strengthened by the logicist school of which Alfred North Whitehead and Bertrand Russell were the chief proponents.[8] The basic assumption here is that mathematics is a

6. These terms are those used by Davis and Hersh, *Mathematical Experiences*, 318, and the descriptions that follow can be attributed to them.

7. Davis and Hersh, *Mathematical Experience*, 319.

8. Whitehead (1861–1947) and Russell (1872–1970) wrote their monumental *Principia Mathematica* during 1910–1913. The basic idea of this work was the identification of much of mathematics with logic by the deduction of the natural number system, and hence of the bulk of existing mathematics, from a set of premises or postulates for logic itself.

branch of logic. All mathematical concepts are to be formulated in terms of logical concepts. This approach arises naturally from the effort to push back the foundations of mathematics as far as possible. Thus, the real number system is pushed back to a natural number system and from there into set theory. This process results in "primitive ideas" and "primitive propositions," which are to be accepted as plausible descriptions and hypotheses concerning the real world. No attempt is made to prove the primitive propositions, since they are rooted in reality. In this view mathematics begins with "self-evident" truths and proceeds by careful reasoning to discover other truths which are not so evident.

Formalism

According to formalists there are no real mathematical objects. Mathematics consists of axioms, definitions, and theorems. It is regarded as a collection of abstract developments in which the terms are mere symbols and the statements are formulas involving these symbols. David Hilbert (1862–1943) is considered the progenitor of the method. It is the axiomatic development of mathematics pushed to its extreme. It is at that extreme that mathematics is in danger of becoming a meaningless game played with symbols.

Constructivism

The philosophy of constructivism begun by L. E. J. Brouwer (1882–1966) is clearly a minority viewpoint among mathematicians. A constructivist accepts as genuine mathematics only that which can be obtained by a finite construction. His thesis is that mathematics is built solely by finite constructive methods on the intuitively given sequence of natural numbers. To prove the existence of an entity, the mathematician must show that it is constructible in a finite number of steps. It is not sufficient to show that the assumption that it does not exist leads to a contradiction. Thus, many of the existence proofs in current mathematics are not acceptable to constructivists.

Mathematics, a Continuing Revelation

In this section we pursue the idea further that mathematics is but a continuing revelation from God. It is a story that begins in the concrete and moves to the abstract. We discuss some of the historical highlights that suggest that such a wonderfully puzzling, often mysterious, and useful activity of mankind, an activity that has continued for thousands of years with remarkable consistency, cannot be mere chance. It must have some ultimate goal, known only to God. The history of mathematics has known many cases where some great discovery is made simultaneously by two or more mathematicians independently in different locations. In other cases, great mathematical discoveries made by one scientist may remain unknown until later reproduced by another with striking precision.

Highlights of Classical Mathematics

The construction of regular geometric figures, counting by means of tally sticks, and a wide variety of other mathematical activities predate recorded history. Mathematical discovery has been a fundamental human activity in virtually every civilization. The Babylonians (about 2000 B.C.) computed some square roots, solved second-degree equations, solved systems of first-degree equations, knew the Pythagorean theorem for certain right triangles, and knew that the distance around a circle was at least 3 1/8 times the distance across it. The Egyptians (about 3000 B.C.) had a surprisingly sophisticated arithmetic and the rudiments of geometry. But it was the Greeks (600 B.C. to A.D. 400) who "created an abstract discipline of power, beauty, subtlety, and rigor such that mathematics as we now know it may fairly be said to have started then and there."[9]

A brief explanation of the terms used here will be helpful. The whole numbers refer to the numbers 1, 2, 3, . . .; numbers expressed as ratios of whole numbers, such as 1/2, 3/4, 17/5, are called rational numbers. An irrational number then is one that cannot be expressed as a ratio of two whole numbers. The Greeks discovered that $\sqrt{2}$ is such a number and that, to their dismay, a square that measures one unit on a side has diagonal length $\sqrt{2}$. Their fruitless effort to compute the exact value of $\sqrt{2}$ led the Greeks to prove that it is an irrational number. The concept of irrational numbers was not fully resolved until the methods of modern analysis were employed in the nineteenth century. They were there all the time, but God chose to reveal them over time as a part of his continuing revelation to human understanding.

The Pythagorean theorem is surely the most famous theorem in the history of mathematics. It is well known to every school child. It states

9. Campbell and Higgins, *Mathematics,* 1.

that in any right triangle the square of the length of the hypotenuse (opposite the right angle) is equal to the sum of the squares of the lengths of the other two sides ($c^2 = a^2 + b^2$). Why is this true? It is not self-evident, but it can be observed on any number of right triangles by measurement. It was Pythagoras in about 550 B.C. who raised this knowledge from empirical observation into what is now called "proof." Pythagoras showed that not only was the relationship true for a right triangle whose sides measure 3, 4, and 5 units, but it was true for every triangle in the universe that contains a right angle. Some historians give the credit for the first proof of this theorem to Euclid some two hundred years later. However, one gets the impression that this relationship is a part of the structure of nature, that God ordained it and over the centuries has revealed it. There are now over 350 known proofs of the Pythagorean theorem.

Geometry was the major part of ancient mathematics. Its origin in antiquity was empirical, that is, rooted in observations and measurements of natural phenomena. For example, nature distinguishes the right angle from any other arbitrary angle. According to Bronowski, "There are two experiences on which our visual world is based: That gravity is vertical, and that the horizon stands at right angles to it."[10] Euclid (about 300 B.C.) is generally credited with the axiomatization of geometry. It was probably he who took those first great steps away from the empiricism that reflects the geometrical nature of the world to formal geometry. His axioms were "self-evident truths" obvious from nature. He then proceeded to deduce from what seemed to be obvious those conclusions that were not.

The impact of Euclid as a model of mathematical reasoning was immense and longlasting. His book, *Elements of Geometry,* has been more widely used, edited, studied, and copied than any other book in history except the Bible. Over one thousand editions have appeared since the first one was printed in 1482. The geometry that is taught in today's schools has a strong resemblance to that of Euclid. This work has dominated the teaching of geometry for over two millennia.

Euclid assumed five axioms, the first four of which were indeed self-evident truths. For example, the first axiom said essentially that there is but one straight line between two points. However, the Fifth Postulate (axiom) was distinctly different from the others

10. Ibid, 63.

in that it was much longer and more complicated. A modern rendering of the axiom would be: Through a given point not on a given line there is at most one parallel to the given line. This statement by its nature, its hint of the infinite, presented mathematics with a problem for more than two thousand years. Mathematicians tried to prove it as a consequence of the other four axioms—to no avail. It was the denial (or negation) of the Fifth Postulate in the nineteenth century that led to the discovery of non-Euclidian geometries, and that in turn opened the way for the modern era of abstract mathematics to begin.

The calculation of pi was an important discovery. The ratio of the circumference of a circle to its diameter is such a significant, almost mysterious, number that it must be mentioned here. A character, Π, of the Greek alphabet has been set aside to represent this number. It is uncanny how frequently \pi turns up in mathematical developments. The ratio is given in round numbers as 3 in the Scriptures (in 1 Kings 7:23 and again in 2 Chron. 4:2), but it was laboriously computed by Archimedes in about 240 b.c. to be about 3.14 by using inscribed and circumscribed regular polygons of some ninety-six sides.

The chronology of \pi includes hand computations of its values to more than seven hundred decimal places. Modern computing machines have produced the computation to more than one billion decimal places, but to print the number would require a stack of computer sheets 125 feet high. In modern times Π has been shown to be first an irrational number and then a *transcendental* number in the sense that it is not a root of any polynomial with rational coefficients. Such magnificent properties from such a naturally occurring number!

Highlights from Modern Mathematics

Eves considers the modern era of mathematics to have two periods, one from 1450 to 1700, the other from 1700 to the present.[11] The examples that follow are from the latter period and are meant to illustrate the continuing understanding of the nature of God's revelation of mathematical concepts.

The mathematics of continuous motion, the calculus, was discovered. Two superb minds of the seventeenth century—Isaac Newton and Gottfried Wilhelm Leibniz—discovered calculus at about the same

---

11. *Introduction,* "The Table of Mathematical Periods," inside front cover.

time. Since the time of Pythagoras it was believed that the laws of
nature were numbers. But now "the laws of nature become laws of
motion, and nature herself becomes not a series of static frames but
a moving process."[12]

Newton was an unquestioning believer in an all-wise Creator of
the universe, and even though he was the greatest mathematician
of his time, he was also a believer in his inability to comprehend
the universe. He wrote,

> I do not know what I may appear to the world; but to myself I
> seem to have been only like a boy playing on the seashore, and
> diverting myself in now and then finding a smoother pebble or a
> prettier shell than ordinary, whilst the great ocean of truth lay all
> undiscovered before me.[13]

It seems clear that Newton considered mathematics to be discovery,
not invention.

Non-Euclidean geometry revolutionized the thinking of mankind. Any
geometry that results from the denial of Euclid's Fifth Postulate is
referred to as a non-Euclidean geometry. It is the same as
Euclidean geometry except for those results that depend on the
parallel postulate. For centuries, Euclid's had been *the* geometry
because it seemed to square with nature—except for that nagging
Fifth Postulate. Then in at least three separate locations and at
about the same time, the idea to deny the Fifth Postulate came to
Carl Freidrich Gauss (1777–1855) in Germany, Johann Bolyai
(1802–1860) in Hungary, and Nikolai Lobachewski (1793–1896) in
Russia.

Harold E. Wolfe quotes Bolyai's father in a letter to his son, in
which he urged Bolyai to make his discoveries known without
delay:

> It seems advisable to me . . . that the publication be hastened: first
> because ideas easily pass from one to another who, in that case, can
> publish them; secondly, because it seems to be true that many things
> have, as it were, an epoch in which they are discovered in several
> places simultaneously, just as the violets appear on all sides in the
> springtime.[14]

12. Campbell and Higgins, *Mathematics*, 71.
13. Eric T. Bell, *Men of Mathematics* (New York: Simon and Schuster, 1937), 90.
14. *Introduction to Non-Euclidean Geometry* (New York: Holt, Rinehart, and Winston, 1945),
45.

So it happened that independently and at about the same time the discovery of a logically consistent geometry in which the Fifth Postulate was denied was made by Gauss, Bolyai, and Lobachewsky.

Modern abstract mathematics relies on assumptions. The discovery of non-Euclidean geometry led to a treatment of geometry that was dependent on the assumptions made instead of on empirical evidence from nature. The resulting geometries proved to be just as consistent as the geometry of Euclid.

E. T. Bell refers to this as the "liberation of geometry."[15] A similar story can be told of algebra, as it moved from self-evident properties to noncommutative algebras. This "liberation" led to the formulation of the abstract systems in mathematics usually referred to as modern algebra and encompassing group theory and ring theory.

The axiomatic development of geometry, first Euclidean and then non-Euclidean, made a powerful impression upon thinkers throughout the ages. The method consists of accepting, without proof, certain propositions called *axioms* or *postulates;* and then deriving from the axioms all other propositions of the system, called theorems, through the process of logical deduction. Thus, in an axiomatic system the axioms and basic theorems need not necessarily be "self-evident." The choice of axioms is restricted by one condition: freedom from self-contradiction. Thus the words *true* and *false* become meaningless. A statement is "true" if it is consistent with the axioms and theorems and "false" otherwise and may have nothing at all to do with reality. This reflects more of the philosophical view of the formalists than that of the Platonists.

Formalism became the predominant philosophy by the mid-twentieth century. It was apparent in textbooks and other mathematical publications. For Euclid, the axioms of geometry were not assumptions but self-evident truths. The formalist, however, makes a distinction between geometry as a deductive science and geometry as a descriptive science.

The mathematics of the twentieth century has been heavily influenced by the emphasis on abstraction. Perhaps nowhere is this more evident than in the writings of a group of mathematicians, mostly French, who write under the pseudonym of Nicolas

15. Howard Eves, *Great Moments in the History of Mathematics after 1650* (Washington, D.C.: Mathematical Association of America, 1983), 76.

Bourbaki. Some thirty-one volumes have been written, and they encompass the content of set theory, algebra, and analysis at the graduate level. Their presentation is characterized by uncompromising adherence to the axiomatic approach.

The formalist style gradually penetrated downward into undergraduate mathematics teaching and even into the high schools and elementary schools under the name *new math*. The intention was that the emphasis on structure could effect considerable economy of thought and aid to understanding.

Davis and Hersh feel that in recent years a reaction against formalism has been growing. In recent mathematical research there is a turn toward the more concrete and applicable and "the signs seem to indicate that the formalist philosophy may soon lose its privileged status."[16]

Formalism should not be written off just yet, however. There is no doubt that the twentieth century has seen more new mathematics discovered, perhaps invented, than all of recorded history prior to this century. Many of the mathematical systems that have been developed axiomatically have turned out to have important applications many years later. Further, the advent of electronic computing has made applicable some of the mathematics that before was only theoretical, because the labor involved in the algorithms can now be done with ease and with great speed. What may have been abstract has become concrete.

Each of the philosophies we have discussed has its own inherent limitations. Constructivists have not gained much acceptance among mathematicians. According to Davis and Hersh "their status in the mathematical world sometimes seems to be that of tolerated heretics surrounded by orthodox members of an established church."[17]

Both Platonism and formalism employ the axiomatic method. It is at the foundations that they part company, that is, at the source of the axioms. Formalism supposes that mathematics is the creation of the human mind and that mathematical objects are imaginary. Platonism recognizes that mathematics has its own laws, which we must obey.

Christian mathematicians can "play the game" of the formalist, studying the abstract systems in which truth is relative. However,

16. *Mathematical Experience*, 344.
17. Ibid, 322.

Scripture tells them that the God of the universe is the Source of all mathematics and that God has revealed this great discipline down through the ages through the genius with which he has endowed various individuals. Shafarevitch says it thus:

> A superficial glance at mathematics may give an impression that it is a result of separate individual efforts of many scientists scattered about in continents and in ages. However, the inner logic of its development reminds one much more of the work of a single intellect, developing its thought systematically and consistently using the variety of human individualities only as a means.[18]

The foundations of mathematics may be a bit uncertain. Platonism pushes the foundations back to set theory, but then the set theory of Cantor has been found to contain some contradictions. Likewise, Kurt Gödel showed in 1931 that the axiomatic method has certain inherent limitations that rule out the possibility that even the ordinary arithmetic of the integers can ever be fully axiomatized. Further, he proved that it is not possible to establish the internal logical consistency of all deductive systems.

What does this dilemma do to mathematics? It says that "no final systematization of many important areas of mathematics is attainable, and no absolutely impeccable guarantee can be given that many significant branches of mathematical thought are entirely free from internal contradiction."[19]

Principles of a Christian View of Mathematics

The basic principle of a Christian view of mathematics is that mathematics is inherent in the structure of God's creation of the universe. Mathematics began empirically, and through the inventiveness and genius of man, God has revealed at the right time and in various places the next chapter of a continuing revelation. It is, at this point, an imperfect system, as is any other branch of knowledge. The fact that the foundations of mathematics are a little shaky simply says that not all the facts are in yet; we do not know the whole truth of the matter. We should accept mathematics as it is: fallible, somewhat tentative, correctable, and very meaningful and applicable.

18. Ibid, 52.
19. Ernest Nagel and James R. Newman, *Gödel's Proof* (New York: New York University Press, 1960), 6.

Christian mathematicians stand in awe of the discipline when contemplating the infinitude of the Mind that stands behind it. They have a better idea than most people of what *omniscient* means after surveying the vastness that is mathematics. Further, the teacher of mathematics at a Christian university must convey that sense of awe to students while imparting mathematical knowledge.

The history of mathematics also says something to us about its pedagogy and perhaps about pedagogy in general. That history has been a journey from the concrete, or obvious, to the abstract, from observation to induction, from induction to deduction, and from deduction to verification. Rigor entered the picture quite late. Abstraction is a necessity, however, because it connects (seemingly) unrelated ideas. Rigor is necessary because it produces agreement as to what is accepted as "proved."

Mathematics, imperfect as it may be, is the key to understanding the universe. Let us recall the statement of Galileo with which we began this chapter: "The universe cannot be read until we have learnt the language and become familiar with the characters in which it is written. It is written in mathematical language." God used mathematics in creating the universe, and he gave us the ability to understand the universe through mathematics.

God is a rational being. He created us in his own image. Thus, we are rational beings. We are able to catch a glimpse of the mind of God through the study of his universe. The Christian mathematician has the distinct privilege of knowing the Creator through his Son, the Logos (John 1:1), and knowing something about the cosmos, the universe, through the science of mathematics.

The Relationship of Mathematics to Other Disciplines

Mathematics occupies a unique role in a university because it is neither a science nor an art—it partakes of both disciplines. In the sciences it is clear that mathematics is a prerequisite to any serious study. Indeed, in the physical sciences it may be hard to know what to classify as applied mathematics and what as theoretical physics.

Applied mathematics has had some rather nasty connotations in the minds of the pure mathematicians. The highest aspiration to a pure mathematician is to achieve a lasting work of art—a monument of aesthetic beauty. If, on occasion, a beautiful piece of pure mathematics turns out to be useful, as is often the case, then so much the better, but utility remains an inferior goal for some.

In recent years, however, there has been a noticeable shift in attitudes predominant among mathematicians. Applied mathematics is enjoying a surge of popularity unknown before due in large part to the advent of computers. Statistics, computer science, numerical analysis, operations research, and other branches of applied mathematics dominate the job market today.

Mathematics is not as apparent in the arts as in the sciences, but it is there. It is there in geometric form in the perspective of great painting and in such ratios as the "golden ratio" of ancient Greece. In a delightful essay entitled "The Music of the Spheres," Bronowski relates the story of Pythagoras as he discovered a basic relation between musical harmony and mathematics.[20] He found that a single stretched string vibrating as a whole produces a ground note. The notes that sound harmonious with it are produced by dividing the string into an exact whole number of parts: into exactly two parts, into exactly three parts, into exactly four parts, and so on. If the still part, the node, does not come at one of these exact points, the sound is discordant. Pythagoras found that the chords that sound pleasing to the ear are those that correspond to the exact divisions of the string by whole numbers. The agreement between nature and number was so cogent to the Pythagoreans that it persuaded them that not only the sounds of nature, but all her characteristic dimensions as well, must be simple numbers that express harmonies. Thus, all the regularities in nature are musical.

The Pythagorean philosophy rested on the assumption that the whole number is the cause of various qualities of both man and matter. According to Eves this led to an exaltation and study of number properties and arithmetic (or theory of numbers), along with geometry, music, and spherics (astronomy), as the fundamental liberal arts curriculum of the Pythagorean program.[21] This group of subjects became known as the *quadrivium* during the Middle Ages. A *trivium* of grammar, logic, and rhetoric was added during that period so that these seven liberal arts came to be regarded as the necessary foundation of an educated person.

We have noted that mathematics is a growing subject. New mathematics is being discovered almost daily and in all parts of the world. Further, applications of mathematics are being made nowadays that were unheard of only a few years ago. Some of the

---

20. Campbell and Higgins, *Mathematics*, 61.
21. *Introduction*, 48.

abstract systems that may have had only aesthetic value to a few people are now being applied in such areas as linguistics. Mathematical models are proving invaluable in economic theory. A cursory examination of the research journals available today reveals such titles as *Mathematical Population Studies* and *The Journal of Mathematical Sociology.*

The growth of mathematics has been likened to a tree: Think of the height of a place on the tree as a measurement of *time,* with early mathematics located near the roots and the most recent advances (and applications) flowering at the tips of the highest limbs.[22]

I have attempted to develop a Christian view of mathematics, presenting the discipline as God-given from its beginnings but as an incomplete, still developing, and very relevant component of all that humanity does. It is not just the language of science; mathematics now contributes in fundamental ways to business, finance, health, and defense. Modern mathematics provides a powerful instrument for understanding the world in which we live.

A recent national report warns that our nation is at risk because of a lack of knowledge by our citizens of the mathematical sciences.[23] The report points out that we not only face a shortage of personnel with the mathematical preparation suitable to scientific and technological jobs but also that the level of mathematical literacy of the general public is completely inadequate to reach either our personal or national aspirations. Mathematical literacy is essential to a social foundation for democracy in a technological age.

The charge is clear, then, for the mathematics department of a Christian university. We must transmit the knowledge, skills, and special ways of thinking that are required in today's world and do it with a sense of awe, excitement, and purpose. That is our responsibility to mankind.

Our responsibility to God is greater. Our response to the Great Commission can be a unique one. We and our students have opportunities to carry the precious gospel of our Lord to the mathematical community. Equipped with a knowledge of mathematics that commands the respect of coworkers and a love for Christ that compels them to share him with others, our students will be able to help change the world and preserve freedom.

22. Campbell and Higgins, *Mathematics,* 73.
23. National Research Council, *Everybody Counts, A Report to the Nation on the Future of Mathematics Education* (Washington,D.C.: National Academy Press, 1989).

10   Health and Sports

Alan Rabe

Since the late 1960s, most institutions of higher education have developed departments of health education or health science, which, in turn, train professionals to address critical health issues such as suicide, weight control, family life education, drug education and many other societal behavioral lifestyle problems. For various reasons Christian colleges and universities have tended instead to emphasize only physical education and athletics. Consequently, secular colleges and universities have had the opportunity to permeate our society with health dogma that neglects the human spirit. While Christian schools have chosen to participate in health-professional preparation programs in a limited form, namely in physical education and athletics, the remaining health professions have been thoroughly dominated by an anti-Christian philosophy and leadership.

In a 1985 survey of health education status and need in over one hundred secondary Christian schools across the nation, this writer found that health education classes covered a variety of health topics. However, most instructors said they did not receive adequate professional preparation to teach those topics in the

Christian colleges and universities from which they graduated.[1] Christian colleges and universities must begin to look at health education as a broad societal need and as a discipline that integrates the components of body, soul, and spirit. Traditional physical education and sports programs are not enough to meet the major health problems that exist in our society today.

Biblical Basis for a Christian View of Health and Sport

The Bible declares that we are loved by a sovereign God who knows our every part and way (Ps. 139:1–16). But because we are members of a fallen humanity in a fallen world, our bodies will deteriorate and wear out even if we treat them with optimal care. Paul wrote, "but we ourselves . . . groan inwardly as we wait eagerly for . . . the redemption of our bodies" (Rom. 8:23). Achieving any positive advantage, even good health, is a struggle against the decay inherent in nature.

Scripture clearly commands us to be responsible for physical, mental, and spiritual health. Paul wrote that the body is "for the Lord, and the Lord for the body" (1 Cor. 6:13). He further stated: "Do you not know that your bodies are members of Christ himself?" (6:15).

What we allow to enter our minds should be subject to God's direction as well. "Finally, brothers, whatever is true, . . . noble, . . . right, . . . pure, . . . lovely, . . . admirable—if anything is excellent or praiseworthy—think about such things" (Phil. 4:8). And we must respond to Jesus' call to refrain from worry (Matt. 6:25–27).

In general, the Christian is commended to form attitudes in godly directions; Christian attitude is an outgrowth of what we think and have learned. Interestingly, Paul used an athlete as an example. Athletes work hard, avoid negative influences, and eventually get the chance to prove their skills in competition. A victor "competes according to the rules" (2 Tim. 2:5). What greater challenge is there for a Christian than to follow the example of an athlete? For this reason, perhaps, Christians are likened to runners in many places throughout the Scriptures. Analogy is usually made to swiftness in a race or effort to attain an end or reward (Isa. 40:31; 1 Cor. 9:24–27; Gal. 2:2; Gal. 5:7; Phil. 2:16; Heb. 12:1).

---

1. Alan N. Rabe, "Health Education Status and Need in Secondary Christian Schools," unpublished paper (Lynchburg, Va.: Liberty University, Department of Health Sciences).

Christian institutions of higher education need to emphasize health and sport so that their graduates will be better able to compete in the world. As they compete, Christians must care for their bodies and minds so as to honor God and to be at their peak performance for as long as possible. The goal of good health must be viewed from a God honoring perspective or it can become a license for selfishness and indulgence in sensual gratification.

The health education and sport program at a Christian university can provide an ethical basis for a healthy body that honors God rather than self. Students not only learn the scriptural basis for exercise and eating correctly but also have the opportunity to practice what they know before a world that is often more interested in the results than in the method. Christians can show that godly ways are better, as Daniel did long ago with respect to his eating habits (Dan. 1:8–15). Developing healthy habits for personal glorification is not the end. For the Christian, the goal is to glorify God.

Sports provide athletes with the opportunity to show how rigorous discipline can honor God. Not every person should be an athlete, but every person should learn how to discipline his or her body (1 Cor. 9:27). Sports provide opportunity for character-building and physical achievement for those in intramural and extramural college athletics. Many times an athlete is respected by others, and at these times God may allow the athlete to be an ambassador for Christ (2 Cor. 5:20), bringing the gospel to people who would not listen to anyone else. Sports at a Christian university should always provide an evangelistic thrust. Athletes must not only lead moral lives but also be personally committed to Christ. For students who are not athletes, the greatest challenge is to show what God has done with their total health—that is, with body, soul, and spirit. As one cares for the body physically, there should be a testimony to God's masterful creation. As one shows high levels of mental, emotional, and social health through wisdom, love, and interaction with others, God is honored. And as one stresses spiritual growth and maturity of walking with God (Gal. 6:1–8) as a priority in life, God is pleased and those around are encouraged to lead godly lives (Gal. 6:9–10).

The Nature of Health and Sport

Throughout history societies have viewed health from a purely physical perspective, defining it as the absence of illness. In 1947,

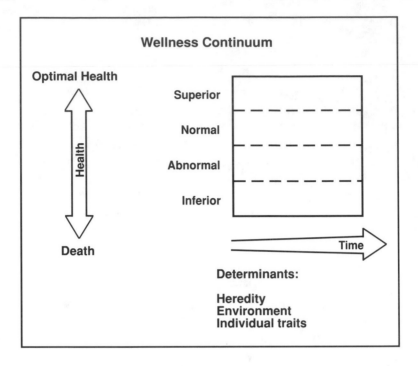

Figure 10.1

the World Health Organization (WHO) defined health as "a state of complete physical, mental, and social well-being and not merely the absence of disease and infirmity."[2] For fifty-two nations to agree upon the definition for such a complex term as *health* was quite a task. This definition motivated the general public to think of health as well-being rather than lack of sickness.

From a Christian perspective some problems exist with this popular definition. Health is a dynamic process that should be viewed as a continuum (see fig. 10.1). Based upon many factors, decisions, and behavior, our health varies from time to time. The first two human bodies were made in optimal condition. However, after the fall, a major change occurred. Human bodies were set on a course of constant and consistent deterioration. Therefore, it is important to work constantly to keep our bodies in a condition that is honoring to God (in contrast to the view that we keep our bodies in shape to honor ourselves.)

---

2. World Health Organization, "Constitution of the World Health Organization," *Chronicle of the World Health Organization* 1 (1947): 29–43.

Second, there is a major error in the definition, since it excludes the spiritual component. Human beings are body, soul, and spirit. Without the spiritual component, there could be no intimate relationship with God. The WHO definition emphasizes a social component, whereas the biblical view emphasizes a God-consciousness component that allows communication between God and human beings.

Health is an Anglo-Saxon term that means complete, whole, together, or sound. Andrew Weil states that "whole" indicates that all the components are there and are arranged in harmonious integration and balance. Health is "wholeness." We have no need for the redundant phrase *holistic health*.[3] However, the phrase is popular and surely needs explanation. Paul Reisser states that "despite the increasing visibility of holistic health, the movement is struggling to define itself, a task hindered both by its newness and its rapid growth."[4] Dennis Warren commented in 1978 that

> the holistic approach is in its embryonic stage. There is no accepted consensus as to the scope of holistic practices, the role of medicine and society. There are no objective standards or guidelines for treatment. There is only a general philosophy of approach to health care. The rest is experimentation and individual implementation.[5]

It would be naive to think that any major refinement has come about in the past ten years. However, there has been a growing emphasis on "new consciousness," and a pervasive form of supernatural-psychic humanism within the movement through the years. New-Age thinking seems to be at the heart of this, and Christians can be completely taken in by pseudo-Christian terminology. When the term *holistic health* is used to express the idea that the components of a human being are dependent upon each other, that would support the biblical view (see table 10.1). However, the other side of the holistic health concept is a different matter. *The New England Journal of Medicine* concludes that "the irrational side of the holistic movement, with its mystical cults and all the paraphernalia of sectarianism," is a great danger.[6]

Throughout history the church has taught that the human body

3. *Health and Healing* (Boston: Houghton Mifflin, 1983), 42.
4. *The Holistic Healers* (Downers Grove, Ill.: InterVarsity, 1983), 12.
5. "Legal Considerations in the Search for Holistic Health," *Journal of Holistic Health* (1978): 104.
6. Editorial, *The New England Journal of Medicine,* 8 Feb. 1979.

Table 10.1
Holistic Health

Components	Input for Growth	Period of Emphasis	Approx. Age of Maturity	Application	Average Birth Age	Average Death Age
Physical (body)	Food, water, sleep, exercise, oxygen, shelter	Adolescence and/or before	21	Vd. ache. cancer	0	70–72
Mental (mind)	Idea, facts, knowledge	? 5–25	35–40	Labeling, handicapped	Early in life	?
Social (will)	Interaction with people	13–40	30–40	Insecurity, guilt, cliquishness	Early in life	Late in life
Emotional (heart)	Love	0–6	? 15–?	Hate, fear, stress, depression	?	Late in life
Spiritual (spirit)	Faith (beliefs)	Late in life, close to death, or traumatic experience	Never in this life	Blame God, lack absolutes, attribute to fate	Anytime	?

Soul

is a sacred vessel that should bring honor to God. For the body to be able to honor God to its maximum, it must be healthy. In the early medieval university, knowledge about health was a by-product of the study of philosophy and the sciences. Over time this transfer of knowledge broke down, and a major problem arose. To understand this problem fully, we must look closely at the development of health and sport in society.

Health and sport has a history as old as the human race. When the earliest societies formed communities, people banded together for protection from enemies and to support each other in food-gathering. Certain individuals were chosen to be soldiers because of their strength and skills. People soon learned that soldiers should undergo an extensive period of physical training designed to increase their proficiency, strength, and endurance. Because of the importance of an army, soldiers were the only group who received any specific training in physical skills.

Sport was first developed as an art by the Greeks.

> Because of their zeal for arts, it was natural that the Greeks should be the first to recognize the possibilities of increasing the beauty and efficiency of bodily movements by means of specific sports and exercises. Consequently, all young males of the upper class received training in the sports and physical skill of the day. After the conquest of Greece by the Romans, sports became almost entirely a means of mass entertainment.[7]

The Olympic Games today derive from ancient Greek festivals. "Timaeus (352–256 B.C.) was the first to date events with reference to the listing of olympic victors, available from 776 B.C."[8] Sports continue to serve as entertainment to this day. However, in recent years the popular emphasis on physical fitness has merged sports and health in a closer relationship.

Much of the early history of health parallels that of ancient theory and practice in medicine and science. The oldest persons in a group were respected for their longevity, since such people were thought to have special knowledge about health. They became the respected headmen or shamans who protected and passed on tradition. From archaeological records John J. Hanlon records later health practices.

7. H. F. Fait, et al., *A Manual of Physical Education Activities,* 2d ed. (Philadelphia: Saunders, 1961), 5.
8. *Encyclopedia International,* 1966 ed., "Olympiad," 414.

The Egyptians of about 1000 B.C., as described by Herodotus, were the healthiest of all civilized nations. They had a marked sense of personal cleanliness, possessed numerous pharmaceutical preparations and constructed earth closets and public drainage pipes. The Jews extended Egyptian hygiene thought and behavior by including in the Mosaic law what is considered to have been the first formal hygienic code. It dealt with a wide variety of personal and community responsibilities including cleanliness of the body, the protection against the spread of contagious diseases, the isolation of lepers, the disinfection of dwellings following illness, the sanitation of campsites, the disposal of excreta and refuse, the protection of the water and food supply, and the hygiene of maternity.[9]

Homer, Hippocrates (the father of modern medicine), Galen, and others added further to medical and health knowledge, but not until the end of the Reformation did medical science and health care begin an age of discovery. "More than anything else this era after 1650 was characterized by the dominance of science and replacement of superstition with the analysis of cause and effect."[10]

A Christian view of health and sport is much needed in our society today. The popular view of health implicitly denies that humans can or should relate to God. The spiritual component, as revealed in Scripture, must be taught if our society is to progress. Holistic health must be just that and not be prostituted by New-Age groups.

Further, Christians must be aware of popular health and sport attitudes. Few Christian institutions of higher education emphasize health, although they usually have a physical education department. A vast difference exists between health education and physical-skill development. Few Christian colleges and universities emphasize sports beyond the traditional intramurals and limited extramurals. The Great Commission exalts us to minister in all areas of life. Ancient and biblical history show good reasons why health and sport has had a mission throughout the years.

The Principles of a Christian View of Health and Sport

People desire high levels of wellness primarily so that living can be devoted to goals beyond food-gathering and fighting enemies. Until rather recently, health and sport have had that common

9. *Principles of Public Health Administration,* 3d ed. (St. Louis: Mosby, 1960), 693.
10. Laurna Rubinson and Wesley F. Alles, *Health Education: Foundations for the Future* (Prospect Heights, Ill.: Waveland, 1988), 4.

rationale and purpose. Today, however, sport generally involves a few select participants who provide entertainment for large groups of spectators. Nevertheless, health theory and practice undergird this high level of skill development seen in athletes.

Every person should achieve his or her highest potential of physical, mental and spiritual well-being. For this reason, everyone should strive for optimal health, that is, to be the best we can under the circumstances and within the components of physical, mental, and spiritual well-being that God has given us. Without a healthful lifestyle, achieving one's potential will be only a dream. Therefore, health education and sports are necessary to the university curriculum so that every person can have the potential to develop to the fullest. Health is not simply the opposite of sickness. Health is that condition which allows us the opportunities to lead physically productive, challenging lives.

A Body of Knowledge

Perhaps the most basic question of a discipline is, What is its distinctive body of knowledge? Health education in the schools is an important part of the discipline because of the direct relationship between schoolchildren's potential to learn and their personal health, their classmates' health, and the healthful environment that surrounds them. In the first edition of his book entitled *School Health Practice* (1956), Dr. C. L. Anderson wrote,

> Health promotion is a recognized component of present-day functional public school education which is designed to prepare each youngster to deal with life's academic, cultural, and practical needs. No phase of the school's activities has more to contribute to the student than does the health program.[11]

He noted that schools became one of the principal agencies of health promotion even before the year 100 B.C. in Egypt.[12] In 1918 the Commission of Reorganization of Secondary Education named health as the first of the cardinal principles of education, and educational emphasis began to shift from physiology-oriented classes to those that emphasized healthful living as a means of conserving health.[13] Even so, "the primary responsibility for the health of the

11. *School Health Practice*, 3d ed. (St. Louis: Mosby, 1964), 7.
12. Ibid., 18.
13. J. Koegh Rash and Morgan Pigg, *The Health Education Curriculum* (New York: Wiley & Sons, 1979), 5.

child rests with the parent, but the school is in a strategic position to contribute effectively to the health of every school aged child . . . the school health program is planned to fortify and supplement the efforts of the parents."[14]

As Christians perhaps it is our responsibility to teach health at home since values so permeate instruction. However, even parents who homeschool must recognize their limited knowledge and resources. Therefore, the Christian school, elementary, secondary, and post-secondary, must provide information and decision-making skill development in areas such as nutrition, sexuality, disease, family life, and substance abuse. The Christian school can provide integration of scriptural principles and the latest knowledge concerning health.

The goals of health education in the schools were once based on the establishment of good health habits and physical activity for students. Through the years the definition of health education has broadened in response to social and environmental changes. The President's Committee on Health Education in 1973 tried to clarify the role of health education by stating that it must promote positive health and stress disease prevention.[15] Health education had its origin in two fields, medicine and education, so it has been at once dominated by medical science with its focus on treatment and control and by education with its focus on individual growth and development.[16] The goal for health education is diverse but must give basic knowledge early in life that provides a base for decision-making later in life.

A profession must contain a body of knowledge that is unique. The roots of health education, physical education, and sport are similar. Sport developed out of physical education in an attempt to provide entertainment and competition at the highest levels. "Physical education and health were held to be identical and, apparently, not until 1910 was there a change in this point of view."[17] Not until the late 1960s did health education truly identify a unique body of knowledge different from physical education. At that time, universities across the nation began to differentiate be-

14. Anderson, *School Health*, 7.
15. "Report of the President's Committee on Health Education" (New York: Xerox Corp., 1973).
16. Rubinson and Alles, *Health Education*, 416.
17. Anderson, *School Health*, 7.

tween health and physical education by forming separate departments, or divisions within departments, whereby health content
could be taught. This separation occurred probably because most
states had different certification procedures and requirements for
health teachers and for physical education teachers in the public
systems.

New content within the body of knowledge that makes up
health education is not as set (as some would prefer) because
health problems and issues are always changing. However, in 1981
the Education Commission of the States recommended minimum
elements of a comprehensive school health curriculum: personal
health, mental and emotional health, prevention and control of
disease, nutrition, substance use and abuse, accident prevention
and safety, community health, consumer health, environmental
health, and family life education. It is significant that none of these
topics has a "home" in any other discipline. Thus, even though the
body of knowledge changes to keep pace with individual and community needs, the general theme of knowledge is a mix of the
social and natural sciences in applied form.[18]

Defining Principles

Principles of a Christian view of health and sport are derived
from the philosophical base already outlined. Numerous major
concepts can be synthesized to formulate the basis for health and
sport at a Christian university.

Health is an applied science. Applied sciences are necessary to put
ideas or principles into action. Scripture is rather specific when it
states, "Do not merely listen to the word, and so deceive your-
selves. Do what it says" (James 1:22). In many ways, it is not until
action takes place that one identifies his own true feelings about an
issue. Learning about eating the proper food is one thing but actually eating the appropriate food is another. Thus, people should
examine their behavior to determine whether they put what they
believe into practice. The essential facts of good health may be
extrabiblical, or they may be obvious in Scripture. For example,
Scripture specifically condemns homosexuality (Rom. 1:26–27).
However, the Bible is not so clear about specific kinds of family
planning. In the latter case one must study the workings of contra-

18. Education Commission of the States, *Recommendations for School Health Education*
(Denver: Education Commission of the States, 1981).

ceptive techniques, integrate this knowledge with scriptural principles, and eventually make a decision.

Health is bringing together knowledge gained in the natural sciences (e.g., biology, physics, and chemistry) and the behavioral sciences (e.g., psychology, sociology, anthropology) to solve human
problems. At Christian universities this takes place through comparison and contrast with biblical principles. The report of the
Calvin College Curriculum Study Committee in 1970 states that
Christian higher education should have core requirements in
selected areas, including a four-semester program in physical education.[19] The committee further states,

> No person, either in or out of college, can perform his tasks well
> unless his body is in condition. Contemporary studies in medicine
> and psychology have shown that this is true in numerous ways
> never before suspected. Thus teaching a young person how to keep
> his body in condition and training . . . is an indispensable part of
> preparing him for his future life.
>
> Certainly it is a part of total Christian education . . . the body is an
> integral facet of our human existence, intrinsically neither better nor
> worse than any other facet.[20]

In 1970 Calvin College had no requirement in "studies of persons and society." However, the curriculum study committee recommended that every college student take at least one course in
"those sciences which deal with the nature and activities of persons
and social groups."[21] Emphasis was placed upon sciences that apply
basic knowledge to man rather than to animals. The committee
concluded by saying, "Furthermore, the biblical revelation
addresses itself very directly to the nature of persons and society;
no integrated and comprehensive Christian vision of reality can
possibly ignore the matters considered by these sciences."[22]

The goal of health education is to foster the merging of sciences
into an applied form of learning about the human body and
human relations. The teacher who has a firm grasp of many disciplines and of the Bible is invaluable to the process of integrating
God's truth.

19. *Christian Liberal Arts Education* (Grand Rapids: Calvin College and Eerdmans, 1970),
77–79, 89.
20. Ibid., 89.
21. Ibid., 79.
22. Ibid.

"Correlation of Christianity with his regular teaching will be natural and intuitive, not forced and calculated."[23] When this happens in the classroom, the student immediately can see the relationships between scriptural principles and scientific discovery and the application of both to his life. This can only take place in a genuine manner when God's truth is seen in the natural and social sciences and then applied to human lives through biblical principles. This can happen only at a Christian university where doctrinal issues are not repressed.

Health and sport are relevant to living. To care for one's body is to keep it effective and efficient for a long period of time. Learning and then testing our basic knowledge of health and discipline in sports will glorify God and strengthen his servants. "Convictions of our faith become more fully our own, as we practice and learn them in the laboratory of daily life and work."[24]

Health knowledge and skills in decision making provide the basis for optimal health as they are applied in the circumstances of our life and work. Exercise and sport allow young people to practice skills in a controlled setting that builds confidence and skills for living life as adults. Health education and sport at a Christian university support godly order in our society and allow students to practice healthful living in an environment of Christian nurture.

The 1978 Bethesda Conference on Health Education stressed three goals of health education today:

1. To foster or facilitate individual and community responsibility for the prevention of disease and the management of optimum health status;
2. To facilitate opportunities among individuals and communities to make informed decisions or intelligent choices regarding health and behavior;
3. To stimulate community interest in health, resulting in the development of consumerism, participation, conservation, and prevention.[25]

These goals amplify the fact that health education is designed to make education relevant to life. Further, sports allow a highly visi-

23. Ibid.
24. Frank E. Gaebelein, *The Pattern of God's Truth* (Chicago: Moody, 1968), 49–50.
25. H. Cleary, "Health Education: State of the Art, Parameters of the Profession," proceeding of the Workshop on Commonalities and Differences in the Preparation and Practice of Health Education, Bethesda, Md., 1978.

ble stage in which God can be glorified through outstanding skill development. In many ways college life and sports could be considered a microcosm of life beyond the ivy-covered walls. What better place to learn about life than at a Christian university where God is rightfully honored in every aspect of living?

The fullness of life is experienced only when one reaches full potential, and for Christians that means building character. Health and sport contribute to this end. Further, the ideas and practice learned in the classroom and on the playing field must be implemented in the real world so that holiness is manifested and the gospel proclaimed to a lost and degenerate people. To promote such goals can not even be thought of at a non-Christian college or university.

In the Book of Colossians, Paul gave the admonition to "set your hearts on things above" and your "minds on things above, not on earthly things" (Col. 3:1–2). Furthermore, we are to "put to death, therefore, whatever belongs to your earthly nature: sexual immorality, impurity, lust, evil desires and greed, which is idolatry" (Col. 3:5). We are exhorted to "let the peace of Christ rule in your hearts, . . . and be thankful . . . and whatever you do, whether in word or deed, do it all in the name of the Lord Jesus, giving thanks to God the Father through him" (Col. 3:15–17). None of this is natural behavior in this world. Individuals must be taught to discipline their sexual desires and eating habits and to practice regular exercise, healthful habits, good grooming, and numerous other health skills, remembering that they may be the only image of God many people will ever see. Similarly, the process of integrating current knowledge with biblical data is not innate but needs to be learned, practiced in a supportive environment, and then tested in larger and greater ways in the world until the person becomes a tried and proven servant of God.

Frank Gaebelein calls such a procedure the "criterion of craftsmanship."[26] The person of God is guided through a process that leads to a job well done. It is a time when motives reach beyond self-advancement to the glory of God.

Sports is an example. Pitching a shut-out game is spiritually fruitless from a Christian perspective unless the way the pitcher responds on and off the field displays the discipline of character. The balance of athletics is summed up by Gaebelein when he states,

The place of athletics, though always subsidiary to the main business of school or college, is a vital one. It is once more a question of method; especially in sports, the manner in which they are conducted is all important. Team-play, the heart of which is self-restraint and self-sacrifice; the moral courage that is good sportsmanship — these can be learned on playing fields in such a way that they become lasting character traits to the glory of God. And the benefit of athletics under Christian leadership is by no means confined to participants; the whole school community may learn group lessons in encouraging the defeated, being generous to rivals, and showing under all circumstances the courtesy that is such an essential by-product of the Gospel.[27]

Life is worth living only when we can say to ourselves (and eventually to God), "I have fought the good fight, I have finished the race, I have kept the faith" (2 Tim. 4:7). The teaching of health and sport can only be done with this result at a Christian university.

It is essential that health and sports be articulated in a Christian university. In every discipline a biblical view of what human beings are must be presented in such a way that the spiritual dimension is seen as a critical component. Sport is necessary to provide an avenue for the select who will discipline themselves in order to achieve high levels of health and skill development. Because of the high visibility of sports at a university, God can use it to bring some to salvation and to promote Christ-like character with individuals who may never identify with God in any other way.

Health education is an applied science, unique from all other areas of study, that bridges many disciplines so that we can apply information and decision-making skills to everyday living, the ultimate goal being healthful and godly behavior. The Christian university is responsible for projecting godly living which is in direct opposition to humanistic lifestyles endorsed and promoted on many secular campuses and in the world. Health and sport, then, are an important part of the curriculum in a Christian university.

27. Ibid., 90–91.

11   Education

Milton Reimer

Unlike many of the classical disciplines that compose a university curriculum, education is a broad, amorphous field of study. There is little agreement among the experts as to what exactly constitutes "education." Definitions range from a broad social science perspective to the narrow view that includes only what occurs in formal, organized school environments.

Furthermore, there is disagreement regarding the nature of the field. Is education a discipline? Is there a clearly defined body of knowledge that can be called "education"? Is education both a process and a content? If so, is the process (teaching/learning) a profession or merely vocational? What is the content of education? It is beyond the scope of this chapter to answer all these questions, but several of them will be addressed.

In the preface to his monumental and highly acclaimed three-volume work *American Education*, Lawrence A. Cremin provides a comprehensive definition of education: It is, he states, "the deliberate, systematic, and sustained effort to transmit or evoke, knowledge, attitudes, values, skills, and sensibilities, a process that is

Opening the American Mind

more limited than what the anthropologists would term enculturation or the sociologist would term socialization, though obviously inclusive of some of the same elements."[1]

By this definition all social institutions, to a greater or lesser degree, serve an educational function and role. Schools and colleges are, of course, major suppliers in the knowledge and learning process. Our society has assigned to them the formal role of inculcating in our youth the cultural patterns that prepare them to function effectively in our adult world.

Often overlooked and frequently neglected are the impact on and critical importance of other social institutions to the educational process. Increasingly schools have been delegated responsibility to provide instruction in areas that previously were the function of family and church. This has occurred partly because families and churches have voluntarily abdicated their roles, particularly in the teaching of values and morality. Ironically, we live in a time when public institutions of all kinds have assumed an amoral stance. Thus, the family and church must attempt to retain their role in teaching the young, even though social forces are contrary.

A Biblical Basis for a Christian View of Education

The Bible has a great deal to say, both implicitly and explicitly, about education. It provides insight into such questions as: Who is primarily responsible? What should be education's main content? And what is its goal? Several key biblical passages allude to all three of these areas.

> For I have chosen him [Abraham], so that he will direct his children and his household after him to keep the way of the LORD by doing what is right and just. [Gen. 18:19]

> These commandments that I give you today are to be upon your hearts. Impress them on your children. Talk about them when you sit at home and when you walk along the road, and when you lie down and when you get up. Tie them as symbols on your hands

---

1. *American Education: The Colonial Experience 1607–1783* (New York: Harper and Row, 1970), xiii. Cremin's effort is a major contribution to American educational historiography. He provides a detailed and fair treatment of the education contributions of families, churches, missionary associations, lyceums and expositions, as well as schools and colleges. These three volumes are recommended reading for anyone seriously interested in American education.

and bind them on your foreheads. Write them on the doorframes of your houses and on your gates. [Deut. 6:6–7]

and how from infancy you have known the holy Scriptures, which are able to make you wise for salvation through faith in Christ Jesus. [2 Tim. 3:15]

Fathers . . . bring up [your children] in the training and instruction of the Lord. [Eph. 6:4]

Clearly, parents are the designated teachers, and the home is the learning environment. This gives parents the primary responsibility, under God, to lay the moral, spiritual, and epistemological foundation of their children's lives.

This does not imply, however, that children should have no teachers other than their parents, or that schools are unbiblical. Formal educational institutions developed in response to existing needs. As culture and society become more sophisticated and complex, so do the educational needs of our children. Formal schools and qualified teachers are needed to present the complexities of an ever more demanding society.

The biblical mandate of parental responsibility for children's education often comes into sharp conflict with the secular notions of states' rights and ownership. Indeed, in most states existing laws already pre-empt many parental rights. Most parents are unaware of such laws because the state usually acts benevolently toward parents and allows them to function as though they have legal control of their children.[2] Paul A. Kienel quotes an Ohio law that illusrates the growth of state control: "The natural rights of a parent to custody and control of . . . children are subordinate to the power of the state to provide for the education of children. Laws providing for the education of children are for the protection of the state itself."[3]

Although formal schools, in concept, are not unbiblical, the idea that children belong to the state is. Therefore, as Kienel notes, "We must do anything possible to preserve our rights as

2. In the state of Minnesota, for example, the law requires state approval before parents can leave their children in another home (e.g., grandparents) for more than three months. This law is seldom invoked; therefore most parents are unaware of the erosion of control they have experienced.

3. *The Christian School: Why It Is Right for Your Child* (Wheaton, Ill.: Victor, 1974), 61.

parents to maintain the custody and control of the children God has given us."[4]

The ultimate content and focus of education is truth: objective, universal, unified truth. The ultimate Source of truth, and by implication, of the curricular content of education, is God himself. This does not mean that Christians have all knowledge just because Christ indwells them or that the Bible is the only textbook that should be studied in a Christian school. Rather, it means that all truth, wherever it is found, is God's truth.[5]

> Whatever we understand about nature is ultimately about His creative wisdom and power; whatever we do in human art and science ultimately comes from the creative and rational potential that God invested in men by making us in His own image. To understand this centrality of Jesus Christ in all knowledge gives perspective to moral and social issues, to interpersonal relations, marriage and work, in fact to everything in all the arts and sciences of men.[6]

To assume that only Christians can know truth and that the secular scientist or sociologist or historian is incapable of discovering God's truth is a fallacy. In spite of most contemporary translators' claims to more accurate rendering, the Authorized Version of Romans 1:18 is instructive: ungodly and unrighteous men "hold the truth in unrighteousness." This implies that unbelieving scholars may not know the source or nature of truth, but the truth they discover is still God's truth.

Although the Bible is not the only textbook needed in Christian education, or the only source of data for understanding the world in which we live, it must serve as a standard for truth—a criterion by which truth from other sources is judged. As this writer has stated elsewhere, "The Christian teacher believes in the authority of the Bible over all human disciplines. Its statements must take precedence over all human pronouncements. In other words, all human wisdom, all professional consensus, all educational/scientific theories, must be subordinate to its authority."[7]

Where the Bible specifically addresses the intended purpose of

4. Ibid.
5. Arthur F. Holmes, *All Truth Is God's Truth* (Grand Rapids: Eerdmans, 1977), 8.
6. Ibid., 12.
7. Milton K. Reimer, *A Brief Survey of Educational Studies: An Introduction to Education from a Christian Perspective* (Minneapolis: Burgess, 1982), 106.

education, it relates primarily to spiritual and moral concerns. Children are to be trained in the way they should go (Prov. 22:6); the Scriptures are to be persistently taught to provide wisdom for salvation (2 Tim. 3:15); and fathers are to provide "training and instruction of the Lord" (Eph. 6:4). According to H. W. Byrne, the primary purpose of education is salvation, and the general purpose is "the perfect man in Christ."[8]

The Christian is admonished to study "to present yourself to God as one approved, a workman who does not need to be ashamed and who correctly handles the word of truth" (2 Tim. 2:15). In the Great Commission Jesus sent his followers forth to teach and to baptize in all nations, "teaching them to obey everything I have commanded you" (Matt. 28:20).

But implicit in the great truths of the Bible is the mandate to prepare people to live effective lives in the world into which God has placed them. To subdue and rule the earth (Gen. 1:28) people must understand its natural and social complexities; to be industrious and earn a living in order to "owe no man any thing" (Rom. 13:8 KJV) and to provide for our families (1 Tim. 5:8) requires job skills and vocational training; to heed the continual admonition to not be ignorant and to renew the mind (Rom. 1:13; 12:2) demands rigorous mental exercises that range across the spectrum of human knowledge. Byrne quotes C. B. Eavey as saying that the true purpose of education is for "each individual pupil to live as he was created to live, in order that he may become what his Creator destined him to be."[9]

The biblical purpose of education "is to help students know the truth, to be conformed to Christ's image, and to learn to live effectively in a world ordered by God's laws—physical, social, moral and spiritual."[10]

Principles and Implications of a Christian View of Education

Several key concepts and principles essential for a Christian view of education have already been addressed. The authority of the Bible over all human knowledge is a fundamental principle that distinguishes true Christian education from that which is merely

---

8. H. W. Byrne, *A Christian Approach to Education* (Milford, Mich.: Mott Media, 1977), 106.
9. Ibid.
10. Reimer, *A Brief Survey*, 30.

good, moral, and conservative. The biblical notion that "all truth is God's truth" provides justification for the pursuit of knowledge and truth at all levels and in all fields. But in addition to these critical ideas there remain numerous others to be considered.

One of the key questions in education, and one which impinges on all aspects of it from methodology to content to purpose, is the question of the nature of humans. The generally accepted secular assumption is that humans are chance products of an evolutionary process. From this follows several secondary assumptions: The person is only quantitatively, not qualitatively, different from lower animals, and there is no transcendent purpose for human existence. Thus humans are related downward to animals and not upward to God.[11]

The consequences of such a view of humanity spin off in many directions. Human life loses its special significance, hence the change in references to human life from its sanctity to its quality. This subtle but substantial change in perspective opens the door to various objectionable practices. Abortion, euthanasia, and the elimination of nonproductive members of society, such as the elderly and the handicapped, are by implication desirable means of improving the quality of life for the remaining majority.

The question of morality becomes absurd. When humans are considered merely sophisticated animals, then there is no reason for them not to live like animals. The question of right or wrong has no meaning for an animal; the "human animal" is thus amoral.

The moral implications of the man-as-animal concept pose a serious dilemma for secular educators. Society needs a common set of values, but there is no logical basis upon which to fashion such a criterion. Pragmatists appealed to social consensus as an answer. John S. Brubacher states that "in the secular school the approach to moral character was educational rather than evangelical. There moral education took its point of departure in the ongoing experience of the child in a social situation. Moral kowledge was the result of choosing between alternate ends of conduct and evaluating them in the light of outcomes or consequences."[12]

Such an approach to morality worked as long as there was what Francis A. Schaeffer called a Christian consensus or a Christian

---

11. Francis A. Schaeffer, *Escape from Reason* (Downers Grove, Ill.: InterVarsity, 1968), 25–26).
12. *A History of the Problems of Education* (New York: McGraw Hill 1966), 330.

memory. This memory has been fading fast in Western culture, and secular humanism has become the dominant worldview.[13] The new humanism, according to James Hitchcock, involves the denial of God and of all moral constraints. Only then, say the humanists, can human beings achieve true freedom.[14]

In such a context educators can only encourage students to clarify their subjective preferences; there are no values to teach. Indicative of the moral wasteland is a poster that hung on the wall of a colleague's office in a state university: "Good is better than evil, because good is nicer!" Such a statement defies objective analysis.

The biblical view of human beings is that they are created in God's image. The question of what it means to be created in God's likeness has been discussed ever since that event. It is generally accepted that this does not have reference to man's physical being. God is a spirit, and only in the incarnation did God take on human form. There are human qualities, however, that clearly set us apart from lower animals—qualities of personhood by which humans are related upward to God rather than downward to animals. It is in the mind—the ability to exercise free choice, the human will—that humans are uniquely God-like. Next to the gift of salvation, the mind is the greatest gift God has given. This God-like quality has the potential to elevate a person to lofty levels of positive achievement and righteous performance and, on the other hand, to plummet a person to an abyss of degradation and degenerative behavior.

That humans can make such awesome choices has been a source of great anxiety and confusion for some people. If God is omnipotent, why does he allow a Hitler or a Stalin or, perhaps, a rebellious child to get his own way? In their desire to assure the ultimate outcome in their children's lives, many parents and Christian educators have taken two false approaches, both of which tend to bypass and negate the quality by which humans are identified as being

---

13. James Hitchcock, *What Is Secular Humanism?* (Ann Arbor, Mich.: Servant, 1982), 33–48.

14. Ibid., 48. See also Jacques Ellul, *The Betrayal of the West* (New York: Seabury, 1978), 68–81. Ellul's thesis is that Western cultures have always lived in tension between eros and agape. In our time eros has triumphed and God has been silenced. Modern Western society no longer needs God. "God's silence means that the world that wanted to be left alone is now indeed alone. It is left to its own dereliction." Man "may continue to fight, but his fists will encounter only empty air and unbounded darkness." "The West is dying because it has won out over God" (80–81).

fashioned in God's image, that is, the human ability to exercise free will and make real choices.

The first error is in mistaking certain biblical instructions (for example, Proverbs 22:6 reads, "Train a child in the way he should go, and when he is old he will not turn from it") as ironclad guarantees that their children will ultimately be saved. Such claims reduce people to the level of unchoosing robots and shatters God's image. Proverbs is better understood as a book of practical wisdom that recognizes the power of enculturation on children. The foundations laid in early life are the ones to which people return when they are ready to build an adult life.[15]

The second error made by many parents and educators is even more ciritical to the present discussion. It has to do with the distinction between training and teaching, and it involves the larger issue of behaviorism as an educational/learning theory.

Many advocates of the Christian school movement have leaned heavily on the concept of training. After all, training is a good biblical term, and it fits well an authoritarian mindset. Some have even argued that the notion of *education* itself is somehow liberal and secular and that only "training" is appropriate in a truly Christian school.

Granted, training is an important process by which certain principles and practices are imparted to young children by parents and teachers. It is important to note, however, that training is closely related to indoctrination and conditioning. It involves a minimum of reasoning and/or intelligence, and it inculcates beliefs and ideas, bypassing choice and will on the part of the child. The motivations for accepting the beliefs and habits acquired by training are usually extrinsic, ranging all the way from physical force and intimidation to positive reinforcement, such as pleasurable rewards and benefits.

The fact that it is appropriate to "train" children at an early age in no way justifies training as a primary methodology in Christian education. Thomas F. Green has pointed out that teaching (as compared to training) must stay within "the region of intelligence," and must "involve reasons, evidence, argument, justification."[16] In other words, the mind must be involved in true education.

Educational practice and learning theory are dominated by

---

15. For an interesting, albeit somewhat irreverent, treatment of the powerful force of value-programming at an early age, I would refer the reader to a lecture by Dr. Morris Massey, "What You Are Is Where You Were When." It is available in most public film libraries.

16. Thomas F. Green, "A Topology of the Teaching Concept," in *Philosophical Essays on Teaching*, Bertram Bandman and Robert S. Guttchen, eds. (New York: Lippincott, 1969), 28–29.

behaviorism. This fact is noted by a professor of education at the University of Pittsburgh. "In education," he says,

> we are already overwhelmed [by behaviorism]. Our schools are now essentially behavioral laboratories, and in many states legislation has made that mode of operation mandatory. Educational psychology has come to mean behavioral psychology, not the study of what children need or how they think, feel or react, but how they can be manipulated. . . . Schools . . . are already firmly entrenched in the behaviorist camp.[17]

The "high priest" of behaviorism is B. F. Skinner, whose research into animal behavior and conditioning has provided much of its theoretical and philosophical framework. The most important tenets of this theory are as follows:

1. Human behavior is predetermined by social and biological factors, hence freedom of choice is an illusion.
2. Knowledge about a person comes from observing behavior; there is no other "window."
3. Human life is qualitatively the same as all other forms of life. Therefore a study of rats or pigeons will yield accurate and usable insights into human behavior and how to manipulate it.
4. The way to manipulate "animal" behavior is by conditioning—providing consistent positive reinforcement for "desireable" behavior.

Behavioristic education therefore produces "desireable" behavior in children, not because they choose to do right, but because they are conditioned to act without choice.

Perhaps on the surface behaviorism seems relatively benign. After all, if children will not choose to do right, is it not better to condition them to do right than to allow them to choose wrong? That, indeed, seems all too frequently to be the rationale behind much Christian training. Parents and educators have been so concerned for the welfare of the children entrusted to them that they have resorted to any and all means to assure products that will be "conformed" to their image of Christ.

17. David Campbell, Review of *People Shapers*, by Vance Packard, *Phi Delta Kappan* (Dec. 1978), 226.

But thinking Christians have issued warnings. Back in 1947 C. S. Lewis anticipated the growing threat of behaviorism. He noted that "the man-molders of the new age will be armed with the power of an omnicompetent stage and an irresistible scientific technique."[18] "By prenatal conditioning, and by an education and propaganda based on a perfect applied psychology, [man] has obtained full control over himself."[19] When that point is reached, autonomous man is abolished, and God's image in man has been erased.[20]

The attraction of behaviorism is that it works! The contradiction of using behaviorism in the process of instilling right behavior is that it ultimately violates the image of God in human beings. The result of narrow training rather than open education is frequently seen in one of two aberrations. First, it can produce people who know all the clichés, have all the pat answers, and refuse to engage in the hard process of thinking through the difficult implications of their faith. Second, there are those who have learned all the "right answers" but have found that they do not apply to most of life's questions. Such people often abandon their simplistic faith and reject the total system.

Christian education must engage the mind; it must confront the person with choices; it must demand commitment and doing what is right because it *is* right. A fact that parents and teachers who advocate training over education are loath to admit is that "right" behavior that is merely a conditioned response is, in reality, merely the path of least resistance. Therefore a person whose behavior is conditioned to be Christian will have no reason to act Christianly when the rewards to act otherwise seem better.

The preceding discussion has already implied a good bit regarding the nature of education. Some further points of clarification, however, are in order, especially as they relate to the definition of

18. C. S. Lewis, *The Abolition of Man* (New York: Macmillan, 1947), 73.

19. Ibid., 72.

20. Skinner agrees with Lewis on this point. However, Skinner approves of the abolition of autonomous man, insisting that we cannot afford a general public that insists on making free choices and thereby messing up the world. According to Skinner, the sooner we can eliminate autonomous humans the better off we will be. See B. F. Skinner, *Beyond Freedom and Dignity* (New York: Alfred A. Knopf, 1971).

Francis Schaeffer joins Lewis in a clear call for retaining human freedom and dignity. We need free, choosing people, he says. "This is the sort of man which Christians must affirm . . . if man is to retain his sense of worth and to have the value of the Bible and the Christian culture which came from the biblical base ascribes to man." Francis A. Schaeffer, *Back to Freedom and Dignity* (Downers Grove, Ill.: Inter Varsity, 1972), 34.

Christian education. The earlier point that "all truth is God's truth" would seem to imply that therefore all education is Christian education. Such is not the case; Christian education is that which is Christ-like; it is consistent with biblical principles.

Integration is a key notion in Christian education. Biblical assumptions regarding God, man, truth, and goodness form the context in which all data is interpreted. Christian education is not merely a teacher opening class with a devotional time of Scripture and prayer. It is not necessarily a teacher quoting Bible verses every few minutes. Rather, Christian education involves a consciousness of God's sovereignty, of human value as well as human sinfulness, of God's redemptive work—past, present, and future—and of the goal of history as it unfolds God's purposes and its ultimate culmination. In this context the same data, the same sources, the same theories, that are used in the secular setting are considered and studied; but the outcomes and conclusions are profoundly different.

In any educational setting teachers are a vital element. They structure the learning environment and determine the curricular focus. They can make Christian education genuinely Christian or merely give it a Christian facade. One can be a Christian teacher or merely a teacher who is a Christian. The teacher who happens to be a Christian may see little relevance between personal faith and one's professional activities. On the other hand, a Christian teacher is one whose commitment to Christ permeates all of professional life.

Fortunately, Christian teachers have a perfect role model—Jesus Christ himself. His teaching methodology—using parables, raising questions, providing a personal touch, showing compassion and ministering to the whole person—provides profound insights for the Christian teacher. The truth he taught gives direction regarding the need for moral and spiritual content, and the goals he pursued are clear indicators of the relative importance of the material world versus the spiritual world. The needs of the present world were addressed but never placed above the ideals of the next.

He was gentle with young children, and he noted their claims to God's kingdom (Luke 18:16). In the effort to address human sinfulness and to provide adequate discipline, Christian educators have sometimes neglected this part of Jesus' model. An acknowledgment of human depravity does not require a belief that there is no redeemable good in children. Indeed, according to Jesus' words, Christian teachers can learn much about God's kingdom from their young students! Jesus' model becomes even more significant in the relationship between a Christian teacher and a child who also is a Christian. In that case, both the adult and the child are members of God's family; the teacher and the student are "siblings." True Christian love (1 Cor. 13) and gentleness encompass such a relationship, even in the administration of discipline.

Education as it Relates to Other Disciplines

The legitimacy of teaching as a profession and education as a discipline has never been fully established to everyone's satisfaction. A department or school of education in a university has far too often been short on intellectual stimulation and long on busywork. This does not suggest however, that education has no place in the university, or that schools of education are incompatible with other academic areas.

Properly understood, education is both process and content. Process includes methodology, techniques, and activities that prepare a person to function professionally in the school system. Content, on the other hand, encompasses the broad spectrum of academic data that are foundational to the process. Where education as a discipline focuses almost exclusively on process, its place in the uiversity is marginal indeed. It is the academic content, the intellectual challenge, that legitimizes education as a course of study.

The academic data that serve as a foundation to teaching are drawn from various disciplines. The primary ones have traditionally been history, sociology, philosophy, and psychology. More recently political science and economics have been added to the list; and for Christian education, theology is equally important. Each of these disciplines provides critical insights and needed background to a process and profession that largely determines the quality and character of the next generation.

One question that remains is this: Is a course such as History of Education "history" or "education," and should such a course be taught by an educationist or a historian? A valid case can be made for either option. At the very least, someone teaching such a "foundations" course should have interest and expertise in both areas. Relatively few educationists have suficient academic background to handle the discipline areas adequately, and equally few strict academicians know or care enough about education to relate their data to professional teaching needs. Where such courses are housed is perhaps less important than the qualifications of the instructor who teaches them. Universities that have large departments or schools of education and also offer graduate courses in the field are usually ready to offer strong foundations courses. They will usually have faculty members who have master's degrees in one of the academic disciplines or perhaps hold doctorates in the foundations of education.

The extent to which the various disciplines support the study of education is not always understood or appreciated. Psychology is usually an exception to the case. Both educationists and psychologists recognize the inseparable relationship between their respective fields. Learning theory, human growth and development, and exceptionality, to name a few, are areas of common concern. Indicative of the close association of the two fields is the fact that in the past it was quite common for education and psychology to be part of the same academic division within a college.

Although often less compatible, other disciplines also share many common concerns and insights with education. Sociology in particular shares a common background with education. Some of the early sociologists were in fact educationists. Emile Durkheim was a professor of pedagogy in Paris before sociology was even recognized as a valid field of study. A major part of his sociological research was focused on the relationship between society and its institutions, especially its schools.[21] Sociology, then, is concerned with the "relationship of education to societal change, cross cultural research, and the social systems of the school and the classroom."[22]

Philosophy, too, is closely tied to education, both by some of the past individuals in the discipline and by the critical insight it gives to the profession. From earliest times philosophers have served as model teachers and have provided intellectual structure for the process of learning. The Socratic method, for example, is recognized by all educators as a powerful approach to in-depth teaching. Most of the great philosophers addressed the question of education at one time or another, and each of the major schools of philosophy provides insight, assumptions, and guidelines that help teach-

21. Jeanne H. Ballantine, *The Sociology of Education: A Systematic Analysis* (Englewood Cliffs, N. J.: Prentice-Hall, 1983), 8.
22. Ibid., 9.

ers deal with the challenges they face in the classroom. Whether they are aware of it or not, all teachers approach their profession in response to their view of the big philosophical questions: What is real? What is true? What is good?

It is significant that John Dewey, who formulated the one truly American philosophy, pragmatism, devoted much of his intellectual energy to understanding the relationship between school and society. Regardless of one's view of Dewey's philosophy, it is impossible to ignore the profound effect it had on American education, particularly in the first half of the twentieth century.

The relationship of history to education is similarly significant. Historians have shed light on institutions, movements, and persons whose impact has been valuable. This has been especially true with the growing emphasis on social and intellectual history. An example, cited earlier, is the three-volume study on American education by Lawrence Cremin.

Nearly as important as the interpretive data on education provided by historians is the contribution of an historical mindset to the pressing problems of contemporary education. Harry S. Broudy, professor emeritus of the philosophy of education, University of Illinois, emphasizes the significance of historical thinking in a statement decrying the lack of it.

> Educational movements, doctrines and personages are vulnerable to obliviscence, in large part because so much of school people's time is pre-empted by the predicament of the moment. Oriented to the present and to the immediate future, their stance tends to be a-historical. This accounts for the frequency and ease with which bandwagons are launched down the corridors of the public schools. Ignorance, or the ignoring of history is the mother of much educational innovation.[23]

Each of these traditional disciplines, along with the more recently emerging ones, has a major role to play in providing a proper and complete understanding of education. In the Christian university especially there needs to be a commitment to the unity of truth. Truth in all these disciplines dovetail into one whole. Education is a part of this whole and recognizes its interdependence with the other disciplines of the university.

23. Harry S. Broudy, "What Do Professors of Education Profess?" fourth annual DeGarmo Lecture, Society of Professors of Education.

The Christian university has an obligation both to maintain its credibility as truly higher education and to produce Christian teachers who can think through their beliefs and intelligently apply them to their professional activities. Teacher education in a Christian university must be much more than the acquiring of certain teaching techniques and vocational skills. Consistent with true Christian higher education, teacher education in a Christian university must challenge the mind, it must clarify purpose and mission, it must engender discernment of truth and error, it must demand justification for methodology and practice, and it must above all else demand a thorough understanding of human nature, of God, and of the relationship between the two. Anything less than this renders education suspect in the context of a Christian university.

The School of Education in the University

A school of education in a university serves the purpose of providing an organizational setting for the preparation and continuing education of teachers. Similar to other professional schools such as business, nursing, law, or pharmacy, its primary emphasis is vocational, focusing on methodology and teaching techniques and skills. Because of this, schools of education tend to be process- rather than content-oriented.

However, teachers do not just teach; they teach something. The liberal arts component is normally the student's major, taken outside the school of education. For the elementary teacher the content is contained in the education courses designed to give the future teacher a broad general background that enables the teacher to introduce students to various learning experiences relative to the different areas of knowledge.

The larger question of whether teaching is truly a profession with a clearly defined body of knowledge is also implicit in this discussion. For the most part, educationists insist that teaching is a profession and that the teacher education program consists of essential and specific professional knowledge that will produce teachers. The near-fanatical commitment that certain educationists have to statistics is related to the claim that teaching is truly a science and therefore has a professional knowledge base. Fortunately, not all educationists or social scientists are as narrow in their perspective as to believe that statistics is the profession's only claim to academic respectability.[24]

For the most part, the courses taught within the school of education are those that lead to teacher certification. There is a common core of courses recognized by most states as requisite. These include "methods" courses in each subject area the student plans to teach. It also includes educational psychology, a course encompassing human growth and development as well as learning theory. A significant focus of the program is on student teaching, a supervised introduction to the professional function of the teacher in an actual classroom. Also included is an introductory course in education, designed to provide general information regarding the profession as a whole.

In a Christian university these courses provide a powerful vehicle for the integration of education and a biblical worldview. Implicit in all these courses is a definite view of human nature, of truth, and of values. The biblical view of human beings as created in God's image, yet possessing a sinful nature, has far-reaching implications relative to discipline and to teaching techniques. Students need direction, constraints, and correction. Teachers must learn to be firm and gentle in providing such direction. Because all humans are made in God's image, there must be respect for one another in the classroom. And where both teachers and students are Christians, the family bond of brotherhood in Christ is a dimension of reality that must be considered at all times. There is no hierarchy of worth, only a differentiation of role and responsibility that separates teachers and students.

Another critical concern in teacher education is how to convey the notion of absolutes in a relativistic society. Methodology implies assumption. Therefore the method courses in the teacher education program cannot indiscriminately mimic the secular style. For example, values clarification techniques may be appropriate if the objective is to identify the student's present perception of good and evil so that corrective teaching may follow, but the student's per-

24. Several noted social scientists have indicated their disapproval of the heavy statistical orientation of their fields. Peter Berger, for example, notes that although statistics may be necessary at times and can provide some necessary data for the sociologist, it is not the whole orientation of the discipline. Indeed it is but a small part of it; the use of statistics, he says, is to sociology what making nasty smells in test tubes is to chemistry. Peter L. Berger, *Motivation to Sociology: A Humanist Perspective* (New York; Doubleday, Anchor Books, 1963), 11–12.

ceptions cannot substitute for Christian values. Subjective preferences, pragmatic considerations, and cultural expectations must all be subjected to the authority of the Scripture as it proclaims the moral standard of a holy God.

A second example is the problem of accurate grading and assessment of students' performance. "Curve" grading, a common procedure in academics, needs careful explanation. An implication of grading on the curve is that there is no absolute right or wrong and that truth is relative to the composite performance of a certain group of students. This, then, sends an erroneous message to the student, unless there is a clear explanation and justification for its use that conforms to the notion of Christian absolutes. Such a justification may be found in the fact that teachers are fallible: they may not have been clear in their presentation, or they may have missed covering certain material in their lectures. God does not grade on the curve, but teachers may need to make some adjustments to compensate for their imperfection.

In most Christian universities, as in their secular counterparts, a primary responsibility of the school of education is to prepare teachers for state certification. If the purpose of the Christian university is to prepare students to permeate society in all possible areas, then the production of qualified and certifiable teachers for both public and private schools is a worthy goal.

All communication from a state department of education relative to program approval and certification standards is directed to the school of education. The dean of the school therefore is the official liaison officer between the school and state departments. The school of education in a Christian university must perform, therefore, a critical role of developing and maintaining a quality teacher education program that reflects both the true goals and objectives of a Christian university and that meets the standards for state certification and approval. This is a formidable task. But the opportunities for influencing society through this channel are so profound that a Christian university cannot afford to neglect this challenge.

Contributors

W. David Beck, dean of graduate studies and assistant vice president for faculty development at Liberty University, received his Ph.D. degree in philosophy from Boston University. He has authored and coauthored several articles and books including "Secular Humanism: The Word of Man" and "Kant" in *Biblical Errancy.* His primary research interests concern the nature of Christian philosophy and the existence of God.

Robert Chasnov is associate professor of physics at Liberty University. He received the M.S. degree in physics and the Ph.D. degree in materials engineering from the University of Illinois at Champaign-Urbana. His specialty was researching hydrogen-metal compounds using x-ray and neutron crystallographic techniques. He has coauthored four journal articles and has contributed to the three-volume collection, *Physics Exam Files.*

Norman L. Geisler holds the B.A. and M.A. degrees from Wheaton College; his Ph.D. degree in philosophy is from Loyola University. He is dean of the Liberty Center for Research and Scholarship and professor of philosophy at Liberty University, and is a noted lecturer and debater. He has authored and coauthored more than fifty articles and thirty books, the latest of which include *The Battle for the Resurrection, When Skeptics Ask, Christian Ethics: Options and Issues,* and *Apologetics in the New Age.* His main interests are philosophy of religion, apologetics, and ethics.

John W. Hugo holds the D.M.A. degree in choral music from Arizona State University and is assistant professor of voice and director of the concert choir at Liberty University. He recently published an article, "French Prosody and Musical Settings: Considerations for Interpretation," in the *Choral Journal*. He is an active composer, regularly publishing choral arrangements.

David Miller received the Ph.D. degree in counselor education/counseling psychology from the University of South Carolina in 1981. He has authored four books, including *Parent Power; A Parent's Guide to Adolescence; Single Moms, Single Dads;* and *Legalism: A Psycho-Spiritual Perspective*, along with more than fifty scholarly and popular articles on the family. He is currently professor of counselor education at Liberty University and is a recognized authority on child abuse and corporal punishment in the home and at school.

J. P. Moreland holds the Th.M. degree from Dallas Theological Seminary, the M.A. in philosophy from the University of California-Riverside, and the Ph.D. degree in philosophy from the University of Southern California. He has published articles in numerous journals, including *The Australasian Journal of Philosphy, Philosophy and Phenomenological Research, The American Philosophical Quarterly, Process Studies,* and *The Thomist*. He has authored or coauthored six books, including *Scaling the Secular City, Christianity and the Nature of Science,* and *Does God Exist?* Formerly associate professor of philosophy at Liberty University, he is currently professor of philosophy, Talbot School of Theology, Biola University. His main interests are in metaphysics, epistemology, philosophy of science, and philosophy of religion.

Alan Rabe, chairman of the department of health sciences and professor of health education at Liberty University, formerly taught at Central Michigan University, Illinois State University, and the State University of New York at Brockport. He holds the Ph.D. degree in health from the University of Utah and the M.R.E. degree from Liberty Baptist Theological Seminary. He has authored books on health education, curriculum, emergency health care, and community development as well as numerous articles. *Be in Health,* a textbook for Christian secondary schools, parents, and youth leaders, is his most recent work.

Milton Reimer, professor of education and social science, formerly taught at the universities of Minnesota and Montana and Southwest State University in Minnesota. Since earning his Ph.D. degree at the University of North Dakota, he has authored more than thirty articles and reviews in such professional journals as *Phi Delta Kappan, School and Society, Journal of Thought,* and *Educational Studies.* He is coeditor of *Christian Perspectives on Sociology* and his primary area of interest is history and philosophy of education.

Paul R. Waibel is associate professor of modern European history at Liberty University. He holds a doctorate in history from West Virginia University, and undertook additional graduate study at the University of Bonn, Germany, as a Fulbright-Hayes Scholar. His previous publications include *Politics of Accommodation: German Social Democracy and the Catholic Church, 1945–1959,* plus numerous articles and reviews in academic journals, periodicals, and reference works.

Bert Wheeler is assistant professor and director of graduate studies in the School of Business and Government at Liberty University. He earned a Ph.D. degree in economics with concentrations in international trade, economic development, and econometrics from the University of Tennessee and pursued further study at Mid-America Baptist Theological Seminary. His most recent publication is "Federal Deposit Insurance: A Regrettable Necessity of an Antiquated Scapegoat."

Branson Woodard, associate professor of English at Liberty University, holds the Doctor of Arts degree from Middle Tennessee State University. His specialty, literary studies of the Bible, is the subject of two recent articles which focus on Jonah and Zephaniah. Currently he is working on a study of biblical inerrancy as a response to post-structuralist assumptions about textual meaning.

Glyn Wooldridge received his Ph.D. degree in mathematics education from the University of Texas at Austin and his M.S.T degree in mathematics at the University of Missouri at Columbia. Presently he is professor of mathematics and chairman of the department of mathematics at Liberty University. He has published various articles in mathematics and mathematics education journals, his specialty being curriculum and instruction in mathematics.

Index of Persons

Index of Subjects

229